D0339715

ORDNANCE SURVEY
LEISURE GUIDE
DEVON
AND
EXMOOR

914.23
C.1

Produced jointly by the Publishing Division of the
Automobile Association and the Ordnance Survey

Cover: Birland Rocks, on the Exmoor Coast near Lynton
Title page: Clovelly
Contents page: The Cygnet, *Exeter Maritime Museum*
Introductory page: on Dartmoor

Editor: Michael Cady
Copy Editor: Sally Knowles
Art Editor: Dave Austin
Design Assistant: Tony Truscott
Picture researcher: Wyn Voysey
Original photography: Andrew Lawson

Editorial contributors: Jan Beart-Albrecht (Food and
Drink and Gazetteer boxes) works for *Devon Life*; Dr
Peter Beecham (Traditional Buildings) is Historic
Buildings Officer for Devon County Council and
Dartmoor National Park Authority; Martyn Brown
(Gazetteer) is a freelance historical writer, researcher and
museums consultant; Derrick Charles (Directory) is a
freelance writer and researcher; Stan Davies (Wildlife) is
the RSPB's Regional Officer for the West Country; Dr
Basil Greenhill (Maritime History) is a Fellow of Exeter
University and was formerly Director of the National
Maritime Museum, Greenwich; Brian Le Messurier
(Walks) works for the National Trust and has written
several books on the West Country; Ian Mercer
(Ancient Landscapes) is the Chief Officer of the
Dartmoor National Park Authority.

Typeset by Avonset, Midsomer Norton, Bath.
Printed in Great Britain by Chorley & Pickersgill Ltd,
Leeds.

Maps extracted from the Ordnance Survey's 1:625 000
Routeplanner Map, 1:250 000 Routemaster Series and
1:25 000 Pathfinder and Outdoor Leisure Map Series,
with the permission of Her Majesty's Stationery Office.
Crown Copyright reserved.
Additions to the maps by the Cartographic Dept of the
Automobile Association and the Ordnance Survey.

Produced by the Publishing Division of the Automobile
Association.

Distributed in the United Kingdom by the Ordnance
Survey, Southampton, and the Publishing Division of
the Automobile Association, Fanum House,
Basingstoke, Hampshire RG21 2EA.

The contents of this publication are believed correct at
the time of printing. Nevertheless, the Publishers cannot
accept responsibility for errors or omissions, or for
changes in details given.

© The Automobile Association 1988
  The Ordnance Survey 1988

All rights reserved. No part of this publication may be
reproduced, stored in a retrieval system, or transmitted
in any form or by any means – electronic, mechanical,
photocopying, recording, or otherwise – unless the
written permission of the Publishers has been given
beforehand.

AA ISBN 0 86145 665 3 (hardback)
AA ISBN 0 86145 655 6 (softback)
OS ISBN 0 31900 138 5 (hardback)
OS ISBN 0 31900 137 7 (softback)

Published by the Automobile Association and the
Ordnance Survey.

AA ref: 55602 (hardback)
AA ref: 55592 (softback)

DEVON
AND
EXMOOR

Contents

Using this Book

The entries in the Gazetteer have been carefully selected to reflect the interest and variety of Devon & Exmoor, although for reasons of space it has not been possible to include every community in the region. A number of small villages are described under the entry for a larger neighbour, and these can be found by using the index.

Each entry in the A to Z Gazetteer has the atlas page number on which the place can be found and its National Grid reference included under the heading. An explanation of how to use the National Grid is given on page 80.

Beneath many of the entries in the Gazetteer are listed AA-recommended hotels, guesthouses, camp sites, garages and self catering accommodation in the immediate vicinity of the place described. Hotels and camp sites are also given an AA classification.

SELECTION

For reasons of space the AA-recommended establishments under some entries are a selection made from the full lists. See the AA *Members' Handbook* and range of AA annual guides for full details.

HOTELS

1-star	Good hotels and inns, generally of small scale and with good furnishings and facilities.
2-star	Hotels with a higher standard of accommodation. There should be 20% with private bathrooms or showers.
3-star	Well-appointed hotels. Two-thirds of the bedrooms should have private bathrooms or showers.
4-star	Exceptionally well-appointed hotels offering high standards of comfort and service. All bedrooms should have private bathrooms or showers.
5-star	Luxury hotels offering the highest international standards.

Hotels often satisfy *some* of the requirements for higher classifications than that awarded.

Red-star	Red stars denote hotels which are considered to be of outstanding merit within their classification.
Country House Hotel	A hotel where a relaxed informal atmosphere prevails. Some of the facilities may differ from those at urban hotels of the same classification.

SELF CATERING

These establishments, which are all inspected on a regular basis, have to meet minimum standards in accommodation, furniture, fixtures and fittings, services and linen.

Details are to be found in the AA *Holiday Homes, Cottages and Apartments in Britain* annual guide.

GUESTHOUSES

These are different from, but not necessarily inferior to, AA-appointed hotels, and they offer an alternative for those who prefer inexpensive and not too elaborate accommodation. They all provide clean, comfortable accommodation in homely surroundings. Each establishment must usually offer at least six bedrooms and there should be a general bathroom and a general toilet for every six bedrooms without private facilities.

Parking facilities should be reasonably close.

Other requirements include:
Well maintained exterior; clean and hygienic kitchens; good standard of furnishing; friendly and courteous service; access at reasonable times; the use of a telephone and full English breakfast.

CAMPSITES

1-pennant	Site licence; 10% of pitches for touring units; site density not more than 30 per acre; 2 separate toilets for each sex per 30 pitches; good quality tapwater; efficient waste disposal; regular cleaning of ablutions block; fire precautions; well-drained ground.
2-pennant	All one-pennant facilities plus: 2 washbasins with hot and cold water for each sex per 30 pitches in separate washrooms; warden available at certain times of the day.
3-pennant	All two-pennant facilities plus: one shower or bath for each sex per 30 pitches, with hot and cold water; electric shaver points and mirrors; all-night lighting of toilet blocks; deep sinks for washing clothes; facilities for buying milk, bread and gas; warden in attendance by day, on call by night.
4-pennant	All three-pennant facilities plus: a higher degree of organisation than one–three pennant sites; attention to landscaping; reception office; late-arrivals enclosure; first aid hut; shop; routes to essential facilities lit after dark; play area; bad weather shelter; hard standing for touring vans.
5-pennant	A comprehensive range of services and equipment; careful landscaping; automatic laundry; public telephone; indoor play facilities for children; extra facilities for recreation; warden in attendance 24 hours per day.

WALKS

The walks in this book have been carefully planned to suit families, but a few need particular care if young children are in the party. Potential hazards are highlighted in the text.

It is always advisable to go well-equipped with suitable clothing and refreshment, and, as an extra precaution, a compass.

DEVON
AND
EXMOOR

Introduction

This guide covers all of Devon, and the whole of Exmoor National Park, including that part which is over the county border in Somerset. This area contains some of Britain's best loved seaside resorts as well as unspoilt cliffs and coasts; gentle, hedged landscapes as well as wild moorland; sleepy villages as well as bustling towns. It is an area to be savoured, and to be returned to time and again. This guide points the way to the best of it, and helps explain what makes Devon and Exmoor so special.

Ancient Landscapes

As ancient landscapes go – in the British Isles at least – the peninsula of south-west England has a double claim to fame. First, an anatomy of the oldest rocks in southern England, escaping the attention of the great ice sheets of the last million years, retains much older surfaces than those to the east or the north. Second, successive waves of settlers, from the Old Stone Age on, moving outwards from the south-east, dug in and survived longer in the far west, imprinting themselves and their organisation upon those same surfaces. Ancient rocks carved into ancient valleys and shorelines have provided a haven for man throughout prehistoric and historic times. Here change has been slow, the agricultural and industrial influence as light as anywhere, never quite obliterating the evidence of each previous age.

Today's Devon labourer is the latest player in the story of making and mending the hedge-banks, linhays and leats of Devon. Here a network of 8,000 miles of lanes stretches from coast to coast, thin and taut over Dartmoor and Exmoor, richer and more dense at lower levels near the sea; whose knots are villages and market towns which owe allegiance to Roman Exeter, or Alfred's Barnstaple, or Drake's Plymouth.

Beginnings

The River Exe roughly separates two great geological provinces. The origin of the rocks west of the Exe lies in a broad oceanic trough which, some 400 million years ago, was steadily receiving sand, silt and clay in quantity from adjacent naked continents – naked in the sense that what primitive vegetation existed was no great protection against the ravages of wind, snow and running water. The resultant vast thickness of sediment slowly solidified and, while still flexible, was squashed from north to south and folded and uplifted by movements of the plates of the earth's crust. This great upheaval – called Armorican, for Brittany suffered likewise – built the Cornubian Mountains. Within them the original sediments were altered, clays to slate and shale, sands to hornfels, and limestones to marble. Into their roots was intruded the Dartmoor granite – and all granites west to the Scillies – and on their flanks volcanic eruptions added ashes and lavas to the geological sequence. All the rocks so far formed are classified worldwide as Devonian and Carboniferous – though Devon is hardly representative of either. Contemporary Devonian rocks are known as Old Red Sandstone in the rest of Great Britain, and Devon's Carboniferous is called the Culm, after a river and various villages,

so different is it from all that limestone and Millstone Grit of the Pennines, or the Coal Measures of south Wales and the north.

There is hardly a quarry, coastal cliff or hollow lane west of the Exe that does not show the distorted and up-ended attitudes of the rocks that are now the mere stumps of those elderly mountains. Their denudation began in a hot, dry climate some 280 million years ago. The early debris from the wearing away, cracking up and stripping down that is the other side of the geological coin, is a deep red, coarse concrete of angular gravel seen in cliffs from Paignton to Dawlish on the south Devon coast. It grades upwards (in time sequence) into red sandstones exposed on the same coast, in the low cliffs that border the Exe estuary, and on from Exmouth to beyond Budleigh Salterton. Tiny outliers of the same stuff lie at Slapton in Start Bay and at Thurlestone in Bigbury Bay. Indeed the Thurlestone itself is a great perforated sea-stack of this red, desert conglomerate.

So begins that second province of rocks, and the east Devon suite – red at its western edge but passing up via the chalk of Beer and Seaton, the Greensand of the Great Haldon, and finally to the flinty gravels that cap all the plateaux and ridges – is but a small sample of the whole family of formations that floor south-eastern England. While not so torn about and distorted as the western rocks, they are a little warped, and all slope away generally eastwards. Conversely, they once extended further west, overlying all that has been so far described; indeed the red soils, for which Devon is well known, are themselves in part a relic of the staining downwards from that red basement, now itself removed.

This then is the structural inventory of the Devon landscape. Basic to its variety, the courses of some of its rivers, and the pattern of its coasts, it is also the source of its building stones, lime for its mortar and its fields, half of its medieval and Victorian wealth, its water and its soils.

Rivers and the sea

Since the last real rock was emplaced, displaced and then settled in its present position, and the first soil formed at its surface, much dramatic activity affecting the contemporary landscape has occurred. The earliest rivers to affect it flowed eastward, on similar lines to the Thames, the Tyne, the upper Dee, the middle Trent. The broad shallow valley of the West Dart in central Dartmoor is the oldest landscape fragment. Its low spurs near Sherberton, Huccaby and Prince Hall bear remnants of former valley floors graded to sea levels hundreds of metres above the present. The great trough in which the Teign estuary lies lines up with it, and miles away in south-east Dorset granite pebbles and that ball-clay derived from weathered granite lie where only an eastward-flowing river could have carried them. That river was suddenly interrupted by a cataclysmic rift in the crust, running from Torbay north-westward through Bovey Tracey to Sticklepath, on through Meeth and Petrockstow to Barnstaple and beyond. The load of the proto-Dart filled up the new lake between Newton Abbot and Bovey Tracey, and ball-clay is still extracted there in quantity and exported out of Teignmouth. West of the rift the whole peninsula tilted southward, a tilt that had a profound effect upon the modern patterns of Devon.

Soon after, the sea flooded the land right up to the edges of Dartmoor and Exmoor, at about 200 metres above its present level. The inundated surface was itself of low relief, as the gravelly plateau tops of east Devon bear witness, but the '200 metre' sea was stable long enough for substantial coastal platforms and strandlines to be etched and to survive to this day. At the south-west edge of Dartmoor, Roborough Down and Plaster Down are extensive samples of these wave-cut benches; Poundsgate sits on the same step above the Dart, and little fragments are recognisable everywhere at the right height. The summits of south and mid Devon, Dartmoor and Exmoor apart, owe their uniformity to successive stages in the withdrawal of this sea, for most are trimmed off to surprisingly similar local heights. The most impressive is that at about 120m, best seen between Start Point and Bolt Tail, where a horizontal plateau stretches for nine miles.

Throughout the sea's retreat, and between these planed-off summits, the rivers of the Devon landscape reasserted themselves, and adjusted their courses a little. That long-established tilt to the south is probably responsible for the fact that the longest – the Tamar and the Exe – both rise close to the northern coastline and flow right across the county to the English Channel. On Dartmoor far more streams flow southwards than in any other direction, and even the two main rivers which flow out at the north coast collect tributaries that flow southward.

Ashburton nestles below the high moor (opposite); Hound Tor (left), an example of Dartmoor's most striking landform; (below) at Saltash, Brunel's 1859 railway bridge and a modern suspension bridge span the Tamar side-by-side

Ice

During this retreat of the sea there occurred the four advances of the Polar Ice Sheet which we call the Great Ice Age. In each of these glaciations, the sea level fell dramatically, and each time rose again but to a successively lower height. After the first it rose to the height of Berry Head at Brixham, after the second to the height of Plymouth Hoe – both planed-off cleanly at 58 and 30 metres respectively – and after the third to seven metres. This last is now the height of a wave-cut platform closely conforming with the present coastline, but with sand and shells on it at Hopes Nose at Torquay, and a ruined fishing village at Hallsands near Start Point. The sea level is still rising from the last glaciation – on a rare day at the equinox, and after a good gale, 4,000-year-old tree stumps, normally buried by sea sand and shingle, can sometimes be seen. They are hard evidence for the continuing post-glacial adjustment of the coastline.

The classic symptom of this most recent rise in sea level is the drowning of the lower reaches of all the main river valleys. If sea level falls suddenly, then rivers are given a new impetus to erode and deepen their valleys, and Devon is characterised for many by deep, narrow, steep-sided valleys and combes. They are on the whole narrower in the older, tougher rocks of the western province, and it is here therefore that their drowning has produced the most dramatic scenery. The Tamar, Plym, Yealm, Erme, Avon and Kingsbridge estuaries all have their devotees; the Dart is to many the most impressive – Queen Victoria called it the English Rhine. The estuaries of the Teign, the Exe, the tiny Otter and the Taw and Torridge in the north all lie in broader shallower vales, and rely on their wide and wild mudflats and curlew calls at low tide for their own special appeal.

There remains one last effect of the Ice Age. Inland, especially on Dartmoor, but also on the higher cliffs and where harder rocks outcrop, the intense cold wreaked havoc as the polar ice butted against Devon's northern coast. The alternate freezing and thawing of the brief summers levered away block after block of rock, narrowing down hilltops and spur ends and corroding the lips of valley sides. In granite the classic result is the tor, with a boulder field below called clitter, but similar features lie hidden in Devon woods and remote fields, where other igneous rocks outcrop. The cliffs of schist around Prawle Point, and of grit in the Valley of the Rocks at Lynton, are all symptoms of that same activity creating the most memorable of landscape details.

Of men

Plants and animals, among them men, filtered back into this newly detailed landscape as the climate improved – some before the English Channel filled up again. By 8000BC Mesolithic men – hunters and gatherers – were living throughout the county,

Prawle Point (below), the extreme southern tip of Devon, an historic observation place; the safe, sheltered harbour at Teignmouth (below left) one of many which have fostered the sea-faring tradition; the spectacular Valley of the Rocks, Lynton (below right)

The hilltop structure known as Hembury Hill Fort was occupied from Neolithic to Iron Age times

and a trace of charcoal in Dartmoor's peat suggests that they may have begun clearing the forest that by then covered most of Devon. Their successors began to farm and continued the clearance. Scattered through the county are sites where these Neolithic people made fields and huts and buried their important dead. But then comes, as far as we can now tell, the great first settlement of the whole landscape. Bronze Age people farmed on Dartmoor over substantial acreages. They built villages, made fields and divided their lands by long parallel banks of stone called 'reaves'. Bronze Age hut circles, singly and in groups, sometimes enclosed in pounds, are still crowded in large areas of Dartmoor, as are stone rows and circles; barrows and cairns are thick on Exmoor and patchy through mid-Devon and on the east Devon commons. Evidence elsewhere is slender but consistent. Burial mounds, tombs and cairns mark routes from Dartmoor to the south coast, and have encouraged speculation about metal trading. What is clear is that these people were the first to take a grip on the landscape; they cleared a good deal of upland forest and forged the first routes through Devon.

Poor, short-lived, building material, unwholesome dank valleys, and man's intensive subsequent use of the land, have all been used to explain the lack of Bronze Age domestic evidence on the lower landscapes. Certainly it is to Dartmoor that we have to look for the detail of the first and most ancient humanised landscape. Holne Moor, between Holne village and Hexworthy, provides easily inspected evidence of the first comprehensive taming of the land. From a terminal reave long parallel boundaries run away north-eastwards at right angles to it; some of the strips so formed are divided by cross banks, single huts sit in field corners, and excavation has revealed wooden fence lines, post holes, and many mole runs – these last proclaiming a bigger worm population and thus a better soil than now. At Merrivale, between Tavistock and Princetown and straddling the B3357, is a dense collection of hut circles (the foundation walls of timber-and-sod roofed houses), with ceremonial stone rows, a cist, and menhir close by. These are mere samples of the densest collection of Bronze Age settlements in

Bronze Age remains at Merrivale on the western edge of Dartmoor National Park

a similar space in north-west Europe. Taken together, they form not just a collection of artefacts, but a tangible Bronze Age landscape.

These people concentrated on, and developed most fully, the upper slopes of the middle valleys of the radiating rivers of Dartmoor. Their cultural successors, Iron Age people whom the Romans eventually recorded as the Dumnonii, seem to have shifted their ground leaving only hilltop structures, and these just at the outer edges of the two great uplands. Away from Dartmoor and Exmoor, some are on isolated hills like Stanborough at the heart of the South Hams; Stoke Hill, Posbury and Cadbury in the Exe Valley; Milber at Newton Abbot; and Berry Castle and Hembury in the north-west. There are three Hemburys on the Iron Age map: the second is small and overlooks the Dart as it leaves Dartmoor; the third, just north of Honiton, is the best known and biggest, and is typical of the largest number of these so-called 'hill-forts', which sit at the edges of plateaux, on coastal cliffs, and on the ends of ridges, always overlooking some lower space. Some seem clearly defensive in site and design, others secure but domestic.

Romans and later

Unlike their difficulties with the Dorset British – at Maiden Castle, for instance – the Romans seem to have talked the Dumnonii into submission, alliance, co-existence, what you will. No signs of battle have yet emerged. Before the Romans brought their hods and trowels to Exeter (Isca Dumnoniorum) there were already trading posts at Mount Batten (Plymouth), Topsham and Stoke Gabriel. Coins that are 300 years older than the Exeter buildings have been recovered from many coastal sites. The few Roman roads occur mostly east of Exeter where there is even the occasional villa, as at Seaton. Almost certainly a road ran from Exeter to North Tawton and beyond, but physical connections have not survived on the ground to link it with Mount Batten in the south-west and Martinhoe on the north coast. Nevertheless there is hardly a market town without its Roman coin.

The Dark Ages were as dark here as anywhere, but as more and more is pieced together about the Anglo-Saxon take-over of southern England, so the Devon settlement becomes more clear. It may well be that population pressure along the south coast, as the south Saxons of Sussex found their woodland clearings merging, caused peaceable immigration on to the 30-mile-long east-facing shore from Exmouth to Start Point. Why else the proliferation of Saxon names – Shaldon, Paignton, Marldon, Brixham, Slapton, Stokenham, Huckham. Saxons may well have been already growing crops and milking here while their military cousins under King Ine were still pushing the British westwards along the proto-A30 (the first defeat of the Cornish at home was at Lifton in 710). Only 100 years later, Aethelwulf – Alfred's father – gave himself some land so that he could give it to someone else for services rendered. That land is detailed in a charter dated 846 and the boundaries of it 'On Homme' (taken to be the first reference to the South Hams) are carefully described, from the Thurlestone near the mouth of the Avon to the Dart at Tuckenhay via Stanborough. This document is not only the oldest West Saxon written record, but its boundary markers include human elements – the 'ditch that Esne dug', the 'old way' and the 'Welsh way'.

Whereas Aethelwulf may have left some domestic mappable detail in one corner of Devon, his son organised the entire area. It was Alfred who decided that four boroughs were what was needed and set up Barnstaple, Exeter, Lydford and Halwell as such. The first three are easily explicable, and two of them have prospered since. In those days Lydford guarded the Dartmoor metals from marauding Celts, and played an important role in the tin industry for much longer. Halwell is a mystery, though Alfred had a mini-fleet at Dartmouth even then and Halwell is on the road out of the town; but within his own lifetime, as a wise town planner, Alfred wrote off Halwell and shifted his patronage to Totnes – lowest bridging point and tidal head of the River Dart – a much better candidate for social, economic and strategic development.

We cannot really be sure what kind of short-list Alfred had from which to choose his boroughs. But only 187 years after his death in AD899, the Domesday record implies by its backward references that most of the villages of present-day Devon were already local centres of Anglo-Saxon activity. They, as manors, were grouped in 'Hundreds' (hundreds of what, is not known) but,

Grimspound, a Bronze Age shepherd settlement, consists of hut circles in a walled enclosure

as with the shires, William found these divisions of the landscape too useful, administratively, to cancel. The Moot of the Hundred was the regular meeting, usually in the same place, of priests, reeves and four reputable laymen from each manor, where taxes were apportioned, minor legal cases determined, and land dealings registered. They survive only, but intriguingly, as the division by which the General Commissioners of Income Tax operate.

So it is to the Anglo-Saxons that we owe the completion of the Devon and Exmoor ancient landscapes. From the Dark Ages to the 19th century there were numerous minor adjustments and minor developments, but the pattern of villages has remained the same, the routes between them are as ancient, and many of the qualities recorded by William's surveyors are still recognisable.

Local differences

Inevitably there were variations across the county. Domesday Book indicates relative wealth, and Devon's second geological province – mostly east of the Exe – with its gentler slopes, softer rocks, deeper soils was clearly the richest. The Romans had given it a bit of a start, no doubt. Here were more mills in the same space than anywhere else, mainly along the Exe and the Otter, but on many minor streams too. The hinterland of Torbay – as far in as Buckfast – and that of the Taw/Torridge estuary were also well off, as was the extension westwards of the Exe valley soils along the Vale of Creedy and on to Okehampton. The South Hams, though well settled, and with more fisheries and salt-pans than anywhere else, is surprisingly below its subsequent capacity level. Dartmoor and Exmoor were inevitably thinly populated, but all the Dartmoor villages but one are recorded as manors in 1086, some modern parishes containing two or three of them.

While all this explains the preponderance of Anglo-Saxon place names throughout Devon and

Exmoor, the names themselves show intriguing variation. Endings meaning home, farm, place and people – ham, ton, ing – are widespread across southern England. Elements related to natural features are more south-western: combe, tor, venn (fen), cleave (cliff); and berry, bury and burgh all seem to be the Anglo-Saxon describing the defensive works of his predecessors. Beare was a Saxon wood, and leigh or ley a clearing in it. A farm called Grimstoneleigh not far from a hamlet called Grimstone is evidence for the pressure to clear some more space for living and cultivation. Barton means corn farm, stoke, cattle farm; cote or cott, worthy and wick all seem to be variations on the farm theme. Cote and cott and worthy dominate on Exmoor and the rest of north Devon, and spill over into Cornwall. Hay and hayne are commonest in east Devon running in from Dorset, leighs on the wooded heavy clays of mid-Devon north of Dartmoor, and tons and hams in the South Hams. On the whole the natural features were named before the Saxons came and used them in their own names for their new villages and farms. Twelve villages at the edge of Dartmoor have the river name incorporated, and five more are river crossings of some kind.

Rivers and roads

The significance of the rivers is very considerable. They were named earlier because they had to be crossed, because they were defensible, they were fisheries, they provided the wherewithal of life itself, and irrigation and power. Mostly they were, and are, difficult of access, so that crossing points and their approaches, being rare, achieve a greater significance than elsewhere. Generalisations are unsafe in the landscape, and each Devon river has its own character, but the Anglo-Saxons confirmed the first farmer's use of the upper slopes, developed the middle reaches where possible – the vale of the Exe, the Dart valley between Totnes and Buckfast, and the left bank of the Tamar – and first

Two old ways of crossing the Barle on Exmoor: Landacre Bridge, Withypool (below), and Tarr Steps

developed any gentler slopes down to the estuaries. The Romans had admittedly sailed up the Exe at least to Topsham, and may have used the Dart to Stoke Gabriel, but Alfred developed Dartmouth, and almost certainly it was the Saxons who began that interrelationship between land and sea possible only where branching estuaries tongue well inland.

However much coastal traffic they generated, the Anglo-Saxons clearly picked up, and used, those old Bronze and Iron Age routes inland. The more important lanes now in use still lie along the watersheds, following the summit ridge very closely, swerving and swaying with it across country between the main streams. It was the Saxon farmers – on regular journeys from farmstead to village, mill, salt pan and lime kiln – who created the denser network of narrower lanes within the prehistoric framework. Right-angle bends on smaller lanes are indicators of ancient fields, since such bends are only necessary to go round an already existing field or boundary. A traditional Saxon property boundary was the ditch dug by the adjacent occupiers side by side, throwing out the spoil on their own side. Many a hollow lane on a parish boundary must be a candidate for this kind of explanation.

Character in the completed landscape

The great Devon hedgebanks, where the hedge itself often seems accidental on the top, may have similar origins. Clearly in a landscape of poor slates and shales weathering to heavy clay, walls are unlikely, so a bank of shillet – the Devon term for slatey sub-soil – is the local answer. That walls do occur whenever the stone lends itself only serves to underline the point. Quite suddenly walls appear, and the discerning traveller will recognise the geological change as he finds walls of schist at the extreme south end of the county, of limestone in the Dart Valley, near Plymouth and Torquay, and more obviously of Dartmoor granite and Exmoor grit. They grow mosses and lichens, liverworts and ferns, and those good south-western indicators wall pennywort and shining cranesbill, but the county-wide earth bank is a wildlife habitat all of its own, and has been a corridor for small mammals and birds for a thousand years. A Devon laneside hedgebank has yellow lesser celandines at its damp base early, and then paler primroses higher up, bluebells, white stitchwort and red campion; in turn followed by cow parsley, hogweed, foxgloves and hemp agrimony in July: a procession which has marched along the lanes since Alfred's henchmen set the stage.

Crowning the hedgebanks themselves is a whole variety of shrubs and trees which like the drainage and can stand the wind. It is claimed that a good hedge gains a woody species every hundred years. Oak, elm, ash and blackthorn; hazel, spindle, holly and elder; sycamore, birch and sallow, dog rose, honeysuckle and even wild service tree, not to mention gorse and bramble; the list itself suggests that the ancient landscape actually brushes the shoulder – or the mudguard – of the passer-by. He cannot help but feel its longevity.

The ancient qualities of the Devon landscape, then, were accredited before the Conquest. The

A disused mine near Warren House Inn

Norman touch was light, even if feudal manor courts slowly cut across the old Hundred Moots as Lords of the Manor exercised more or less benevolent power over the tenancy. Remoteness from the metropolis and regal government helped ensure that 'ancientness' survived. As in much of southern England, a population explosion occurred in the 12th and 13th centuries and many villages became boroughs; but by the end of the 14th century the Black Death had taken its toll, the Peasants' Revolt had sent its ripples into Devon, and boroughs like Torrington were asking to be let off the obligation of sending representatives to Parliament. Nevertheless Saxon villages grew into the small towns of today for a number of reasons: tin mining in Dartmoor needed control and marketing, cloth industries developed in mid and east Devon, and the French connection meant that south-western ports were needed commercially and militarily. So the erstwhile villages of Ashburton, Plympton and Tavistock, Tiverton, Honiton and South Molton flowered; and Plymouth and Dartmouth brought others together. The wool, the tin, and the corn economy of east Devon underpinned the monastic industry of the south and east. Soon after Henry VIII dissolved the monasteries, Drake and the other great 16th-century seamen were developing Devonport, bringing potatoes to Moretonhampstead and beginning the re-organisation of Dartmoor's water for the benefit of growing urban populations.

All this has implications for the landscape, as does medieval to 20th-century tin working, china clay, turnpikes, canals, railways and agricultural grant aid. But nothing has come within an ace of masking the geological provision of the anatomy and the prehistoric and Saxon surface layout of Devon and Exmoor.

Wildlife

The rich wildlife of Devon and Exmoor owes much to the tremendous variety of habitats occurring in the area.

From the remote, high moorlands of Dartmoor and Exmoor through the deep river valleys with their hanging oakwoods down to the wide open bird-rich estuaries; from the sheer cliffs of Hartland Point in north Devon to the gorse-covered heathland of east Devon, there are places for a wealth of different plants, animals and insects. Across the whole area there are also many thousands of acres of farmland, sheltered valleys, scattered small woodlands and copses and, unlike some parts of England, there are still miles of hedges, many on raised banks.

Spring comes early to the sheltered south-facing valleys and by early February banks of snowdrops can be seen on the wooded sides of fast-flowing streams. By March the woodland is carpeted with clumps of primroses and wood anemones, soon to be followed by the swaying yellow heads of wild daffodils. Even close to towns and villages the sight of wild primroses and daffodils growing in the hedgebanks makes a spring drive an enjoyable experience.

Coasts

Over large stretches of the north and south coast there are high cliffs which are home to a variety of wild flowers. Drifts of pink thrift mix with the delicate blue of spring squill and the yellow of golden samphire to carpet the clifftops in colour. Butterflies are attracted to the wild flowers: pearl-bordered fritillaries and small tortoiseshells are regular, and scarce summer migrants include painted ladies and clouded yellows. The limestone headland of Berry Head near Brixham has a range of special plants related to its underlying geology, as do the chalk cliffs of Beer Head in the east of the county. Berry Head is a country park with one of the main seabird breeding colonies of Devon. Nesting guillemots can be found in their hundreds on the cliff ledges from April until July. A few pairs of razorbill also breed here, and there is also a sizeable kittiwake colony. Another concentration of breeding seabirds can be found in north Devon at Woody Bay.

Some seabirds are more widely distributed around the whole coastline, especially herring and lesser black-backed gulls, and also fulmars. These are members of the petrel family which look superficially like a gull but fly very differently on stiffly-held wings in the manner of a small glider. Among the other nesting seabirds is the shag, a smaller version of the cormorant with greenish-black plumage and a distinct crest.

A day visit to the island of Lundy in early summer, by passenger steamer from Bideford, provides the best opportunity to see the widest possible range of Devon's seabirds. Lundy is a Norse word meaning 'puffin island' and puffins can still be found here.

Coastal wildlife: a puffin carries sand eels on Lundy; red campion thrives in hedgerows; painted lady butterflies are summer visitors

Below the cliffs, rocky shores provide shelter from the rough seas for a wide variety of seaweeds and sea animals. Rock pools at low tide are fascinating places for children to explore, for anemones, hermit crabs and shore fish.

In the mouths of two of the larger estuaries – the Taw and the Exe – the effect of wind and currents have combined to create sand dune systems which have their own special wildlife interest. A range of plants thrive in the shelter behind the foredunes, particularly orchids such as marsh helleborine and autumn lady's tresses. Due to their special wildlife both Braunton Burrows in the north and Dawlish Warren in the south are designated as nature reserves. Dawlish Warren has one plant which grows nowhere else in the entire British mainland, a diminutive crocus which flowers in short turf. Tree lupin and evening primrose – two of the most obvious plants – are, surprisingly, introduced species and cause problems due to their invasiveness.

Estuaries

Estuaries, where the fresh water of the rivers meets the salt water of the incoming tides, are important places for wildlife, and Devon possesses some outstanding examples. The Exe, the Taw/Torridge and to a slightly lesser extent the Tamar complex around Plymouth have wide expanses of mudflats and sandbanks. Smaller, sheltered and more compact estuaries occur all along the south coast of Devon, the majority in narrow drowned valleys where woodland comes right down to the shoreline.

The mudflats that remain when the tide recedes are not always as highly valued as they should be, for they provide the home for millions of tiny organisms which in turn are the food for migratory birds. Wading birds and wildfowl are attracted in their thousands to Devon's estuaries for their rich feeding grounds. For sheer numbers and variety the Exe estuary is perhaps outstanding, but most of the typical birds can be found on every estuary, even the very smallest. Mid-winter on the Exe sees peak numbers, with over 4,000 Brent geese arriving from arctic Russia to feed on eelgrass, a plant which grows beneath the waters of the estuary and is exposed for grazing at low tide. Other wildfowl feeding on the grass include wigeon and pintail. Wading birds feeding on ragworms and larger shellfish such as cockles and mussels include curlew and the more obvious black and white oyster-catchers. Smaller waders running across the surface of the mud to pick up food include dunlin, ringed plover and sanderling. At least 15 different kinds occur regularly, with several others only during spring and autumn migration. Of special interest is the elegant avocet, a mainly white wader with a delicate upcurved bill. Devon is one of its primary wintering sites in the whole of Britain and well over 100 can be found during most winters on both the Exe and Tamar estuaries. Special boat trips to see avocets are organised annually by the Royal Society for the Protection of Birds – whose emblem they are.

At high tide most waders collect together at undisturbed roosts until the tide drops, and this is an ideal time to view them. On several estuaries

Marsh helleborine – orchid of damp places

hides are provided; at Dawlish Warren a large hide overlooks the main roost site and is well worth visiting at any time of year. During the summer months the sheer numbers of wading birds are reduced but there are always a few to be found together with summer visitors like the terns. These striking white sea-swallows hover and dive for sand eels off the estuary mouth and then come in to roost with the remaining waders. By July, when the beaches are thronged with holidaymakers, the waders have already begun their autumn migration and this can be one of the best times to visit high-tide roosts.

In some sheltered places the gradual build-up of mud allows patches of salt marsh to gain a foothold and here a range of salt-adapted plants occurs, initially glasswort and spartina, but eventually the more colourful sea aster and sea lavender, all adding to the wonder and wealth of wildlife in the estuaries of the county.

Moorland

Moorland areas, with their wide vistas, have special landscape qualities which are enhanced by the wildlife. In spring the flight song of the skylark fills the air while in the distance can be heard the bubbling calls of curlew. Over the nearby valleys the mewing of buzzards is carried on the wind as the birds circle in currents of warm air.

Devon is fortunate to have two large moorland blocks, Dartmoor and Exmoor (shared with Somerset). The fact that both are cared for as national parks is an added bonus. Dartmoor is much the larger of the two and also the higher,

Ring ouzels are found where jagged tors rise from heather-clad slopes

with an upland blanket bog system on its high plateau. Moisture trapped in the deep covering of peat provides ideal growing conditions for wetland plants; the swaying white tufts of cotton-grass along with the colourful tints of purple moor grass are good indicators of where these conditions occur. These areas of Dartmoor are the only places in the West Country where golden plover and dunlin breed regularly.

Heather was once much more widespread on both moors and it is still most important as the basic plant on which much moorland wildlife depends. The richest areas of heather are the best places to see many of the special moorland birds. For example, the ring ouzel, a shy moorland blackbird with a small white bib, is often found in remote heather-clad gullies. Red grouse have become relatively scarce with the decline of heather through overgrazing and overburning. If you disturb them listen for their distinctive 'go back' calls as they fly ahead of you.

The granite tors of Dartmoor are the places to look for ravens; the largest members of the crow family, they are best distinguished by their wedge-shaped tail and harsh call. One bird that the visitor is almost certain to notice in summer is the wheatear. Most often found in areas of short grass with scattered stones, these small migrants show a prominent white rump as they fly away. Over two thousand pairs nest on Dartmoor and they are also common on Exmoor.

Exmoor is a much more compact area with a softer feel to the landscape; its best heather areas are in the east around Dunkery Beacon, its highest point. It possesses the West Country's largest population of red deer and anyone spending some time on the moor stands a good chance of seeing Britain's biggest wild animal. They can be found out on the open moor or, towards dusk, feeding amongst scattered trees on the moorland fringe, but they do spend a good deal of time 'lying up' in combes. Late summer on Exmoor when the heather is in flower is a good time for a visit. It is worth exploring the sheltered combes where bracken and gorse slopes attract many small birds such as winchat, stonechat, yellowhammer and linnet.

Streams, rivers and lakes

The narrow valleys on the high moors carry the shallow streams which are the headwaters of most of Devon's major rivers. Some, such as the Exe, Dart and Teign, flow south, while the Taw and Torridge wind generally northwards. The Tamar, which is the boundary between Devon and Cornwall, begins its life almost on the north coast and joins the sea on the south coast at Plymouth.

All the rivers support populations of migratory game fish – salmon and sea trout – which return from their hazardous ocean journeys to fight their way upstream in late summer. Sadly, river pollution has much reduced their numbers, but still the sight of a massive fish jumping the rapids is one of the magic moments of nature. Otters make their homes on Devon rivers, but they are shy creatures and seldom seen – footprints in the muddy banks are often the only evidence of their presence. The River Torridge was the river of *Tarka the Otter*; nowadays the introduced mink is more likely to be seen and is frequently confused with the much larger otter.

Where the rivers gain momentum and rapids occur is the place to look for dippers. These bobbing brown birds with striking white breasts are famous for their habit of walking under water. They often make their nests under bridges, and these are good places to watch for them. Another typical bird of the fast-flowing stretches is the grey wagtail, a bird which is constantly on the move, with attractive lemon-coloured underparts and flickering tail.

As the rivers slow and widen, the waterside vegetation increases and yellow iris and purple loosestrife can be found at the right season. Here the meanders form low banks which are hollowed out by sand martins and kingfishers to create nest holes. Where areas of reed occur other birds are attracted to breed; these might include reed and sedge warblers and reed buntings.

There are relatively few natural lakes in Devon, but water supply reservoirs have been created by damming rivers, especially on the two moors. They are not always outstanding places for wildlife because of their acidity and exposed situation, but

Red deer haunt the wooded combes and open moors of Exmoor

may still be worth exploring for wetland birds. The two Tamar lakes in the north-west are among the better ones and lower Tamar lake is also a nature reserve. The largest natural body of water in the county is Slapton Ley, on the south coast, a long lagoon enclosed by an extensive shingle ridge and divided in two by a road bridge. The main ley is the best breeding site in Devon for great-crested grebes, and the scrub alongside the higher ley is a sure place to hear the powerful song of Cetti's warbler, a fairly recent colonist.

Woodland

Some of the richest woodlands for wildlife are found on the sides of the river valleys as they run down from Exmoor and Dartmoor. These are mainly mixed oakwoods with other hardwood trees such as ash, beech and sycamore and are generally on steep slopes unsuitable for easy cultivation, one reason why the woods have survived here. The ground flora of the open woodland is fairly low growing and conditions are ideal for bluebells, primroses and wood anemones. The moist conditions encourage many varieties of fern and a wealth of fungi in late summer. The fresh unpolluted air is good for the growth of lichens and these occur all through the woods. There are many woodland butterflies; some common examples are the speckled wood and the brightly coloured brimstone, which is often found along woodland rides as early as March.

These deciduous woods boast some birds not commonly found in the east of Britain. The wood warbler occurs in great numbers and its trilling song carries well in May and June beneath the gradually increasing canopy of leaves. Other summer visitors include the hole-nesting redstart and pied flycatcher; the population of the latter has increased with the introduction of nestboxes.

Especially recommended places to visit in order to see some of these species are Yarner Wood or Steps Bridge on Dartmoor, and the Barle valley or Horner Wood on Exmoor. Throughout the county most woodlands are home to typical woodland birds, including woodpeckers, nuthatches and tree-creepers; look out, too, for birds of prey such as sparrowhawks and buzzards.

Conifer plantations are widespread in Devon with some very large blocks established on Dartmoor. While they do not support the wide range of wildlife of the traditional woods they still hold some wildlife interest. In many places the Forestry Commission has established car parks and nature trails, with Haldon Forest near Exeter a good example. These woodlands do have certain unusual breeding birds such as crossbills and siskins, but the casual visitor is much more likely to find the commoner coal tits and goldcrests.

Heathland

Lowland heaths, with a unique mix of plants, animals and insects, are superb places for wildlife. Several types of heather and two different species of gorse can be found on the open heath. Where wet conditions occur they are joined by specialised plants including sundews, which use their sticky tendrils to catch insects for food, several orchids and the bog asphodel. These wet areas support a number of scarce damselflies and dragonflies. A warm summer day is the best time to look for them; two of the largest are the emperor, usually only found over the pools, and the golden banded, which flies more widely over the open heath. In summer the heaths are outstanding places for butterflies with the silver studded blue and the grayling among the specialities. The bird population includes several, such as the Dartford warbler and the nightjar, which are usually only found on heathland. Nightjars are mainly nocturnal, but a late evening visit in calm conditions provides the chance to hear the churring song of this summer visitor. It can sometimes be seen in the fading light hawking low over the ground in search of moths. The best areas to visit for heathland wildlife are the pebble-bed commons of east Devon (collectively known as Woodbury Common); they are crossed by a main road and there are several large car parks close to the open heath.

Two attractive and often-seen inhabitants of West Country rivers: grey wagtail (top) and dipper. Both birds eat insects – the dipper searches for them under water! The main picture shows a Dartmoor scene with western gorse in the foreground

Buzzards are quite common in the West Country. Usually, they are seen soaring or gliding, sometimes being mobbed by other birds – as here. A buzzard at the nest (below) is a much less usual sight

Tawny owl (above) and barn owls. Although there are more tawny owls than there are barn owls, the latter are more likely to be seen, since they often hunt in broad daylight as well as at night

Farmland

The majority of the countryside of Devon is farmland and its wildlife is the most obvious to the visitor. Typical Devon farms are livestock and dairy and most farmland is pasture with much less arable cropping than is usual further east. Although many miles of hedgerow and hedgebank have been lost in recent years a high proportion remains, forming the basis of much of the wildlife interest. In spring and early summer the wild flowers of the Devon lanes are still rich and varied. Primroses give way to speedwell and red campion with a host of other plants. The insect life of these sheltered sun traps includes butterflies, grasshoppers and crickets. The green rolling countryside still includes many farm woodlands and copses, so that the general appearance is of well-wooded country.

Of the birds the hedgerow species are still to be found in good numbers – whitethroat, yellowhammer, chaffinch and many others. In the sheltered farmland of south Devon there is one national speciality. This is the cirl bunting, a hedgerow bird now almost entirely restricted to this area, with the majority of its British population of 130 pairs in the coastal strip between the Exe and the Tamar. It relies on thick hedges and mild winters to survive in this country. Farmland has always been good country for owls, and barn owls still occur, although they are now rather scarce; tawny and little owls are commoner. The largest of the farmland birds is the buzzard; it occurs widely throughout Devon and can be found circling lazily over almost any small farm woodland at any time of year.

Several mammals are widespread in the countryside; rabbits and, to a lesser extent, hares are common, as are the less commonly seen badgers, foxes, stoats and weasels. Even the shy roe deer is well distributed and can be seen out in the open fields especially towards dusk.

In recent years many factors have affected the wildlife of Devon: pollution, roads, industry, intensive agriculture, all have played a part in the decline and loss of some species. Clearly much still needs to be done to conserve and enhance the county's flora and fauna. It is also clear that concern for the future of our wildlife is growing as more and more people learn of the wealth which still remains. All of the specialised habitats of Devon and Exmoor are in need of conservation. Some are already nature reserves, others are being managed sympathetically, and so, as knowledge of the wildlife resource grows, the chances for its survival grow also. A high proportion of the visitors to this very special area of Britain come for the natural beauty it contains; with a little effort by all concerned there is no reason why that beauty should not be enhanced rather than diminished.

Traditional Buildings

Farmhouses and farm buildings, humble thatched cottages, small colour-washed houses in the village street, town houses of the larger historic settlements, seaside architecture, structures of local industry: these local buildings are worth much more than a passing glance. The interested visitor, armed with a few basic clues about what to look for, can use them to explore the ways of life of many past generations in Devon.

Farmhouses

Ancient farmsteads are scattered thickly over the Devon countryside, many on sites recorded in Domesday Book. They represent the basic dispersed pattern of settlement in rural Devon into which the villages were later incorporated, though many villages are mere hamlets and few are, historically, of very impressive size. It is the farmstead which dominates the landscape of Devon, and it is the farmhouse which is one of Devon's greatest historic treasures. Hundreds of farmhouses are at least 500 years old and were built as 'hall houses', scaled down versions of the large medieval house, the supreme example of which in Devon is Dartington Hall. Like Dartington, these houses usually began as single-storey, open to the roof and with a version of the 'screen's passage', in this case a cross-passage through the building with doors at either end; there was also a similar plan with the cross-passage dividing off a service room from the 'hall' (the principal living room) and a more private room beyond the hall, later to become the parlour.

These houses are solidly built (not partly timber-framed as is the case in some Devon towns) and have thatched roofs, making them attractive to look at. But the roof is often an important clue to the story of a house's development. For the hall house was heated by an open hearth fire in the centre of the hall from which the smoke rose to percolate out through the thatched roof, blackening the whole of the underside of the thatch and the roof carpentry with soot. It is both remarkable and fascinating that hundreds of Devon houses retain their 500-year-old roofs, complete with 500-year-old thatch, because the

15th-century Devon farmer and his successors over the next 200 years retained the older house and simply adapted it to meet their increasingly sophisticated requirements. In response to the need for more privacy and greater comfort, chambers were inserted at first-floor level, staircases built, chimneys constructed and new wings or extra rooms added, all within or around the basic medieval structure.

From the outside it is still possible to see much of this history even though these farmhouses are so heavily disguised. The basic pattern will be obvious enough, the cross-passage dividing the building unequally between hall and parlour one side and service room on the other; often the main chimney stacks will be placed against the cross-passage wall or on the most prominent external wall. In either case they may display considerable decoration in patterned stonework and conscious architectural

The thatcher's art has hardly changed through the centuries. Cockington (below) looks much the same today as when this picture was taken

A Dartmoor longhouse (above), with quarters for humans to the left of the cross-passage entrance, and stabling for the animals to the right. Left – a 15th- or 16th-century farmhouse with a massive chimney stack. Proud owners often used plaster to decorate their homes (below left). This example is at Dartmouth.

The Dartmoor longhouse

Dartmoor has its own distinctive farmhouse, known as the longhouse. Although it looks superficially similar to other farmhouses of the county it is fundamentally different in being a dual purpose building: a house combined with animal shelter. Here the cross-passage divides the hall and parlour from the cow house, or shippon as it is known locally. Excavations on Dartmoor have shown that much earlier houses were also of this dual kind; it is possible for the visitor to see some of these excavated earlier buildings at Houndtor medieval village. Although the combination of human and animal shelter seems primitive, in fact longhouses are highly sophisticated buildings with all the creature comforts of their neighbours in the rest of Devon. Such houses are well known on the Continent today although they remain a great rarity in England, Dartmoor being the only area where they are found, with only about 100 examples still preserved today even here.

The distinctive nature of the longhouse is emphasised by its construction in granite, often in large square blocks and using site boulders in the foundation courses. Longhouses are also buried deep into the hillside for shelter from the harsh upland climate with orientated downslopes to aid drainage from the shippon. Inside the shippon you may see the central drain, stone mangers and tethering posts, and large beams for the hayloft above – as at Uppacott, Poundsgate, a longhouse purchased by the Dartmoor National Park Authority for preservation and display to the public (by appointment in conjunction with the guided walks programme).

Farm buildings

The specialist buildings of the farmstead are usually not as old as the farmhouses themselves but they are impressive testimony to the history of the mixed economy of the Devon farm. They are also one of the visual delights of Devon, for unlike the houses, their walls are usually unrendered and so

design, sometimes complete with a date plaque and the initials of the owner, all specialities of West Country building; the top may sometimes be round, especially in north Devon and on Exmoor. A bulge in the wall will indicate a staircase or a large oven or smoking chamber for cooking and curing food. Windows may often be replacements but many 17th-century ovolo (quarter round) moulded, mullioned windows survive, and even the very rare, small wooden medieval window. Porches and cross-wings were added in the 17th century, by which time many houses were being newly built as two-storeyed houses with increasing attempts at symmetry and more centralised plans.

If you are lucky enough to stay in one of these houses, many signs of the sophistication of the 15th–17th-century farmer are visible. The farmer seemed to reserve the best ornament as a surprise, to be appreciated only when the visitor was favoured by an invitation inside. There are beautifully carpentered oak stud-and-panel screens, ceiling beams (and roof carpentry if you can see it), rich plasterwork ceilings and over-mantels, and much stencilled or painted decoration especially around the fireplace.

display the constituent textures, colours and patinas of their walling materials, which are numerous variations of stone and cob. The striking diversity of the local building stone gives them – like the grander features of the farmhouse such as the fireplace and chimney stack – their distinctive local character: granite on Dartmoor, slatestones and schists in the South Hams and west Devon, red sandstones in central Devon and part of south and east Devon, purple volcanics around Exeter, flints, cherts and limestones in east Devon and parts of south Devon.

Cob – the local name for the mud wall – is probably Devon's most widespread traditional building material and is used in the humblest construction of the farm, such as a garden wall, and in the most substantial medieval farmhouse. Because it is built simply of a mixture of local sub-soil and straw, its colours naturally reflect the soil so that the farm buildings are the same colour as the fields.

Each building has its special function. The most common building is the linhay or linney, an open-fronted shelter shed for animals with feed storage above; the open side is constructed of timber framing or stone. The barn is the largest building, with the threshing floor between large opposing doors. Roundhouses were often added to the barn, originally providing a circular walk for a horse to provide power to drive machinery in the barn. The shippon, or cow house, can be a separate farmyard building as well as being incorporated in the lower end of the longhouse. Stables, dovecotes, granaries and ash-houses (small circular buildings near the house for the storage over winter of ash to be used on the fields in the spring) are worth looking for, as is that most important specialist building of the Devon farm, the pound house, where the cider was made; some still retain the apple-crushing machinery.

Farm layouts show regional variation and

Cob (above) was used throughout the area until recent times. Many old cob buildings are now falling into ruin because of neglect and ill-treatment, but there are signs of a revival in cob-building. Below: part of a mid 19th-century farm layout, grouped round a yard

development in plan form in response to the agricultural improvements of the 18th and 19th centuries. Many small Dartmoor hill farms have extensive grazing on the open moor and have few farm buildings other than shelter sheds for animals, while at the other extreme the larger farmsteads of east and central Devon often include double courtyards of specialist buildings. Farm buildings were originally rather informally grouped around the house, but gradually they became more separate from it and more formally organised on courtyard layouts from the 18th century onwards, particularly on the great estates. For example, all over the countryside between Exeter and Sidmouth are examples of Mark Rolle's late 19th-century rebuilding programme of farms and village cottages on his large estate: his initials MR and a date such as 1876 are easily seen in this area.

Right: the Cherub, one of Dartmouth's finest surviving timber-framed buildings.
Below: Exeter's Cathedral Close, with a glorious mixture of houses from many centuries; harmony is provided by the red stone

Town Houses

Just as the farmhouses were the homes of wealthy and substantial yeoman farmers, so the traditional houses which survive in many of Devon's historic towns were the homes of prosperous merchants and traders. But they differ from their rural counterparts: they are of different construction (solid stone side walls with timber-framed front and back walls), later in date (usually later 16th and *c*17th centuries at the earliest rather than medieval) and of more varied yet distinct plan. Since every merchant required a frontage on to the main street there was a premium on space in the small crowded town centres, and so the houses were squeezed on to very narrow long plots of land called burgage plots – plots of land held by a burgher of the town. Consequently the houses are built in blocks: a front block containing the shop and superior house rooms, separated by a courtyard from a back block, and sometimes by another courtyard from another block. Access was provided by internal or external side passages, and linked by galleries at first floor level: this latter feature is highly unusual and is unique in England to Devon towns. Interiors were enriched with superb plasterwork (especially in Barnstaple, Totnes and Exeter, which seem to have been centres of plasterwork skills in the 17th century) and the exterior to the street was sometimes highly decorated to show off the prestige of the owner, often jettied out at successively higher levels over the street. Some houses are actually built out right over the pavement to provide colonnaded walks.

Totnes has one of the most outstanding collections of 16th- and 17th-century houses of all these types anywhere in England, with other excellent groups in Dartmouth, Topsham, Exeter, Plymouth, Barnstaple, Plympton and Kingsbridge. But most Devon towns have some early houses, and others of slightly later date which display

additional interesting features like the patterned slate hanging of the Ashburton houses, especially the fish-scale decoration of 31 East Street and the pack of cards pattern of 10 North Street.

Later in the 17th century some planned estate development of town houses began, as in Bridgeland Street, Bideford. The following two centuries saw much more such planned development on even larger scales. Even after its grievous wartime losses, Exeter still has splendid examples of 18th-century brick building in Baring and Colleton Crescents and the terraces of Southernhay and Dix's Field. During the mid and later 19th century, the larger estate owners began to develop extensively in the urban centres, like the Courtenays in Newton Abbot, the Rolles in Exmouth and the Palks in Torquay; some town development was carried out by local architects like Foulston in Plymouth and Gould in Barnstaple. Perhaps the most spectacular piece of 19th-century planning in Devon which survives complete is the Duke of Bedford's remodelling of the town centre of Tavistock: impressive civic buildings in local green Hurdwick stone incorporate remains of the monastic buildings of Tavistock Abbey, while spacious stucco villas line the new road from the centre to Plymouth.

Seaside architecture

Devon's attractive coastline and warm temperate climate has long attracted people seeking relaxation and recreation, so the buildings which embody the history of the seaside resorts are of particular and varied architectural interest.

The earliest resort development began in the 19th century with the building of seaside houses by the wealthy classes, as classically represented by the extraordinary appearance of the 'cottage ornée', an exaggerated architectural expression of the dream of the rustic idyll. Sidmouth, Exmouth, Dawlish,

Top: Exmouth's extraordinary A la Ronde
Above: Fairlynch, one of Budleigh Salterton's early
19th-century gothick villas
Right: Regency elegance at Sidmouth; few towns
have so much careful detail so close together

Shaldon and Torquay on the south coast and Lynton on the north coast have excellent examples of these eccentric houses with ornate thatched roofs, gothic pointed windows, elaborate barge-boards and oddly-planned interiors like the octagonal À la Ronde in Exmouth.

Then came the building of the crescents, terraces and villas of the seaside resorts like Fortfield Terrace in Sidmouth, the Beacon in Exmouth, Hesketh Crescent in Torquay and Hillsborough Terrace in Ilfracombe. Among the pleasures of these buildings are their intricate tented verandahs and balconies with delicate ironwork, especially in Sidmouth where one group is actually named, aptly, Elysian Fields. Eventually the extensive development of the larger resorts, especially in Torquay and Ilfracombe, occurred in large detached houses as well as in hotels and other municipal buildings. Even in the early 20th century, the resorts still inspired well-known architects: Lutyens' Drum Inn at Cockington in Torquay was to have been but part of a planned development; in Budleigh Salterton Ernest Gimson built a splendid Arts and Crafts tradition house entirely in cob and roofed in thatch at Coxen, and E S Prior an inventively planned house with re-interpretations of local materials at The Barn, Exmouth.

Industrial buildings

Though industry is not naturally associated with Devon, the county has a rich and diverse history which stands recorded in many historic structures, even if some have been converted to new uses from their original purpose. For example, Devon's distinguished maritime history is represented in the survival of the Quay area at Exeter with its Customs House, its 17th-century transit sheds (recently discovered and restored), its impressive 19th-century warehouses (of national fame as the location for much of the television series, *The Onedin Line*), and its maritime museum. Devon's national maritime role is preserved in the Royal Dockyard at Plymouth with some of the most dramatic and monumental buildings of English nautical history.

Devon's wealth from the middle ages to the 19th century was largely based on the woollen industry. Textiles still survive at Heathcoate's Factory in Tiverton, moved to the town by John Heathcoate from the Midlands after Luddite troubles in the early 19th century. The woollen mill at

Main picture: these warehouses are now part of Exeter's Maritime Museum. Inset: mill at Bovey Travey

Coldharbour, Uffculme, has now been re-opened as a working museum, and woollen industry buildings survive at Buckfastleigh and Ashburton. Water mills for various purposes can be found in many places because Devon abounds with potential water power. Many, such as Otterton and Bickleigh, now find new uses as recreation and craft centres. Mineral extraction has been one of the most enduring of Devon's industries, and the small buildings of the former mining industries of Dartmoor and Exmoor can still be discovered thickly overgrown with vegetation. At the other end of the scale the supreme example is the now-restored Morwellham Quay area on the Tamar, a monument to the spectacular growth of the copper mining industry of the second half of the 19th century. Paper-making is still undertaken at Hele and Ivybridge but the impressive paper mill at Tuckenhay near Dartmouth is now converted to housing. Brewing is also a traditional local industry, though sadly many local breweries have been demolished: one in Paignton has been converted to residential use, and another at Dartmouth is now used as a pottery.

The history of transport has left its mark. Though sadly truncated, much of the railway network in the county is a monument to Brunel's engineering genius; it also includes Brunel's glorious failure of the projected atmospheric railway represented by the Pumping House at Starcross. Elsewhere many former railway stations deep in the heart of the country have been converted to houses and still evoke something of the former geographical glory of the railway age which penetrated so much of this large rural area. Canal architecture can be seen at Tiverton (the Union Canal), and at Exeter around the Maritime Museum. Deserted canals can be found in other – sometimes highly unlikely – places, such as the remnants of the Bude–Holsworthy canal.

Industrial housing was also given priority by some of the great estate owners. An especially interesting example is the extensive industrial housing of the late 19th century in Tavistock where there are several groups of terraced cottages, all retaining most of their original features. Few 20th-century buildings yet seem distinguished enough to note, but perhaps we are still too close to them to appreciate their worth: one of the exceptions is the fine extension to Clyst St Mary's 18th-century Winslade House.

Food and Drink

Wickedly fattening cream teas, and scrumpy to make your knees buckle; farmhouse cheese and butter and moorland honey; fresh crabs and mackerel and fine salmon and trout: Devon is a county with a long tradition of producing good things to eat and drink. Farming and fishing of all kinds have been its main concerns for centuries and, despite changing times, remain a fundamental way of life to many. Between Devon's towns and moorland lie vast areas of rich, fertile farmland where vivid red soil lends its goodness to the lush green grass.

There is no doubt that times have become more difficult or at least more complicated both for the farmer and the fisherman in recent years; they are no longer simply producers of food, their way of life has become a political issue. The imposition of milk quotas has had far-reaching effects on the lives of farmers, as has the introduction of fishing limits on the trawlermen. In many cases, farmers have had to diversify into other areas of food production and this has led to an upsurge of interest in farm produce; this, coupled with a general demand for healthier, natural, additive-free food, has resulted in a unique organisation for the identification and promotion of the county's produce: Devon Fare.

Originally set up under the auspices of Devon County Council, Devon Fare has since become a limited company which counts among its 80 or so members almost anyone who has anything to do with the production of fine food in the county – because, at the end of the day, it is the taste that counts, and Devon's food and drink is tasting as good as ever.

Pure meat

Modern farming methods have tended to put the emphasis on production rather than on the welfare of the animals, but there are those who believe that happier animals make better meat. Some also believe that the old-fashioned breeds of animals have been ignored for too long; for example, Heal Farm in north Devon is approved by the Rare Breeds Survival Trust, and its collection of Gloucestershire Old Spots, Middle Whites, Berkshires and Tamworths produces some of the best pork around, as well as sausages, cooked and smoked meats, patés and salami. The pigs are allowed to roam the open fields and are reared on a diet free from artificial growth promoters.

The same criteria apply to the members of the Pure Meat Company of Moretonhampstead, farmers whose meat reaches the exacting standards of the Guild of Conservation. This requires that no additives, chemicals or growth hormones are given to the animals. So the animals produce better-tasting, healthier meat.

Dairy riches

Out of its rich array of dairy produce, Devon's most famous export must surely be its clotted cream. To attempt to describe this thick, golden, crusted delicacy to anyone who has never tasted it is almost an impossible task: quite simply, it is the richest, most fattening, most delicious cream in the world. Although to describe it as a delicacy is perhaps the wrong word, for generations of Devon farmers were raised on it as part of their staple diet. It is indispensable with apple pie, and unsurpassable with scones and jam, the Devonshire cream tea. A childhood variation is bread and cream with treacle or golden syrup, known as 'thunder and lightning'. The best clotted cream is made from the milk of Jersey cows who have grazed Devon's lush pastures; it is simply heated gently over a long period of time and the cream forms a thick crust on top, which is skimmed off after being allowed to cool.

Devon is benefiting from the imposition of milk quotas in the plethora of alternative dairy produce which is appearing: yoghurt is now being made on many farms, as are cheeses of all shapes, sizes and varieties. There are blue cheeses, camembert-type cheeses, goats' cheeses, sheep cheeses, traditional farmhouse semi-soft cheeses, all of which add greatly to the county's reputation for fine food but, despite its universal bastardisation, a genuine cheddar cheese takes some beating. Although the name comes from neighbouring Somerset and Cheddar Gorge, real cheddar is made in Devon and one of the best is that of J L Quicke & Partners of Newton St Cyres, near Exeter. Their mature cheddar revives memories of how real cheese ought to taste and furthermore it looks like real cheese ought to look: round, and with a naturally-formed rind.

To watch real cheese being made is to watch craftsmen at work. Once the rennet has been added to separate the curds and whey, knowing when to cut the curd is a matter of some precision. The slabs of curd are then turned by hand, releasing more whey until the correct levels of acidity and moisture are reached. The cheese is then milled into small bite-sized pieces; salt is added and mixed by hand, which helps preserve the cheese and encourages more whey drainage. These pieces are then shovelled into the traditional round 60-pound moulds, lined with larded cheesecloths; they are pressed for three days and then left to mature in a cool storeroom for any length of time from two months to a year, depending on how tasty the finished product is to be. The naturally-formed rind allows the cheese to breathe as it matures, a far cry from the plastic-wrapped, factory-produced blocks.

Cider

Another traditional farm product is, of course, cider, or scrumpy as it is known in the West Country. This was formerly never intended for retail sale; each farm had a cider orchard and would have made cider for the consumption of family, friends and farm labourers, part of whose wages were paid in cider, even in this century. The cider made on farms by the simple traditional method is as different from the carbonated, bottled version as real cheddar cheese is from factory-made slabs; it is still, available in a wide range of tastes from mouth-puckeringly dry to honey sweet (the best idea is to mix to your own taste) and its strength should not be underestimated.

Devonshire cider is made from two types of apple, known as bittersharps, which are high in both acid and tannin, and bittersweets, which are lower in acid but still high in tannin. They are simply milled together, made into a 'cheese' layered with straw or cloth and pressed. The juice is collected in barrels and allowed to ferment naturally. There are still farms in Devon where cider is made by this traditional method, and it is well worth buying direct from such places; they will generally allow you to taste before you buy and to decide on your own blend of sweet and dry.

So important was cider in the past that the apple orchards were wassailed to ensure that a good crop appeared each year. This process involved driving away evil spirits from the trees and encouraging good ones, and took place on old Twelfth Night, 16 January. The Wassail Queen was carried into the orchard, mulled cider was drunk from a large two-handled cup, and pieces of toast soaked in the cider were placed in the branches of the oldest tree. The other wassailers would fire shotguns into the tree's branches and make a noise to frighten away evil spirits. This tradition is still carried on in a few places.

Beer

Although not indigenous to the West Country to the same degree as cider, some fine beers are brewed on a small scale here, such as the prize winning Exmoor Ale. The Golden Hill Brewery at Wiveliscombe, Somerset, has been producing real ale since 1980, made from locally grown malted barley, hops and yeast and that is all – no chemicals, no preservatives. Not only is the flavour of beers like this vastly superior to their kegged cousins, but they are much less likely to give you a hangover, despite their strength. Many of Devon's small pubs are bowing to popular demand in dispensing with their easy-to-serve keg beers and returning to the traditional barrels behind the bar.

Wine

A new taste in alcoholic beverages to come out of Devon in recent years has been in the form of English wine, although strictly speaking it is not new at all; the Romans practised viticulture in this country, as did the Normans and, bearing in mind Devon's temperate climate, it is not unreasonable to suppose that wine was made in Devon many centuries ago. Today there are half a dozen or so vineyards in the county whose growers are in the serious business of making English wine. The majority of Devon's wines are light, fresh and flowery, using German grape varieties which are more suited to our unpredictable climate, although one grower, Gillian Pearkes of Yearlstone Vineyard, near Tiverton, is making a delicious Chardonnay as well as a red wine, which is rare to find in this country. She has studied the art of viticulture throughout Europe and is putting her knowledge to good use in Devon's rolling countryside. Several of Devon's vineyards are open to visitors and, despite production being still in its infancy, several wines from Devon are already prizewinners.

Opposite: main picture – a 'cheese', where juice is squeezed out of apples at the start of the cider-making process. Inset top – real cheese maturing at Quicke's. Inset bottom – wassailing the apple trees at Carhampton on old Twelfth Night with the help of shotguns and toast

The mackerel catch is traditional at West Country harbours. Lobsters are much less common, and are, therefore, a delicacy

Mead

It would be wrong to leave the subject of the county's alcoholic drinks without a mention of one more, and this one predates even the Romans: mead. One of the most famous places that this sweet, heady drink can be found is at Buckfast Abbey, Buckfastleigh, which keeps more than 300 hives of bees, and which has become world famous for its knowledge of the subject. During the early years of this century, a disease swept Europe which almost wiped out the bee, but Brother Adam at Buckfast was determined to rebuild his stock and accordingly travelled many thousands of miles to search for new strains of bees. The resulting Buckfast bee is particularly gentle and gives abundant honey, the most prized of which is moorland heather honey from Dartmoor.

Fishy fare

So much for the produce of the land; Devon's rivers and the seas off her coasts also have much to offer. The rocky north coast offers few opportunities for fishermen to land their catches on any scale; the major fishing ports are on the south coast with the two main fish markets at Plymouth and Brixham, which once boasted the largest fishing fleet in the country. This is where the trawlers can be found, although there were many smaller fishing villages, places as tiny as Beer, in east Devon, which once had a thriving fishing industry. There is an old saying in the village, that 'Beer made Brixham, and Brixham made the North Sea' and it is true that the first men to trawl from Brixham were men from Beer.

The sailing trawler reached its peak just before the First World War when the life of the fisherman was extremely arduous; even today the hours are long, the work is hard and dangerous, and there is little stability or great financial reward.

Mackerel is one of the most plentiful and one of the cheapest fish – in former times it was pilchard, which used to be spotted in great shoals off the coast by special watchmen known as 'huers', hence the expression 'hue and cry'. There is no end of other delicious varieties which are now beginning to be appreciated, thanks to the efforts of people like the irrepressible Keith Floyd. Crab is another delicacy and south Devon contributes something like a third of the nation's crabmeat from such ports as Dartmouth, Kingswear and Salcombe.

Finally, a word on the area where food gathering becomes a leisurely activity and, for some, reason enough to take a holiday in Devon: game angling. Devon boasts many fine rivers, as well as several stocked reservoirs, for the taking of trout and salmon, and the sport has seen an upsurge in popularity over the past decade. There is even a centre near Torrington which holds courses in the skills of fly-fishing. Recently some reservoirs have been stocked with brown trout instead of the customary rainbow.

During the Middle Ages salmon was so plentiful in the River Exe (the Roman name for Exeter, Isca, means 'a river teeming with fish') that the fish were held in specially constructed salmon pools; working people used to eat it as often as three times a week, so it was hardly considered to be the delicacy that it is now. It is found in the Dart, the Torridge and the Tamar, to name some of the great estuary-rivers of Devon, although to a lesser degree now in the Exe, and many of the county's top restaurants offer locally caught trout and salmon.

Indeed, the most successful restaurants in Devon are those which recognise that the best meals are made with local, fresh, seasonal produce, and what better way to sample some of Devon's fare. For those who care about the good things in life, the future of Devon's food and drink has never looked healthier.

Maritime History

Devon's two coastlines are very different in character. In the north much of the seaboard is precipitous with a few small harbours – Clovelly, Ilfracombe and Lynmouth and Porlock Weir (over the Somerset border, but still under the shadow of Exmoor) are the best of them. It is a hard country and only the common mouth of the rivers Taw and Torridge provides a relatively big area of deep sheltered water; even here access is made difficult in bad weather and, in all but good tidal conditions, by the shifting sands of Bideford or Appledore Bar. On the rivers are five ports and shipping places: Appledore and Bideford, Braunton, Fremington and Barnstaple. Of these Appledore, Bideford and Barnstaple have played a great part in Devon's maritime history.

In the gentler south there are many sheltered harbours, some of them, like the great and historic ports of Plymouth and Dartmouth, deep enough for big modern ships. They each have their 'creeks' or sub-ports, like Morwellham and Totnes. Some southern harbours provide good berths for smaller vessels, as do Salcombe, Teignmouth and Exmouth, while the Yealm and its creeks and the Erme and the Avon were used by small vessels serving villages, farms and big houses. Sidmouth, Seaton and Beer have beaches from which fishing boats have been worked for many generations.

With such a coastline Devon men have used the sea as a means of livelihood from the earliest times. The sea has played a great role in the history of the county and it is not perhaps surprising that the University of Exeter has recently set up a project group which is preparing a maritime history of Devon to be published in two volumes – the most comprehensive study of a county's maritime history ever to be undertaken.

Early days

The story begins in pre-history, and although there is little archaeological evidence to tell us specifically about Devon maritime activity then, shipbuilding and shipping activity of various kinds undoubtedly went on right through the so-called Dark Ages. From the evidence of place names and what is known of their movements generally, it is evident that the Vikings did land on the northern coast and perhaps used the area as a base for some time. They also penetrated the Tamar on Devon's western border.

Seafaring is an integral part of West Country life. The days of the great explorers may be gone, but thousands of little boats still ply the seas. These are at Beer

Medieval times

Merchant shipping activity increased from the 13th century and Exeter, Dartmouth, Plymouth and Barnstaple (which then included Bideford) became relatively important ports of Britain. Networks of contacts both at home and abroad were developed, with business systems which were sophisticated for the period. Research work has revealed a great deal of the working of Devon's international trade, of the shipowners, and even of individual merchants, of this distant period. Meanwhile customs accounts show the great extent of shipping activity, even as early as the 1300s, including trading contacts between south Devon ports and Portugal and Andalusia in the west and south, and eastwards to the Netherlands and as far away as the Baltic. There was a thriving trade, mainly in fabrics, from the Channel Islands, which became increasingly concentrated on the south Devon ports.

North Devon was somewhat different. Here the trade was with Ireland and up the Bristol Channel to Bridgwater and to Bristol itself. This trade between the shipping places of the Taw and Torridge and Bristol and the ports of South Wales and the upper Bristol Channel was to persist until the middle of the present century.

All Devon ports shared in the great growth of shipping activity which took place in the 14th century. One of the more important trades was that with wine from Bordeaux. In the middle 1300s Devon vessels accounted for no less than 43 per cent of English shipping activity at that important port. Devon vessels also entered into the general carrying trade, taking cargoes from abroad to Bristol and Bridgwater and to Southampton and Hull. They also played a prominent part in the transport of pilgrims from south Devon and Cornish ports to Spain.

Contemporary engraving of a 15th-century ocean-going three-masted sailing ship

Piracy

A strong privateering tradition was built up in Devon. Privateering comprised the licensed operation of armed private ships against the merchant vessels of an enemy country. Clearly, the line between this kind of activity and piracy was a fine one, and in fact piracy was an important Devon business in medieval times.

In due course, with the development of what is known technically as the 'skeleton built three-masted sailing ship' of the 15th century, the first type of ship ever to be built which was capable of sailing anywhere in the world, oceanic voyaging developed in Portugal and Spain and in due course, slowly, in Britain. By the mid-1500s there were what John Appleby has described as 'years of hectic legalised depredation; interspersed with decades of piratical activity'.

The Elizabethan Age

This period saw the emergence of the leading privateering ports – Dartmouth, Exeter, Barnstaple and Plymouth – and the great West Country names, many of them from inter-related families: Grenville, the Gilberts, Raleigh, Hawkins, Drake, and the lesser known figures, Oxenham, Sparke, Cock and Parker. Historians today see this age less as a period of imperialist expansion – whatever the propagandists of the time and subsequently may have claimed – than as a long period of experimental overseas ventures which only too often ended in failure and disaster and which certainly were not a main preoccupation of the monarch in the age of the first Elizabeth. In the successes – Drake's brilliant voyage around the world, whatever its origins may have been, the opening up of trade with what was to become Russia, the defeat of the Spanish Armada – Devon men played a leading part.

Drake's celebrated game of bowls on Plymouth Hoe

This great period in Devon history has left its spectacular relics to be seen today. Of these the most impressive is Buckland Abbey, a Cistercian Foundation which, after the Dissolution of the Monasteries by Henry VIII, was bought from the King by Richard Grenville for £233 3s 4d. Its first occupant as a private house was Roger Grenville, destined to die in the loss of the *Mary Rose*, which he commanded. It was his son Richard who was largely responsible for the conversion of the abbey into a private house – possibly using in part money made with the privateer *Castle of Comfort*, which he shared with another famous Devon figure of the era, William Hawkins. Grenville was to play his leading part with Raleigh in the first attempts to found a colony – or a privateering base – at Roanoke on what is now the Sounds of North Carolina before he died in the *Revenge* off Flores in the Azores. But by then he had gone from Buckland to return to his family's roots in the Bideford area, and Buckland had been sold to a man whose new fortune had been made with the round-the-world voyage, Sir Francis Drake. Today it is in the care of the National Trust.

When the expeditions towards North Carolina set out from Bideford 400 years ago they sailed down the Torridge past what was then a triangular-shaped creek, now long filled in, penetrating the land to the west just south of where Appledore Quay begins today. On the north bank of this was another religious foundation, a fragment of which still survives at the back of a small courtyard. Now known as Docton House, it has served various industrial and storage purposes for at least a century; as the only building still standing on the waterfront which saw Grenville's vessels sail towards North America, it deserves a better fate.

Sir Francis Drake, leading light in Devon's maritime history; his drum, on display in a Drake, Naval and West Country Folk Museum at Buckland Abbey

Deep-sea fishing

Behind all this overt activity of the later 16th century there are shadowy indications, perhaps becoming less shadowy as a result of the Exeter studies, of a different kind of overseas maritime enterprise, of even greater importance in its long-term effects than the well-known historic voyages. The great fisheries resources of the western North Atlantic had already drawn Europeans and Britons for a century or more when the first faltering attempts at British settlement on the coast of North America were made in the 1580s. The islands and headlands of the New England coast, particularly those of the state of Maine, provided land bases for, by the standards of the time, intensive fishing activity. At present, for example, nobody knows when the island of Appledore in the Isles of Shoals in the extreme south of Maine received its name, but it could have been a base, at least in summer, for north Devon deep-sea fishermen before Raleigh's ill-fated colony at Roanoke was established in 1586.

Devon's seafaring connection with the fishery of the coasts of north-eastern North America persisted right through the next four centuries and indeed ended only in 1930 with the sale abroad of the last British sailing vessel engaged in the trade of bringing salt-preserved dried codfish to Europe from Newfoundland. She was the schooner *Lady St Johns* of Salcombe. Devon merchants and financiers became deeply involved in this hard trade, which involved taking sailing vessels little larger than modern ocean-racing yachts, and not remotely so well-equipped, backwards and forwards across the wild North Atlantic at all seasons of the year. There are still numerous indications in Newfoundland speech of the Devon origins of many of the settlers there over the centuries. This was a business in which north Devon, and particularly Bideford, excelled, and at times it seems there were more Bideford ships in this trade than those of any other port in Britain except London. Devon men and women did not go only

Yesterday – pilchard trawlers at Plymouth

to Newfoundland. Through the 17th and 18th centuries there were attempts, some successful, at colonisation promoted by Devon merchants and financiers, and these resulted in sizeable emigration of Devon people to various parts of the eastern coasts of the North American continent, and especially to Virginia. Here Devon factors operated in the old plantations and an extensive trade in tobacco grew up between Devon ports and the early colonies.

The role of the Navy

Other Devon maritime activities over the centuries included smuggling, the revenue service and the inshore fishery; particularly important were the roles of the Royal Navy, the great Brixham and Plymouth Fisheries, 19th-century overseas trade and the last of the sailing coasters. Plymouth Dock, which was to grow into Devonport Naval Base, was founded in the last decade of the 17th century. It grew rapidly, acquiring ordnance, victualling and hospital facilities and, in the 19th century, great yards specialising in steam machinery and steamships. Thus it was that Devon played an important role in the fascinating process by which the Navy was given a steam screw battlefleet in what today seems an incredibly short space of time. The first such fleet to have existed in the history of the world, this was an entirely new weapon which, as historians are now beginning to recognise, played a key role in the war with Russia from 1854 to 1856 – the so-called Crimean War. Devonport Dockyard was at times the largest employer in the south-west and was to play a very important role in the development of the City of Plymouth. The Navy itself, both as an employer and because of the retainer paid to fishermen and coasting seamen who were members of the reserve, played an important direct part in the economies of many coastal communities. Devonport's fortunes are still of great importance for West Country jobs.

Brixham and Plymouth fisheries

Though fishing took place over the centuries from many beaches and small havens, notably from Clovelly on the north coast and Beer, Sidmouth and Hallsands on the south, large-scale fishing enterprise has been associated with Brixham and Plymouth, though at times Teignmouth played a big part in the herring fishery. The development of the use of the beam trawl in deep water, which seems to have taken place at Brixham in the second half of the 18th century, changed a scattered domestic industry supplying local markets into an industry of national significance marketing its products widely in the south of Britain. Two hundred years ago Brixham was already supplying fish in relatively large quantities to London as well as to Bath and Bristol. With the development of the railways in the 19th century expansion was rapid and by 1860 nearly two hundred big powerful sailing trawlers were owned in Plymouth and Brixham. New fishing grounds were discovered and the sailing trawlers ranged far and wide in the North Sea and on the Atlantic coasts. But the ports of the east coast of Britain with their more favourable geographical locations rapidly developed, partly as a result of the migration to them of Devon fishermen, and Devon played a less significant part in the fishing industry, though today inshore fisheries are busy again.

The establishment of the naval dockyard on the Hamoaze in 1691 resulted in Devonport's development as the navy quarter of neighbouring Plymouth. Changing scenes (below and left) – warship design changed for ever with the introduction of steam driven 'iron-clads'. Today (above) the dockyard still builds warships, but the dictates of modern warfare have dramatically altered their design

The Susan Vittery *in full sail*

Overseas trade

With the expansion of industry and the successful development of iron shipbuilding and of marine steam engines in the 1860s, Devon's shipbuilding and shipowning, still using local resources and local capital, became less and less significant in the national scene. Prior to that, however, especially after the end of the Napoleonic Wars, there had been a great expansion of merchant seafaring activity in the ports on both coasts. To take just one well-documented example: from the 1820s onwards Bideford and Northam merchants played an increasing part in the exploitation of the timber resources of Canada and the development of the Canadian shipbuilding industry. This development was of national importance because it led the way to the marketing of large numbers of Canadian-built wooden sailing ships in Britain, and until the 1870s these vessels were to play an important role in the great development of British merchant shipping. After the building of the Richmond dry dock at Appledore in 1856, which remains an important industrial monument, Bideford became one of the principal centres for the sale of new Canadian-built ships of medium tonnage to British shipowners.

This business was largely responsible for the development of Appledore which, almost submerged as it is today in modern housing development, remains in its core around Market Street and Bude Street and in parts of West Appledore a delightful relic of a 19th-century seafaring community.

Another very important Devon seafaring business of the 18th and 19th centuries was the trade with oranges from the Azores and soft fruit from the Mediterranean to England. Most of London's oranges were brought to the capital in fast schooners built and owned in south Devon, their carefully-stowed cargoes literally ripening in their holds, tearing up the Channel under a cloud of canvas in what must have been one of the most spectacular forms of seafaring ever. One of these fast schooners, the *Susan Vittery*, built at Dartmouth in 1859, survived in the coasting trade until the middle of the present century.

As might be expected of a county which became steadily less and less important industrially in the later 19th century, old resources continued to be utilised as long as they could be made to make a small profit. It was these circumstances which led to the survival of the wooden sailing vessel in the coasting trade on both coasts of Devon until well into the present century. This was a phenomenon particularly associated with Appledore and Braunton on the north coast. As late as the outbreak of the Second World War there were some 40 to 50 of these schooners and ketches still sailing over Appledore Bar, sentimentally regarded as romantic and beautiful anachronisms by landsmen, to their owners a means of grinding a hard living using fortuitously surviving obsolete equipment. The last of them ceased sailing with cargoes at sea only in the early 1960s. Three of them, the *Kathleen & May*, the *Irene* and the Devon-built *Garlandstone*, still survive as museums or cruise vessels and as important monuments to Devon's great history on the sea.

The Barbican (1890): Plymouth's original port, history is enshrined in its stones

DEVON
AND
EXMOOR

Gazetteer

*Each entry in this Gazetteer has the atlas
page number on which the place can be
found and its National Grid reference
included under the heading.
An explanation of how to use the National
Grid is given on page 80.*

*Above: the tomb of Lady Dodderidge (died 1614)
in Exeter Cathedral*

Pretty fishermen's cottages and narrow, traffic-free streets add to the charm of Appledore

Appledore

Map Ref: 85SS4630

The 'little white fishing village' described by Charles Kingsley, Appledore is built on a steep hillside facing east across the estuary of the Torridge to Instow.

The village is picturesque and quaint. It is set on a hillside criss-crossed by narrow cobbled lanes closely packed with cottages, many of which are called Opes, as they open onto the Quay.

West Appledore, towards the mouth of the estuary, consists of one street, Irsha Street, of small two-up and two-down cottages backing directly onto the river. On the shore side are a series of courts, with even tinier cottages facing each other across cobbled yards; these were the homes of fishermen and shipwrights, but many are now holiday homes – the fate even of the old Custom House, beside the Lifeboat Station and slip. The lifeboat is now moored permanently in the river.

Appledore is an appropriate place for the North Devon Maritime Museum, situated towards the top of the town in Odun Street with fabulous views over the estuary. It is full of nautical memorabilia, each room portraying an aspect of maritime life.

AA recommends:
Hotel: Seagate, 2-star, *tel.* (02372) 72589
Guesthouse: Red Lion (inn), 15 The Street, *tel.* (023383) 206

Ashburton

Map Ref: 93SX7569

A real country town of brogues and shooting sticks on the southern edge of Dartmoor, set among rolling hills in the valley of the little River Ashburn. The river tumbles through the town centre to join the Dart below Dart Bridge. Moor and tors rise above the town to the north.

The origins of Ashburton go back to a Saxon settlement, perhaps some sort of enclosure or market, when a Portreeve – or chief officer – was appointed by the King to oversee sales of property and cattle and to preside over the Court Leet, a judicial court. The tradition continues to the present day, when on the fourth Tuesday in November the officials gather at the Chapel of St Lawrence. The Court Crier, resplendent in colourful uniform, announces the proceedings and the Ale Tasters, Bread Weighers, Pig Drovers and Viewers of the Watercourses are sworn in to undertake their duties.

The town's prosperity relied on the tin and woollen trades. In 1285 Ashburton became one of the four official stannary towns in Devon, where tin from the Dartmoor mines could be weighed and stamped, and the duty paid. The tinners brought trade and merchants to the town, and they purchased their provisions here before heading back to the mines. The cloth industry also attracted merchants and industry, with the Ashburn powering a number of fulling mills in the valley. Ashburton cloth was exported by the East India Company to China.

The Parish Church of St Andrew reflects the medieval prosperity of the town; the church was almost totally rebuilt in the 15th century as clothiers vied with each other over the generosity of their gifts.

AA recommends:
Hotels: Dartmoor Motel, 2-star, *tel.* (0364) 52232
Holne Chase, 2-star, country-house hotel, *tel.* (03643) 471
Tugela House, 68-70 East St, 2-star, *tel.* (0364) 52206
Self Catering: Apartment 1, Lent Hill House & The Lodge, *tel.* (0364) 52511
Guesthouses: Gages Mill, Buckfastleigh Rd, *tel.* (0364) 52391
Bremridge (farmhouse), Woodland, *tel.* (0364) 52426, (2m E unclass towards Denbury)
Campsite: River Dart Country Park, Holne Park, 3-pennant, *tel.* (0364) 52511
Garage: Chuley Road, *tel.* (0364) 52670

Axminster

Map Ref: 91SY2998

Set originally at the intersection of two Roman roads, the Foss Way and Icknield Street – although archaeological remains from the neighbourhood suggest an even earlier foundation – Axminster is now a busy country town on the A35 between Honiton and Dorchester.

Axminster's famous carpets were not made in the town until 1755. A local cloth weaver, Thomas Whitty, was visiting Cheapside in London when he saw a carpet from Turkey measuring 36ft by 24ft; he puzzled over how such a large carpet could have been woven without a seam until eventually on Midsummer's Day 1755 he produced the first Axminster carpet. Whitty's process was so painstaking and laborious that it was said 'carpets were made by the pliant fingers of little children', and on completion of a carpet the church bells were rung and the carpet was carried in procession to the church for blessing before despatch.

It is not all that surprising, therefore, to find a large modern Axminster carpet in the church together with a sample of one of Thomas Whitty's original carpets. The business prospered until 1835, when manufacturing ceased, but it has now been revived and visitors are welcomed at the new carpet factory in Woodmead Road, just past the railway station.

AA recommends:
Hotels: George, Victoria Pl, 2-star, *tel.* (0297) 32209
Woodbury Park Country House, Woodbury Cross, 2-star, *tel.* (0297) 33010
Self Catering: CC Ref 764OL, Dalwood (house), *tel.* (03955) 77001
The Lodge, *tel.* (0297) 33294
Garages: Hunters Lodge, Charmouth Rd, *tel.* (0297) 32737
Masters, Charmouth Rd, *tel.* (0297) 32100
Musbury Garage, Musbury, *tel.* (0297) 52292
West End Mtrs, West St, *tel.* (0297) 32143
Wilson Allen Mtrs, West St, *tel.* (0297) 33723

Axmouth

Map Ref: 91SY2591

High above the village on the north side, the Iron Age hill-fort on Hawkesdown Hill, haunted by a ghostly warrior with a fire-breathing dog, towers over the starting point of the great Foss Way. In Roman times the River Axe filled the estuary and the largest ships could navigate safely up the river on the flood-tide to moor at Axmouth.

The shingle and pebble bank at the mouth of the river gradually confined the Axe to the east side of the estuary and salt marshes replaced the tide-washed mud flats. In the 16th century John Leland found 'Seton towne but a meane thing' and Axmouth 'an olde and bigge Fischer towne on the est side of the Haven'; Axmouth certainly was much larger then than it is now, as excavations in the neighbourhood have proved.

The church is particularly interesting, with substantial Roman remains, some medieval frescoes and the tomb of the vicar, Roger Hariel, who died in 1324.

On sea cliffs about a mile south of Axmouth a great landslip occurred at Christmas 1839; a chasm ¾ mile long, 300ft wide and 150ft deep formed when 8,000,000 tons of earth crashed in one night. The resulting jungle of foliage offers a rich habitat and is now a protected nature reserve.

Bampton

Map Ref: 87SS9522

Bampton is situated at the junction of the main road from Exeter to Exmoor and the through route from Taunton to Barnstaple, the A361. Here the narrow valleys of the moors begin to broaden and the countryside breaks into gentler rounded hills; it is rich pasture land grazed by sheep and cattle. The little market town leaps into life in late October for the annual Exmoor Pony Sale. Otherwise it is a delightfully peaceful place on the banks of the River Batherm, with pleasant streets of stone and rendered cottages, mostly Georgian in style, plain and practical.

The 14th-century parish church, St Michael's, at the heart of the town, was much enlarged in the 15th century when the north aisle was added.

AA recommends:
Hotel: Bark House, Oakford Bridge, (2½m W A396), 2-star, *tel.* (03985) 236
Self Catering: JFH Ref FM915A, JFH Ref FC1114B. *tel.* (0271) 66666
Guesthouses: Bridge House Hotel, Luke St, *tel.* (0398) 31298
Holwell (farmhouse), *tel.* (0398) 31452
Hukeley (farmhouse), *tel.* (0398) 31267

Barnstaple

Map Ref: 85SS5533

The principal town of north Devon, Barnstaple lies on the east bank of the River Taw at the point where it broadens into the estuary. As at Bideford, there was probably a ford here before the first bridge was erected in the late 13th century; the present bridge, 700ft long, with 16 pointed arches, dates from the 15th century but has been widened and altered many times.

By Domesday, Barnstaple was one of the four boroughs in Devon, with a mint and a regular market. It was walled and fortified in the 12th century – the castle mound is opposite the Civic Centre.

Pottery has been an important industry in Barnstaple since the 13th century; Cross Street was originally Crock Street. Royal Barum Ware continues to be made and the pottery, in Litchdon Street, is open to visitors.

Fairs and markets have underlined the economic success of the town. The Pannier Market building, between the High Street and Boutport Street, covers 45,000 square feet, more like a railway station than a market hall. It is open on Tuesdays and Fridays.

Church Lane, off the High Street, retains the school building erected in 1659 by Alice Horwood for '20 poor maids' – it is now a coffee house. Next door are the

Barnstaple's 15th-century bridge spanning the River Taw

Barnstaple has produced fine pottery for centuries; the tradition continues today

almshouses founded by her husband, Thomas, with a charming flower-filled courtyard behind a heavy black oak door. The lane leads to the parish church, St Peter's, dark and gloomy and of more interest for its monuments than its architecture. Its oddly twisted spire is attributed to a lightning strike in 1010. In the churchyard, St Anne's Chapel has been used as a school; John Gay the poet and dramatist was educated here, and it is claimed his school chair survives. The Chapel is now a small museum.

The Guildhall, in the High Street, is opened regularly for tours; it was built in 1826 in Grecian style. Apart from various corporation portraits, there are exhibits of civic plate and regalia, and a punch-bowl donated by the notorious MP, Thomas Benson.

Modern Barnstaple is very much the administrative and commercial capital of the region, the natural focus for education and local government offices.

AA recommends:
Hotels: North Devon Motel, Taw Vale, 3-star, *tel.* (0271) 72166
Roborough House, Pilton, 3-star, country-house hotel, *tel.* (0271) 72354
Downrew House, 2-star, red-star, country-house hotel, *tel.* (0271) 42497
Restaurant: Lynwood House, Bishop's Tawton Rd, 3-fork, *tel.* (0271) 43695
Guesthouses: Yeo Dale Hotel, Pilton Bridge, *tel.* (0271) 42954
Halmpstone, Bishops Tawton (farmhouse), *tel.* (0271) 830321
Home, Lower Blakewell, Muddiford (farmhouse), *tel.* (0271) 42955
Rowden Barton, Roundswell (2m SW B3232) (farmhouse), *tel.* (0271) 44365
Campsite: Midland Caravan Park, Braunton Rd, Ashford, 3-pennant, *tel.* (0271) 43691
Garages: Ace Mtrs, Abbey Rd, Pilton, *tel.* (0271) 42413
Ray Nicholls Mtrs, Barn Close, Land Wey Rd, Newport, *tel.* (0271) 76071
North Devon Mtr Co, Pilland Way, Pottington Ind Est, *tel.* (0271) 76551

This is a selection of establishments; see page 4.

Thatched roofs and pretty gardens make Bickleigh a popular beauty spot

The unusual site of St Michael's

Brentor

The tiny church of St Michael at Brentor can claim the distinction of being the fourth smallest parish church in the country. It stands 1,100ft above sea level and although services are only held in the five months from May to September, it can be visited at any time of the year and provides a splendid panorama of the surrounding countryside: Plymouth Sound can be seen to the south, Dartmoor stretches away to the east and Cornwall to the west, while 40 miles to the north the hills of Exmoor are visible.

Why this stark and exposed spot on the western edge of Dartmoor was chosen as a site for a church is unclear. One legend relates that the Devil had a hand in it: apparently the foundations were originally laid at the foot of the tor, but each day's work was undone by the 'Prince of Darkness' who carried the stones to the summit by night. Another more plausible story tells of a wealthy merchant who was caught in a storm at sea and, fearing for his life, vowed he would build a church on the first land he saw if he escaped the tempest. Brentor is visible from the sea and is sometimes used by sailors as a landmark, although it would only be the first land to be seen if the lower land was covered by fog.

The first church at Brentor was built in 1130; it was rebuilt at the end of the 13th century, when the tower was added. Embattled in the 15th century, it was most recently restored by the 9th Duke of Bedford in the late 19th century at a cost of £728. The walls are only 10 feet high but are built to withstand the elements, being of three-feet-thick volcanic stone taken from the tor on which they stand.

Beer

Map Ref: 91SY2289

A traditional and very picturesque fishing village where the cottages tumble down the steep valley sides to meet the sea at a sheltered bay.

The main street is flanked by cottages and shops in cob and thatch and the famous Beer stone. Beside the pavement a stream runs down a culvert to the sea and on the higher valley sides detached villas look out to the broad horizon.

Beer stone has been quarried since Roman times; in Devon it is particularly regarded for its use in Exeter cathedral. Part of the quarry,

Beer beach is pleasantly littered with boats and fishing paraphernalia

about a mile west of the village, is now open to the public. Here cavernous underground chambers, their walls marked by ancient tools, are supported by great square pillars of stone, like subterranean cathedrals in themselves.

AA recommends:
Hotels: Anchor Inn, 2-star, *tel.* (0297) 20386
Dolphin, Fore St, 2-star, *tel.* (0297) 20068
Self Catering: CC Ref 7600 (house), *tel.* (03955) 77001
Guesthouse: Bay View, Fore St, *tel.* (0297) 20489

Berry Pomeroy

Map Ref: 93SX8261

The ruins of Berry Pomeroy Castle surpass the wildly romantic images of *Boys' Own* magazine; they are sinister and fantastic, ivy-covered and dripping with undergrowth. The castle stands on a rocky limestone crag beside the steep-sided valley of the Gatcombe Brook, 2½ miles north-east of Totnes.

The castle dates from the 14th century when the gatehouse and massive curtain wall were built; inside the quadrangle are the ruins of a great Tudor house, with a hall nearly 50ft long. In 1548 Edward Seymour, Duke of Somerset, purchased the castle and a fortune was spent on the house.

In the 17th century, another Edward became Speaker of the

House of Commons. He made his home at Maiden Bradley in Wiltshire, and Berry Pomeroy was abandoned; less than 100 years later it was falling into decay.

Bickleigh

Map Ref: 90SS9407

A picture-postcard village of whitewashed cottages with thatched roofs in the valley of the River Exe. On either side of the 16th-century bridge the slopes rise to 700ft or so, steep and wooded.

The river powers the water-wheel at Bickleigh Mill and the internal milling machinery. The mill has been developed as a popular craft centre where craftsmen and women can be seen in action. The adjacent 19th-century farm, stocked with rare and traditional breeds, uses its splendid shire horses and oxen for power. Within the farm a museum depicts Devon rural life at the turn of the century.

Across the river from the village, **Bickleigh Castle**, so called, was a moated and fortified manor house; the gatehouse and small chapel date from the Norman period having survived the destruction that followed the Civil War. Visitors to the Castle today are invited to experience 900 years of history from the earliest features of the buildings to the largest collection of original World War II spying and escape gadgets.

AA recommends:
Hotel: Fisherman's Cot, 2-star, *tel.* (08845) 237
Self Catering: CC Ref 679 (cottage), *tel.* (03955) 77001
Guesthouse: Bickleigh Cottage, *tel.* (08845) 230

Bideford

Map Ref: 85SS4526

Bideford is on the west bank of the River Torridge at the point where it begins to widen into the estuary, before joining the River Taw to enter Bideford or Barnstaple Bay. Bideford, 'by-the-ford', developed on an important highway along the north coast. A wooden bridge was built about 1300; over and around this a stone bridge was erected in the 15th century and much of its remains, although it was widened five times between 1793 and 1969.

The Quay runs north from the bridge and bustles with fishing vessels, cargo and pleasure boats. MS *Oldenburg*, Lundy's passenger and supply ship, sails from here and Ilfracombe – depending on times and tides.

The parish church of St Mary stands on the site of a Saxon church which was later replaced by a Norman building; only the tower (*c*1260) and font (*c*1080) survive, the rest was rebuilt in 1865.

AA recommends:
Hotels: Durrant House, Heywood Rd, Northam, 3-star, *tel.* (02372) 72361
Orchard Hill Hotel & Restaurant, Orchard Hill, Northam, 2-star, *tel.* (02372) 72872
Royal, Barnstaple St, 2-star, *tel.* (02372) 72005
Yeoldon House, Northam, 2-star, country-house hotel, *tel.* (02372) 74400
Self Catering: JFH BK6B (cottage) JFH BW4D (house), *tel.* (0271) 66666
CC Ref 574L 1-6 (cottages & bungalow), *tel.* (03955) 77001
Heale Lodge, Yeo Vale, *tel.* (02372) 77292
Guesthouses: Kumba, Chudleigh Rd, Fast-the-Water, *tel.* (02372) 71526
Mount Private Hotel, Northdown Rd, *tel.* (02372) 73748
Pine's Farmhouse Hotel, Eastleigh, *tel.* (0271) 860561
Sonnenheim Hotel & Restaurant, Heywood Rd, *tel.* (02372) 74989

This is a selection of establishments; see page 4.

Bovey Tracey

Map Ref: 93SX8178

An ancient market town and the 'gateway' to Dartmoor. Though small, it is surprisingly well supplied with shops. There was a Saxon settlement here above the River Bofa or Bovey. After the Norman Conquest the de Tracey family, from Traci near Bayeux, took over land in the neighbourhood. One, Sir William de Tracey, was among the party that murdered Thomas à Becket in Canterbury Cathedral in 1170.

The parish church dates from the 14th and 15th centuries – the carved screen, the stone pulpit and the font are particularly fine.

On the west side of the town, beyond the old railway station, Parke is the headquarters of the Dartmoor National Park Authority. Part of the grounds is used for a Rare Breeds Farm, but it is the woodland and riverside walks which are a delight, especially in the spring. Shaptor and Furzeleigh Woods, managed by the Woodland Trust, in the Wray Valley, lie within the National Park, and are similarly a pleasure to explore.

AA recommends:
Hotels: Coombe Cross Hotel, Coombe Cross, 2-star, *tel.* (0626) 832476
Edgemoor, Haytor Rd, 2-star, country-house hotel, *tel.* (0626) 832466
Blenheim, Brimley Rd, 1-star, *tel.* (0626) 832422
Self Catering: Stickwick Farmhouse Cottage, and Stickwick House, *tel.* (0626) 833266
Guesthouse: Willmead (farmhouse), *tel.* (06477) 214
Garages: Glen Lyn, Newton Rd, *tel.* (0626) 832265
Mid Devon Auto Electrical, Bluewaters Est, Pottery Rd, *tel.* (0626) 832595

Branscombe

Map Ref: 91SY1988

Branscombe is a scattered village of pretty stone and thatched cottages that snuggle in the three deep combes of the tributaries of the little stream that flows out through the shingle at Branscombe Mouth.

Eastwards the chalk cliffs rise to over 400ft, westwards to over 500ft. At Hooken Cliff, between Branscombe and Beer Head, a dramatic landslip occurred in 1790 when 10 acres of land dropped 200ft towards the sea, creating a wilderness of columns and pinnacles now tangled in undergrowth.

There is no village centre, but the ancient church of St Winifred, perched on the hillside of the westernmost combe, has been a focus of life here for at least 800 years. It has an unusual 18th-century three-decker pulpit, and a few fragments of a medieval wall painting, probably representing Belshazzar's Feast.

AA recommends:
Restaurant: Masons Arms, 2-fork, *tel.* (029780) 300
Guesthouse: Bulstone, *tel.* (029780) 446

Exquisite thatching in Branscombe; nearby, an ancient forge is still in use

Braunton

Map Ref: 85SS4836

St Brannoc, the Welsh missionary, founded a chapel here in the 6th century on a spot, revealed to him in a dream, where he found a sow and a litter of pigs; the present church, probably on the same site, is largely 13th-century, and one of the carved roof bosses shows a sow and her farrow. The carved bench ends, dating from the 16th century, are amongst the finest in the country. Braunton is a sprawling village, an odd mixture of narrow ancient streets on the hillside, and large areas of modern suburban housing estates.

Braunton Great Field is an unusual relic of medieval open-field cultivation: 350 acres divided into strips separated only by grass balks. Beyond the field, reed-fringed ditches, with hump-backed bridges for access, surround a marshy meadow.

The track ends at Braunton Burrows, a wild and natural moonscape of mountainous sand dunes four miles long and over a mile wide. The wind-blown sand has been captured and held by the roots and stems of the marram grass; it is a paradise for botanists.

AA recommends:
Hotel: Poyer's Hotel & Restaurant, Wrafton, 2-star, *tel.* (0271) 812149
Restaurant: Otter's, 30 Caen St, 2-fork, *tel.* (0271) 813633
Guesthouses: Brookdale Hotel, 62 South St, *tel.* (0271) 812075
Denham, North Buckland (farmhouse), *tel.* (0271) 890297
Campsite: Lobb Fields Caravan & Camping Park, Staunton Rd, 2-pennant, *tel.* (0271) 812090
Garage: Braunton, Exeter Rd, *tel.* (0271) 812064

Brixham

Map Ref: 93SX9355

The town and harbour of Brixham, on the southern horn of the crescent that forms Torbay, are protected by the promontory of Berry Head and by the great arm of the breakwater that extends nearly ½ mile out to shelter the port from north and north-easterly gales.

For centuries life and work have revolved around the sea. It was always a precarious and dangerous existence, as recalled by a monument in the churchyard to 100 sailors who perished in a storm in 1866, when 40 ships were driven on to the rocks. By the middle of the 18th century Brixham was sending fish to London, Bath and Exeter; and by the early 19th century it was the most noted wholesale fish market in the west of England. Fish was carried up to 50 miles inland on pack-horses, but the London-bound fish was sent by sea to Portsmouth and thence overland. In 1900 there were more than 300 fishing boats at the port. The arrival of steam trawlers and the radical changes in fishing techniques left a permanent scar on the long tradition of fishing from Brixham, and by the end of the Second World War the fishing fleet was practically extinct. On the quayside in the restored Market House, the British Fisheries Museum records this story with models and illustrations.

Permanently moored in the harbour is a full-sized replica of the *Golden Hind*, the ship that took Francis Drake around the world between 1577 and 1580. At the southern end of the inner harbour stands the statue of Prince William of Orange, who landed at Brixham in 1688 to claim the British throne from James II.

South of the town, footpaths lead up to Berry Head, now a nature reserve where colonies of seabirds nest on the spectacular limestone cliffs. Berry Head has been fortified since the Iron Age; the construction of the existing Napoleonic fortifications destroyed traces of a Roman camp.

AA recommends:

Hotels: Quayside, King St, 3-star, *tel.* (08045) 55751
Smugglers Haunt, Church St, 1-star, *tel.* (08045) 3050
Restaurant: Elizabethan, 8 Middle St, 1-fork, *tel.* (08045) 3722
Self Catering: Georgian Cottages, Mount Pleasant Rd, and Winkle Cottage, Roseacre Ter, *tel.* (08045) 2625
Halfway House Holiday Flats, Heath Rd, *tel.* (08045) 3845
Headland Court Holiday Flats, Lower Rea Rd, *tel.* (08045) 7361
Guesthouses: Harbour Side, 65 Berry Head Rd, *tel.* (08045) 58899
Raddicome Lodge, 105 Kingswear Rd, *tel.* (08045) 2125
Ranscambe House Hotel, *tel.* (08045) 2337
Sampford House, 57-59 King St, *tel.* (08045) 7761
Garages: Central, *tel.* (08045) 2474
Hillhead (Dart Auto Marine Services), Higher Brixham, *tel.* (08045) 3887

This is a selection of establishments; see page 4

Buckfast

Map Ref: 93SX7467

The restoration of the abbey at Buckfast is one of the wonders of the 20th century. It was, unbelievably, just six monks – only one of them with any experience of masonry work – who started work in January 1907 and completed the magnificent Abbey Church, now the centre-piece of this living monastic community, in 1937.

The original monastery was founded here in 1018; under the Cistercians, who arrived in 1147, it prospered on their success at sheep-farming on Dartmoor. At the Dissolution the monks were forced to leave, and gradually the buildings fell into disrepair and dereliction. It was not until the end of the 19th century that a small group of Benedictine monks from France, headed by Abbot Anscar Vonier, contemplated the idea of restoration.

The crowning achievement of the new church is the great east window, in the Chapel of the Blessed Sacrament, the work of Father Charles, an acknowledged master craftsman in stained glass.

The village of Buckfast is dwarfed by the great abbey and its surroundings.

Buckfastleigh

Map Ref: 93SX7366

An attractive little market town on the old main road between Exeter and Plymouth. The original settlement was at Buckfast, about a mile up river; Buckfastleigh was 'the clearing at Buckfast', and was probably founded in the 13th century. Up 196 cobbled steps, on the north-east side of the town, the views from the church are breath-taking.

In the churchyard are the ruins of an old chantry chapel, and a strange mausoleum erected over the tomb of Richard Cabell in 1677 to contain his unquiet spirit – he was thought to have been in league with the devil. Tales of fire-breathing black dogs howling round this tomb are believed to have been adapted by Conan Doyle when he was researching for *The Hound of the Baskervilles*.

Wool processing was the major activity until only 50 years ago and woollen mills once lined the banks of the River Mardle. In the 16th

Brixham harbour: now home to many pleasure craft as well as fishing boats, and site of a statue of William of Orange (left)

century the place was heavily industrialised with at least seven woollen mills, a tannery and paper mill, and quarries and mines nearby. The local limestone quarries provided good building stone, and supplied a number of limekilns for producing lime to enrich the poor acidic soils of Dartmoor. There are also a number of caves in the local limestone scenery. The William Pengelly Cave Studies Centre in Higher Kiln Quarry is used for scientific research, and is also the haunt of the greater and lesser horseshoe and Natterer's bats; the Studies Centre and museum are open only when voluntary stewards are available. All the caves in the area are extremely dangerous and should only be entered with an approved guide.

The Dart Valley Railway runs from Buckfastleigh to Staverton and Totnes, with clouds of steam and piercing whistles, a memorable and nostalgic ride (also see page 59).

AA recommends:
Hotel: Bossell House, Plymouth Rd, 1-star, tel. (0364) 43294
Guesthouse: Black Rock, Dart Bridge, tel. (0364) 42343
Campsites: Buckfast Abbey Caravan Park, 2-pennant, tel. (0364) 42479
Beara Farm, Colston Rd, tel. (0364) 42234

Budleigh Salterton

Map Ref: 90SY0682

The beach at Budleigh stretches from Straight Point to Otterton Ledge, a distance of more than 2 miles. It is a coarse shingle ridge of fat round pebbles, 'like buns or muffins', shelving steeply into the water; bathing is strictly for swimmers rather than paddlers.

Sir John Everet Millais lived for a time at The Octagon, at the west end of the Parade, and painted his well-known picture *The Boyhood of Raleigh* there; it was exhibited at the Royal Academy in 1870. Raleigh himself was born a couple of miles away at East Budleigh.

Opposite Mackerel Square stands the Fairlynch Museum and Arts Centre, an odd thatched building with a little thatched dome on its roof. Displays here illustrate the history of the town, and there are regular exhibitions.

Three miles north, on the A376, falcons, fuchsias and farm implements make up some of the popular attractions at **Bicton Park**. The gardens are sub-tropical, verdant and lush, dotted with palms; the Hall of Transport and James Countryside Museum have outstanding collections.

AA recommends:
Self Catering: Cliff House Flats, Cliff House, Cliff Ter, tel. (03954) 2432
CC Ref 6034 (house), CC Ref 7023P (house), CC Ref 7690 (cottage), tel. (03955) 77001

Burgh Island

It was with no expense spared in 1929 that the eccentric millionaire Archibald Nettlefold built the luxury hotel on his recently-acquired 28-acre Burgh Island which lies off Bigbury-on-Sea on the south Devon coast – in fact it was not so much a hotel as an enormous guest-house where he could entertain his business associates and friends. It became known as a jet-set isle, the exclusive hideaway of the rich and famous, a tradition which is continued today. It recently changed hands and is being restored to its former art-deco glory by the new owners, who are offering get-away-from-it-all holidays there.

Famous guests in the past have included Noel Coward, who came to stay for three days suffering from nervous exhaustion and ended up staying three weeks; Agatha Christie wrote six of her books while staying on the island and one of them, *Evil Under the Sun*, is actually set there; the Duke of Windsor and Mrs Simpson stayed there; Kirk Douglas was a more recent visitor, as were the Beatles.

Burgh Island is only a true island at high tide and, as currents around the island make a boat trip hazardous, the problem of transport at all times of the tide is solved by the sea tractor, an extraordinary and unique machine which is designed and built in Newton Abbot. It is able to operate in up to seven feet of water.

Most of the island is a public right of way and it is well worth a visit, if not to the hotel itself, then to the 14th-century Pilchard Inn, haunted by the ghost of a smuggler, or to the crest of the island where the Huer's Hut stands for keeping watch for shoals of pilchards; a 'hue and cry' was raised when they were sighted.

Burgh Island's ancient hostelry

The corner house called The Octagon, where Millais lived, is typical of Budleigh Salterton's Victorian villas

Guesthouses: Copperfields Hotel, tel. (03954) 3430
Long Range Hotel, tel. (03954) 3321
Tidwell House, tel. (03954) 2444
Willowmead, tel. (03954) 3115
Garages: East Budleigh, tel. (03954) 5595
Knowle, tel. (03954) 5327

Chagford

Map Ref: 89SX7087

A traditional moorland town where the whiff of heather and sheep is never far away and where the cottages lie snug and sheltered under a wooded hill. The name means *gorse ford* from the old dialect word *chag* for broom or gorse; the ford was over the River Teign, now crossed by a bridge.

Chagford was one of the three original stannary towns to which tinners brought their metal for assay and stamping.

The Three Crowns Hotel was built as a manor house by Sir John Whiddon in the 16th century. The tragic death of Mary Whiddon in 1641, at the altar of Chagford Church, is said to have inspired R D Blackmore's *Lorna Doone*.

Two miles east **Castle Drogo** looms on its rocky crag over the Teign valley; it is a marvel of the ingenuity of the architect Sir Edwin Lutyens. The house was built during the early part of this century and not fully completed until just before World War II. It contains much to fascinate all the family: magnificent craftsmanship combining the grim splendours of a medieval castle with the luxuries required by the Drewe family, including the castle's own telephone and hydro-electric systems.

AA recommends:
Hotels: Gidleigh Park, 3-star, red-star, country-house hotel, 1-rosette, tel. (06473) 2367
Mill End, Sandy Park, 3-star, country-house hotel, tel. (06473) 2282
Teignworthy, Frenchbeer, 3-star, country-house hotel, tel. (06473) 3355
Easton Court, 2-star, tel. (06473) 3469
Self Catering: Coach House, Granary, Mews & Tackery, tel. (06473) 3313
Guesthouses: Bly, tel. (06473) 2404
Glendarah, tel. (06473) 3270
Globe (inn), tel. (06473) 3485

Chittlehampton

Map Ref: 85SS6325

The 'farm of the dwellers in the hollow' was the centre of the Saxon colonisation of this and surrounding parishes. It is a beautiful spot, ringed by rolling pasture and sheltered by gentle hills.

The little village is dominated by the church with the finest tower in the county. The Square, or town place, slopes up to the churchyard and lych-gate.

The church is dedicated to St Hieritha – or Urith – who was born at Stowford, a mile north of the church, and was martyred by the villagers of Chittlehampton who cut her to pieces with their scythes:
'Where the holy maiden fell
Water gushed forth from a well,
And the dry earth blossomed.'
St Urith's Well can still be seen at the east end of the village. She was buried nearby and sometime later the first church was built around her grave.

A tunnel of pollarded lime trees leads up to the south porch of the present church, which dates from the late 15th century; the pulpit is of that period, and is richly carved in stone with figures of five saints, including St Urith on the north side, holding the palm branch of martyrdom and the foundation stone of the church. The tower, 114ft high, is crowned with delicate tracery; there is a local saying:
'Bishop's Nympton for length,
South Molton for strength, and
Chittlehampton for beauty.'

Chudleigh

Map Ref: 90SX8679

St Martin's Church is mainly 14th-century. The carved bench ends are particularly interesting and there are numerous memorials – that to Sir Pierce Courtenay is especially fine. Next to the church, the old Grammar School is now a private house; it was founded in 1668 by John Pynsent.

On the south side of the ridge, at the bottom of Clifford Street, the old town mill has been imaginatively converted into the Wheel Craft Centre. Visitors climb a steep staircase up through the floors of the mill to see craft workshops and crafts for sale alongside the mill machinery; there is also an excellent restaurant.

AA recommends:
Self Catering: Cider, Stable & Swallow Cottages, *tel.* (0626) 853334
Campsites: Finlake Leisure Park, 4-pennant, *tel.* (0626) 853833
Holmans Wood Tourist Park, 3-pennant, *tel.* (0626) 853785

Clovelly's half-mile-long cobbled street tumbles to the sea lined with cottages, some now catering for tourists

Chulmleigh: St Mary's splendid screen stretches 50ft across the nave and aisles

Chulmleigh

Map Ref: 86SS6814

A sleepy country town on a hilltop above the Little Dart River, Chulmleigh has the sense of having seen better days and of having been left behind in the rush for development.

Local legend claims that Isabella de Fortibus, Countess of Devon, endowed the parish church to provide a prebend for each of seven sons born at one birth to the wife of a poor man of the town. Lady Isabella rescued the children from their harassed father who proposed to solve his family problems by drowning the babies in the Little Dart. Certainly this was formerly a Collegiate Church supporting seven prebends. A fragment of a Celtic cross over the door in the south porch suggests an ancient foundation, but the present building dates from the 15th century.

Although a fire destroyed many of the old houses in 1803 the character of the town was not lost in the rebuilding. A pleasing mixture of architectural styles and courts of cottages around quiet squares make it a delight to explore.

Clovelly

Map Ref: 84SS3124

This is the picture-postcard village of north Devon, familiar as a Christmas biscuit-box lid, and remarkably living up to its reputation in reality. The lower part of the village, tumbling over the precipitous cliffs, was saved from development by the Hamlyn family of Clovelly Court. Clovelly was

only discovered as a tourist honey-pot in the second half of the 19th century, after the publication of *Westward Ho!* by Charles Kingsley – whose father was rector here from 1830 to 1836 – and *A Message from the Sea* by Dickens (1860), both of which described the wildly romantic and picturesque scenery of this part of the north coast.

The policy of the Clovelly Estate Company has maintained the place, against all odds, as a living village. There are no holiday cottages and the weekly delivery of supplies by sledge, on Friday mornings, continues throughout the winter. Apart from the donkeys (now just for the tourists), sledges are the only form of transport, and most of the houses have one, conveniently parked outside the front door.

The dense collection of white cottages, piled almost one on top of the other either side of the stepped and cobbled lane, rises from the harbourside to the summit of the cliff; in places one can literally see down the chimney of the cottage below. In the summer, the place is a blaze of colour as villagers vie for the best display in their window-boxes and tubs. Giant fuchsias and honeysuckle nearly cover the walls of some of the tiny cottages.

Although Clovelly was settled long before, it was a 16th-century lawyer, George Cary, who really established the village by building the stone pier, thus making the only safe harbour between Appledore and Boscastle. Huge sea-worn boulders, wedged by timber stanchions, make the quay, which once sheltered 60 fishing boats; but the herring season has waned and only a handful of boats continue to operate out of the harbour, together with a lifeboat that is stationed here.

For those who cannot face the long haul back up the steps, a Land Rover service operates from behind the Red Lion Hotel.

AA recommends:
Guesthouses: Burnstone, Higher Clovelly (farmhouse), *tel.* (02373) 219
New Inn, Main St (inn), *tel.* (02373) 303
Red Lion, The Quay (inn), *tel.* (02373) 237

Combe Martin

Map Ref: 85SS5846

Charles Kingsley's description of Combe Martin as 'the mile-long manstye' can scarcely be applied to the present village. From the classic U-shaped bay, shielded on both sides by high cliffs, the main street follows the valley of the River Umber inland for nearly two miles, lined by houses and cottages; the street changes its name five times – Borough Road, King Street, High Street, Castle Street and Victoria Street – before running out towards Blackmore Gate.

The village's sheltered aspect has made it famous for early market garden produce and spring flowers – Combe Martin strawberries are amongst the first of the season.

The church of St Peter ad Vincula is about a mile inland, with a little stream bubbling by the churchyard wall. It is a mostly 15th-century building in rose-coloured sandstone with a fine tower. The southern door has a Sanctuary Ring which criminals could clutch to save themselves from arrest on condition that they confessed their crime and left the country – a privilege abolished in the 17th century. The rood screen is finely carved in Spanish chestnut, the panels painted with figures of saints.

In the High Street, the hotel The Pack of Cards was built on the winning streak of an 18th-century gambler, George Ley. The odd

Combe Martin's sheltered combe in its beautiful setting; 1929 Brough Superior in the Motorcycle Collection (right)

construction resembles a child's card house and each floor has 13 doors, for the 13 cards in each suit, and the whole building has 52 windows, the number of cards in a pack.

There are two attractions in the village, the Combe Martin Motorcycle Collection in Cross Street – a nostalgic museum of British bikes, petrol pumps and garage signs – and the Wildlife Park and Monkey Sanctuary on the A399. Three miles towards Ilfracombe, Watermouth Castle, beside a natural harbour usually busy with sailing craft, has been developed as an entertainment complex for all the family; it includes a model railway, cycle museum, and dungeons.

AA recommends:
Hotels: Rone House, King St, 2-star, *tel.* (027188) 3428
Britannia, Moory Meadow, Seaside, 1-star, *tel.* (027188) 2294
Self Catering: Bay View, Woodlands, *tel.* (027188) 2522
Beachside, *tel.* (027188) 3321
Drake Flat, Boronga Rd, *tel.* (027188) 3321
Loverings Maisonette, *tel.* (027188) 3613
Guesthouses: 'Almaza', 3 Woodlands, *tel.* (027188) 3431
Channel Vista, *tel.* (027188) 3514
Mellstock House, Woodlands, *tel.* (027188) 2592
The Woodlands, 2 The Woodlands, *tel.* (027188) 2769
Campsite: Stowford Farm Meadows, 4-pennant, *tel.* (027188) 2476
Garage: Glen Lyn (S G Irwin & Son), Borough Rd, *tel.* (027188) 2391

This is a selection of establishments; see page 4.

Crediton's red sandstone church has Norman remains and dominates the small town

Combe Sydenham

Map Ref: 87ST0736

On the eastern fringe of the Exmoor National Park, Combe Sydenham is cossetted in the bottom of a valley between the little villages of Elworthy and Monksilver. The soft pink hue of the lime-washed walls of the big house and cottages matches that of the earth, so that the whole place glows with warmth against a backdrop of steeply wooded slopes.

The present house was erected on medieval foundations by Sir George Sydenham in 1580. One wing and three of the four original towers were probably demolished during the Civil War, before partial rebuilding after the Restoration in 1660. The place is undergoing a fresh revival by its present owners, who are determined to restore the buildings and grounds to their former magnificence.

Legend records that, in the 16th century, the heiress Elizabeth Sydenham was courted by Sir Francis Drake, after the death of his first wife. The Sydenham family did not rate Drake too highly as a suitor, but when the time came for him to return to sea he had managed to extract a promise from Elizabeth that she should wait for him, no matter how long he was absent. After many months, if not years, of waiting Elizabeth became betrothed to another. On the wedding day, as the bridal party was about to enter the church (it is thought Stogumber), there was suddenly a blinding flash and a great ball hurtled from the sky to fall between the bride and groom. The portent was unmistakable, and Elizabeth refused to go through

with the ceremony. Drake soon arrived in Plymouth and hurried to Combe Sydenham where they were finally married in 1585.

In the hall of the house the great black ball can still be seen; it weighs over 100lb and is some sort of meteorite.

The estate includes a series of fish ponds, laid out in the 16th century and recently restored and stocked with trout; a leat through the Secret Valley to the mill; the deserted hamlet of Goodley – left to decay after the Black Death; and walks through wooded combes to the High Viewpoint at 1,000ft with views to the Welsh coast and the island of Steepholm.

Crediton

Map Ref: 89SS8300

Crediton takes its name from the River Creedy that flows near the town in a sheltered, shallow valley running east–west with the High Street on the south side. The blood-red rock and soil of the area has coloured both the building stone and the local bricks. It is a fertile region once famed for its cider apples, but now mainly pastoral. The town and shops have a distinctly rural flavour and cater for a wide agricultural hinterland.

The principal blot to the town is the main road, the A377 from Exeter to Barnstaple. Luckily the main street is wide enough to cope with thundering lorries, but the planned bypass will bring welcome relief. Off the main road, side streets reveal delightful cottages in cob and brick. The town suffered from disastrous fires in the 18th century, so few of the medieval buildings

Holy Boniface was born in Crediton

have survived; only in quaint and narrow Dean Street, opposite the church, can examples of the old red sandstone cottages which survived the fires be seen.

Winfrith, better known as St Boniface, was born here *c*680 and is commemorated by a statue in the park. He became Abbot of Nursling, and with great fervour spread the Christian message through Europe. He was the first Christian preacher to visit central Germany, where he founded the famous monastery of Fulda.

In the 10th century, a cathedral was built here with Eadulf as the first bishop; it was not until 1050 that the ecclesiastical headquarters was moved to Exeter, to be within the protection of the walled city. Though the present parish church is much later in date, its grandeur reflects Crediton's religious history. It is to be found at the east end of the High Street, built in the local red sandstone with a tower reminiscent of Exeter Cathedral.

AA recommends:
Self Catering: CC Ref 5009L Shobrooke (flat), *tel.* (03955) 77001
Guesthouse: Woolsgrove, Sandford (farmhouse), *tel.* (03634) 246
Garage: Moore Bros, High St, *tel.* (03632) 2074

Cullompton

Map Ref: 90ST0107

The main road between Exeter and Taunton used to drive its way through Cullompton High Street, following the gentle valley of the Culm River, a tributary of the Exe. The M5 now roars through the valley on the opposite side of the river, leaving the bright little market town to enjoy relative tranquillity. The town consists of one main street, called variously Fore Street, High Street and Upper High Street, with narrow courts running off.

Cullompton was one of the great woollen manufacturing towns of Devon. Daniel Defoe listed Cullompton with Tiverton and Bampton 'and all the north east part of the county, which . . . is . . . fully employed, the people made rich, and the poor that are properly so called, well subsisted, and employed by it (woollen manufacturing)'. Such prosperity is conspicuous in the magnificent parish church, St Andrew's, tucked away in a close off the main street.

There was a collegiate church on this site before the Norman Conquest, but the present building dates from c1430. The west tower, 100ft tall in red sandstone with white Beer stone pinnacles and carvings, is the town's landmark. Inside, the wagon roof is richly gilded and decorated against a faded blue background; there is a Jacobean gallery in oak, one of the longest in Devon, and a brightly painted rood-screen. The south aisle was added in the 1520s by John Lane, a clothier, to rival a similar aisle built by his friend John Greenway at St Peter's, Tiverton. The roof is superbly fan-vaulted, and there are carvings of sheep shears, a teasel holder, and John Lane's merchant's mark. A rare survival, displayed in the aisle, is the 'Golgotha' or 'Calvary', which originally stood on the rood-loft: a great tree trunk rudely carved with skulls, bones and foliage.

AA recommends:
Guesthouse: Five Bridges (farmhouse), *tel.* (0884) 33453

Dartington

Map Ref: 93SX7863

The creative restoration of Dartington Hall from a derelict farmyard to an exquisite garden was the brainchild of Leonard and Dorothy Elmhirst, who purchased the estate in 1925 for an experiment in the reconstruction of rural life. The breadth of their

St Andrew's Church, Cullompton, considered one of the finest in Devon, has a 16th-century, pinnacled west tower and a glowing rood screen

concept is illustrated by the series of banners hanging in the Great Hall. Woven by Elizabeth Peacock, they represent symbolically the work of the estate: farming, forestry, gardens, masonry, education, the arts.

On the main road, the A384, at Shinner's Bridge, the Cider Press Centre houses the retail arm of the organisation. Here a range of high-quality craft items are sold, many by local craftsmen, and there is an excellent vegetarian restaurant, Cranks.

The other activities of Dartington are focused around the Hall and its adjacent buildings, including the College, set in a great bend of the River Dart with glorious gardens covering some 25 acres. The Hall was built in the 14th century by John Holland, Duke of Exeter, a half-brother to Richard II; when the Elmhirsts bought it, it was open to the sky and derelict. The Hall now provides a magical venue for concerts.

Cobbled and paved paths lead through neat lawns into the restored Tiltyard, like an amphitheatre with high-stepped grassy banks; a reclining figure by Henry Moore watches from under a canopy of chestnut trees. There are rose borders, a camellia walk and an azalea dell to enjoy, and other sculptures – like the little donkey – to find among the plants. The parkland of the estate, dotted with specimen trees, extends to the banks of the river.

AA recommends:
Guesthouse: Cott (inn), *tel.* (0803) 863777

Dartmeet

Map Ref: 92SX6773

From its source on the boggy plateau of northern Dartmoor the River Dart flows for 46 miles to its mouth on the south Devon coast. The Dart and its tributaries drain a major area of the Moors. East Dart Head (the source of a river on the Moors is known as the 'head') lies a couple of miles to the north of West Dart Head. The two rivers leave the high moorland at Postbridge and Two Bridges respectively and flow through shallow valleys bordered by ancient farm holdings.

At Dartmeet the East Dart flows past Badgers Holt to unite with the West Dart just beyond the road bridge. Then, as the 'double Dart', the river tumbles on its boulder-strewn path, past New Bridge and Holne to Buckfastleigh.

In 1240 the two rivers were referred to as *Derta* and *aliam Derta*, the Dart and the other Dart; by the 17th century they had become Easter and Wester Dart; the name Dartmeet does not appear until 1616.

Dartmoor

The southernmost national park in Britain, Dartmoor covers an area of 365 square miles and rises to a height of over 2,000ft. Attitudes to it have changed from the 16th century when William Camden described Dartmoor as 'Squalida Montana'. Today it is guarded by the National Park Authority and the watchdogs of the Dartmoor Preservation Association as an area of 'outstanding natural beauty' and the 'last great southern wilderness'.

The A30 and the A38 delineate the boundaries of Dartmoor, north and south, the distance between Okehampton and Ivybridge being 26 miles; within lies a great dome-shaped mass of granite. 250 million years ago this was molten magma which cooled and cracked at great depth. The overlying blankets of sedimentary rocks have been eroded to expose raw granite, weathered and etched into monstrous piles and weird shapes, the famous Dartmoor tors, which crown many a hilltop.

In more recent geological time, the last 16,000 years, peat beds have grown from the debris of old vegetation, covering large areas of the high moor like a black sponge; this natural reservoir feeds the rivers which radiate off the moor.

Dartmoor has long enjoyed a reputation for its dampness. One of Devon's first topographical writers, John Hooker, wrote: 'this one thinge is to be observed that all yere through out commonly it rayneth or it is fowle wether in that more or desert' (*Synopsis Chronographical of Devonshire*, c1599). The annual rainfall is indeed high, 60in, twice that of the Devon Riviera at nearby Torbay, and parts of the most exposed westerly fringes of the moor average as much as 100in per year.

Despite such disparaging statistics, by the 19th century the wild beauty of Dartmoor was attracting poets and painters, writers and other visitors.

Scattered over the moor is a rich hoard of prehistoric remains that have survived largely thanks to the durability of granite as a building stone. Bronze Age settlers divided up the moor between themselves; the complexity of their network of long low banks or *reaves* is now scarcely understood. They cleared much of the forest and built hut-circles (those at Grimspound are particularly impressive); their culture demanded ceremonial stone circles, stone rows, menhirs and burial cists (the Stall Moor–Greenhill row may be the longest prehistoric stone row in the world).

As the climate deteriorated during the Iron Age, the population living on Dartmoor decreased. The Britons circled it with hill-forts; the Anglo-Saxons began to people its valleys and built the first long houses, a style of house design that persisted until the 17th century. King John retained the heart of the moor as a royal forest or hunting ground until 1204.

There is considerable evidence for the piecemeal re-settlement of the moor during the medieval period. Several of the farms around Postbridge, for example, are still working within the ancient tenements carved out of the wild moor in the 13th century; but for a vivid impression of life and work on Dartmoor at that time, the deserted medieval village at Houndtor is the place to visit.

From the 12th to the 20th century tin has been extracted from the moors. Medieval tin 'streamers' dug over nearly every valley floor; their Tudor successors opened up vast gullies and drove adits into the hillsides. Sir Walter Raleigh, a Lord Warden of the Stannaries (tin mines), described the Dartmoor tinners as 'the roughest and most mutinous men in England'. In the 18th century vertical shafts were dug and around the moorland fringe lead, copper, iron and arsenic were all mined. The moorland scenery has been pock-marked and battered by such industry, but the scars, now healed and covered by bracken and heather, can be read to reveal a rich palimpsest of man's activity.

Granite for building was initially lying about in such abundance on the surface, conveniently broken into manageable chunks, that no

quarrying was necessary. As demand increased for high-quality stone of specific dimensions, so quarries were opened. Dartmoor provided stone for Nelson's Column, many of the Thames bridges, including the former London Bridge transported to Arizona in 1970, and more recently for the Holborn Viaduct and New Scotland Yard.

The 18th century brought agricultural improvers to Devon, optimistically intent on developing the farming economy of the moor. Intending to demonstrate the scientific management of stock, they built new farms and began to enclose great chunks with dry stone walls. These 'newtakes' can often be seen, the enclosed ground still rough moorland pasture. The efforts of these men encouraged other entrepreneurs to invest in the moor. Turnpike Trusts were established and the first roads built. Previously transport had been on foot or by horse, following rough tracks, with well-worn routes marked by crosses; now carts, wagons and coaches could cross the wilderness.

During the 19th century an increasing number of visitors began to explore Dartmoor. Hotels were opened in Chagford and Moretonhampstead and guides offered their services to lead parties to places of interest. The first of the Dartmoor letter-boxes was placed at Cranmere Pool in 1854, and by 1908 the visitors' book collected 1,741 signatures in a year. At the same time the army was taking a growing interest in the moor as a training ground and local authorities were planning reservoirs in moorland valleys.

Such conflicts of interest led to the formation of the Dartmoor Preservation Association in 1883, initially to protect antiquities, rights of way and common rights, but increasingly it has played a wider role and is now fighting for the protection of the moor as a whole.

The various natural habitats on the moor are home to numerous species of flora and fauna. Lichens appreciate the unpolluted air and the white tassels of bog-cotton wave in the wind on the high moor; heather, whortleberry, bracken, gorse and tough grasses cover the hills, with broad-leaved woodland in the more sheltered valleys. Much of this natural vegetation is carefully managed, by selective burning and grazing, to prevent dominant species from taking over.

Golden plover and dunlin breed on the blanket bog and woodlark on the moorland fringes; many other birds can be spotted and summer walkers will find the air filled with the sound of birdsong, mostly skylark and pipits, with the occasional bubbling curlew.

Dartmoor ponies have been around on the moor since the 10th century at least, when they were mentioned in the will of the Saxon bishop, Aelfwold of Crediton. Apart from the annual autumn drifts, when they are rounded up and branded, they live wild off the poor moorland vegetation, surviving the atrocious winter weather. The cattle most commonly seen are the hardy black or dun-coloured Galloways and the belted Galloways with a distinctive white band around their middles. True Dartmoor white-faced sheep have been largely displaced by northern mountain breeds like the shaggy Blackface and Cheviot, whose breeding ewes can spend the winter on the moor.

The National Park Authority has produced a number of excellent publications for visitors requiring more specific details of aspects of Dartmoor. There are information centres at Tavistock, Princetown, Okehampton, New Bridge, Postbridge and Steps Bridge, useful for local information and often the starting points for guided walks. The Authority's headquarters are at Parke, near Bovey Tracey.

N.B. The Ministry of Defence uses some 33,000 acres of Dartmoor for training, mostly on the northern part of the moor. Access is available over most of the area at weekends, but before planning a route into a training area, be sure to check the firing times. Red flags are used to warn the public when firing ranges are in use.

Several typical views of Dartmoor, with (in the background) Haytor Rocks, the most accessible of the moor's jagged tors. Dartmoor is now a place of wild, sparsely-populated and mostly uncultivated beauty, but it was not always so: few places in southern England have so many prehistoric remains

Two Lovers of Dartmoor

There are few names as highly respected when it comes to writing about Dartmoor as that of William Crossing. Although it is almost 60 years since he died in Plymouth, the town of his birth, his books remain as popular as ever, a fitting tribute to his life's work.

Despite plans for him to follow in his family's footsteps in the sailcloth trade, the call of the moor was dominant in his life and he devoted himself to the exploration and documentation of the great wilderness to the exclusion of almost everything else. Born in 1847, he published his first book, *The Ancient Crosses of Dartmoor*, in 1884; all his life he found it difficult to support himself and his wife Emma, despite the later success of *One Hundred Years on Dartmoor* (1901) and *Gems in a Granite Setting* (1905). His life's work was brought to fruition in the massive and comprehensive *Guide to Dartmoor* (1909) which remains one of the authoritative guides to the moor today. He died in 1928 after suffering from crippling arthritis for many years, brought on by the rains and mists of his beloved moor. He is buried with his wife in Mary Tavy churchyard.

A contemporary of Crossing, but famed for his pictorial rather than written records of Dartmoor is Robert Burnard who, with his father Charles, was a founder member of the Dartmoor Preservation Association. He was among the first to realise that if Dartmoor were unprotected it would be lost to the ravages of time, a sentiment fiercely defended by his granddaughter Lady Sylvia Sayer. Burnard's photographs, dating from the early days of that science, were published in four volumes between 1890 and 1894 at his own expense, in limited editions of no more than 200.

Blackerton, one of Dartmoor's ancient crosses

Dartmouth and Kingswear

Map Ref: 93SX8751

Both towns are dramatically sited on the steep hillsides rising on either side of the estuary about a mile from the mouth of the River Dart. Houses cling to the slopes, tier above tier, forming a backdrop to the boating activity offshore.

Kingswear – on the west bank – is the railway terminus and embarkation point for the ferry between the two towns.

On the opposite bank, Dartmouth has expanded on to flat land along the valley side. Behind the church in the old part of town original cottages remain, perched one above the other and linked by almost vertical cobbled steps. The New Quay was constructed in the 16th century and the New Ground, north of the little enclosed harbour, in the 17th century.

The town was well-established as a port by the 12th century when both the Second and Third Crusades assembled and departed from here, and there was considerable trade with Bordeaux and Spain, wine being the chief import. Two houses, incredibly, survive from the 14th century – Agincourt House at Lower Ferry and The Cherub in Higher Street.

Bayards Cove gives the best impression of the old river front; the cobbled quay was used as the film set for *The Onedin Line*. The Pilgrim Fathers put in to this quay en route from Southampton to the New World in the *Mayflower* and the *Speedwell*. They rested a while then set off again on 20 August 1620; 300 miles west of Land's End they realised that the *Speedwell* was unseaworthy and hastily put back to Plymouth, leaving the *Mayflower* to sail alone and eventually arrive at Cape Cod on 21 November.

The artillery fort at the southern end of the Cove was built in 1509–10 by the Dartmouth Corporation as additional protection for the harbour. Behind the fort narrow and precipitous steps climb up to Newcomen Road, named after Thomas Newcomen, inventor

Dartmouth Castle guards the estuary

14th-century iron leopards grace the south door of St Saviour's, Dartmouth

of the steam pumping engine, who was born in Dartmouth in 1663. A working example of one of his engines can be seen in the Engine House by the Mayor's Avenue car park.

The main shopping street, Duke Street, leads into Victoria Street. The Butterwalk, shaded under a timber-framed arcade, was built in 1635–40; it was badly damaged by bombs in 1943, but has been beautifully reinstated. Encrusted with wood carvings, it is jettied, four storeys high.

There are impressive castles towards the mouth on both sides of the estuary which protected the deep water anchorage; a chain could be drawn between them in times of war. Dartmouth Castle was begun in 1481, and was one of the first castles to be designed for artillery.

The harbour remains alive with a busy fishing fleet, the ferries, numerous pleasure boats and cruisers, and particularly as the on-the-spot training ground for the Royal Naval College which was opened in 1905 and overlooks Dartmouth.

AA recommends:
Hotels: Dart Marina, Sandquay, 3-star, *tel.* (08043) 2580
Royal Castle, 11 The Quay, 2-star, *tel.* (08043) 2397
Royle House, Mount Boone, 2-star, *tel.* (08043) 3649
Stoke Lodge, Cinders Ln, Stoke Fleming, (2m S A379), 2-star, *tel.* (0803) 770523
Restaurant: Carved Angel, 2 South Embankment, 2-fork, 1-rosette, *tel.* (08043) 2465
Self Catering: Britannia Cottage, and Longford Cottage Mews, *tel.* (080425) 389
Redwalls (Flats 1-3, 5, 6 & 8), Townstal Rd, *tel.* (08043) 4222
Second Flat, *tel.* (08043) 4585
Guesthouse: Orleans, 24 South Town, *tel.* (08043) 2967
Campsites: Deer Park Holiday Estates, Stoke Fleming, (2m S A379), 3-pennant, *tel.* (0803) 770253
Little Cotton Caravan Park, Little Cotton, 2-pennant, *tel.* (08043) 25581
Garages: Dartmouth Mtrs, Mayors Av, *tel.* (08043) 2134
Premier, Dartmouth Rd, Stoke Fleming, *tel.* (0803) 770324
Townstal Road (Dennings), Townstal Rd, *tel.* (08043) 2610

On the Exe estuary at Dawlish

Dawlish

Map Ref: 93SX9676

A pretty seaside resort, once genteel and select enough to have attracted both Jane Austen and Charles Dickens. The first houses were not built on the Strand until 1803, but within a few years the sea front, cliffs and valley sides were transformed by neat rows of sedate villas and boarding-houses.

The sea is hidden from view by the railway which arrived in 1846. Brunel's line follows the coast from the Exe estuary right down to Newton Abbot, and here it crosses the seafront on a granite viaduct, with an arch leading to the beach. The station itself is a fine period-piece, an attraction in its own right.

The beach, over a mile long, is a mixture of sand and red shingle; on either side craggy red cliffs rise almost vertically from the sea and present constant hazards to the railway as chunks frequently collapse during the winter storms.

The old village was up by the church, nearly a mile inland, to be safe from raiders; a handful of thatched cottages survive. Elsewhere the gracious villas are white-painted with decorative wrought iron on balconies.

AA recommends:
Hotels: Langstone Cliff, Dawlish Warren (1½m NE off A379 Exeter Rd), 3-star, *tel.* (0626) 865155
Charlton House, Exeter Rd, 2-star, *tel.* (0626) 863260
Self Catering: Gaycourt Holiday Flats, 8 Marine Pde, *tel.* (0626) 862846
High Trees (flats), *tel.* (0626) 863113
Lisburne Holiday Flats, Westcliffe, *tel.* (0626) 863385
Oak Park House (flats), *tel.* (0626) 863113
Guesthouses: Broxmore Private Hotel, *tel.* (0626) 863602
Lynbridge Private Hotel, *tel.* (0626) 862352
Mimosa, *tel.* (0626) 863283
Radfords Hotel, *tel.* (0626) 863322
Campsites: Lady's Mile Farm, (1m N off

A379), 3-pennant, tel. (0626) 863411
Peppermint Park, Warren Rd, 3-pennant,
tel. (0626) 863436
Garages: Dawlish Mtrs, Richmond Pl,
Dawlish Rd, tel. (0626) 862113
Marine, Exeter Rd, tel. (0626) 863298

Dawlish Warren

Map Ref: 93SX9878

The Warren is a sandy spit that
extends over a mile across the
mouth of the Exe estuary, almost
blocking the river's exit to the sea.
It is a wild area today, bleak and
windy in the winter but perfect on
a sultry summer's day.

All the amenities are near the
railway station – campsites, caravan
parks, ice cream vendors, pubs and
hotels, as well as seaside gift shops
bulging with buckets and rubber
rings – but even on the busiest days
there is plenty of room for
everyone and the crowds rapidly
thin out towards the northern end
of the spit.

Two miles north, at the village of
Starcross, Brunel's old pumping
house has been opened to the
public to show his invention of the
atmospheric railway. Brunel
thought that locomotives alone
might not be able to haul trains up
the steep inclines of the South
Devon Railway between Newton
Abbot and Exeter. He devised an
atmospheric system for the track,
consisting of a continuous pipe, laid
between the rails, in which ran a
piston fitted to the leading vehicle
of the train; pumping houses at
regular intervals along the line
sucked the air out of the pipe,
forming a vacuum. The exhibition
includes a working model, using
vacuum cleaners to represent the
pumping houses, and amazingly a
volunteer visitor is propelled up and
down the track to demonstrate the
efficacy of the invention.

In reality the system was beset
with problems, not least that of rats
chewing the leather seals on the
pipes, and in 1848 it was
abandoned, with losses in the region
of £½ million.

Dulverton

Map Ref: 87SS9127

Dulverton shelters in the deeply cut
and wooded valley of the River
Barle, on the boundary between the
wilds of the high moors and the
gentler rounded countryside of
Haddon Hill and the Brendon Hills
to the north.

At the top of Bank Street, All
Saints Church overlooks the little
town and the valley through its
lych-gate. At the opposite end of
the town, down by the river, the
old workhouse has been converted
into the headquarters of the
Exmoor National Park. There is an
information centre here.

AA recommends:
Hotels: Carnarvon Arms, Brashford,
3-star, tel. (0398) 23302
Ashwick House, 2-red-star, tel. (0398)
23868
Three Acres Captain's Country, 2-star,
tel. (0398) 23426
Self Catering: John Fowler Holidays, tel.
(0271) 66666
Garage: Stuart Fords, Unit 14, Exbridge
Ind Est, tel. (0398) 23025

Dunster

Map Ref: 87SS9943

The village sits under wooded hills
at the head of the beautiful Avill
valley, dominated by the
battlements of Dunster Castle. The
main street is unusually wide, with
the Yarn Market at one end, built
in 1609 by George Luttrell; here
local cloth, described as a soft
kersey, called Dunsters was sold. At
the opposite end of the street, the
road narrows to squeeze past the
old Nunnery, a 15th-century
building, jettied and tile-hung. In
between, the shops cater
predominantly for the seasonal
influx of visitors.

The 15th-century priory church
of St George has a superb wagon
roof and is famous for its tuneful
bells. The 13th-century dovecote
belonged to the Priory; it is a
circular stone building with a
revolving wooden ladder inside to
give access to the 500 or so nesting
holes built into the walls.

Dunster Castle on its wooded hill

The known history of Dunster
Castle begins after the Norman
Conquest when the manor was
granted to William de Mohun.

The castle was held by the
Mohuns until 1376, when it was
sold to Lady Elizabeth Luttrell. For
600 years it remained with the
Luttrells, who finally gave the castle
to the National Trust in 1976.
Very little, if any, of the Norman
masonry is visible today. The oldest
part is the entrance gateway within
the splendid gatehouse, dating from
the time of Henry III. Most of the
fortifications were demolished after
the Civil War, and the living
accommodation was remodelled in
the second half of the 19th century.

On a neighbouring hill called
Conygar (the old coney-warren of
the castle), another tower rises from
the woods. It is a folly, designed in
1776 for the Luttrells by Richard
Phelps; the expenses for building it
included £54 for the workmen's
cider.

Below the castle, at the end of
Mill Lane, is Dunster Water Mill.
This is an original 17th-century
working mill with unique twin
overshot wheels; stone-ground
whole wheat flour is for sale.

AA recommends:
Hotels: Luttrell Arms, High St, 3-star,
tel. (0643) 821555
Exmoor House, 2-star, tel. (0643) 821268
Self Catering: Clover Cottage, 3 St
George Street, tel. (0643) 862233
Garages: Luttrell Arms, The Steep, tel.
(0643) 821284
Pikes Mtr Repairs, 9 St Georges Street,
tel. (0643) 821237

Exeter

Map Ref: 90SX9292

The county capital of Devon and mother-city of south-western England, modern Exeter is the thriving administrative and cultural centre for the region.

The site was occupied 200 years or so before the arrival of the Romans, when the line of the present High Street was already established as part of an ancient ridgeway. The inhabitants, the Dumnonii, were tribal Celts who named the river *Eisca*, a river abounding in fish. Isca Dumnoniorum clearly appealed to General Vespasian; the Roman settlement was on a plateau 100ft above the lowest ford across the river, a natural boundary on the west. Trading vessels could negotiate the river to a landing place at a convenient break in the cliffs, where the Custom House now stands.

The Romans imposed a grid-iron street plan on the plateau and surrounded the settlement first with a bank, and later with a wall – fragments of the Roman wall can still be seen in several places, topped and buttressed by later medieval reinforcements. They built a great bath-house, excavated in the 1970s at the west end of the cathedral, a basilica and market place.

An abbey was founded in 670 by King Cenwealh, on the site of the present cathedral, and several of the small red sandstone churches that dot the centre of Exeter are of Saxon foundation – St Martin squeezed into the corner of the Cathedral Close, St Petrock slightly askew on the High Street and St Olave. In the 9th century the Danes ransacked the growing city, but were thrown out by Alfred, who improved the defences and established a mint.

In 1050 Bishop Leofric transferred his see from Crediton to Exeter, and the abbey, rebuilt after the Danish attack, became a cathedral.

A plaque on the wine shop in Longbrook Street commemorates William the Conqueror's siege of the city. The Normans quickly took command and built a castle – Rougemont – on the volcanic hill at the north-east corner of the walled city; the towering gateway still stands at the top of Castle Street.

Most of the Norman cathedral was completed by 1206. The present building dates predominantly from the 14th century, although the Chapter House and Lady Chapel are earlier. The choir stalls have superb misericord carvings – one shows a crocodile swallowing its prey, another an elephant between a monk and a crusader. In the nave the clustered piers rise like trees in a forest to spread, 60ft up, into fans of fine masonry. The gallery of sculpture in the niches on the west

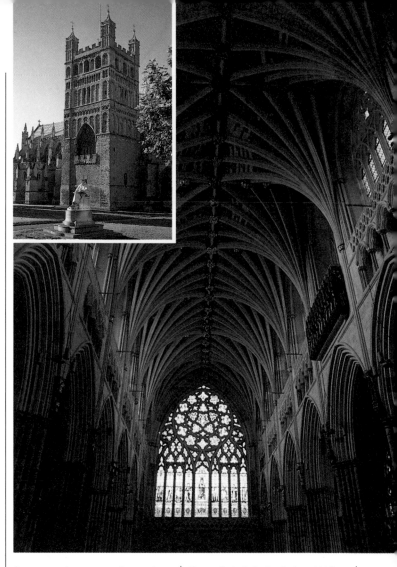

Exeter Cathedral: the glorious 300ft view down the nave, and (top) one Richard Hooker sitting reading his Bible in front of the North tower

front, netted to protect the carvings from pigeon droppings, reads like a Saxon and Norman *Who's Who* – Alfred, Athelstan, Canute, Ethelbert, William.

Cathedral Close is a pleasant green encircled by buildings in a delightful array of architectural styles from medieval to modern. There are ancient arched doorways revealing glimpses of private courtyard gardens and secluded corners of mellow red brick adorned with wistaria and ivy.

Other buildings round the city recall the extent and character of medieval Exeter, with its thriving cloth trade and wine imports. The Guildhall on the High Street is one of the oldest municipal buildings in the country. The hall was built in 1330, though remodelled in the 15th century, the arched and braced roof timbers resting on carved bosses of bears holding staves. The portico over the pavement is Elizabethan. Civic silver fills a cabinet in the gallery and the walls are hung with portraits of Exeter worthies; at the back are the old cells. Beyond the Guildhall a pedestrianised shopping precinct surrounds St Pancras Church.

Beneath the city centre a rat-run of underground passages was constructed in the 14th and 15th centuries to bring water into the city from springs outside the walls. The entrance, near the top of Princesshay, resembles that of the

nearby public lavatories – but visitors are welcomed and can explore the stone-vaulted caverns with a guide.

Stepcote Hill, the cobbled and stepped medieval way into the city, climbs steeply up beside St Mary Steps Church; until 1778 this was the main road into Exeter from the west. Facing the church is the timber-framed Tudor building, 'The House that Moved'; in 1961 it was in the way of a new road, so was strapped and jacked and rolled to its present site to preserve it for posterity.

From Stepcote Hill it is a short distance to the Quay. After the downfall of the Courtenays in 1538 the city fathers made every effort to restore Exeter's position as a sea-port; in 1564 work began on the canal. The impressive Custom House was built in 1681.

The old fishmarket, at the water's edge, now shelters a lifeboat, just one of a world-wide extended family of boats collected and displayed by the Exeter Maritime Museum. On this side of the quay boat sheds house Portuguese working boats; the ferry then transports visitors across the Exe to the principal exhibition area. The collection includes a junk and a sampan, dhows and coracles, Brunel's dredger from Bridgwater and a steam launch. The great pleasure of the museum is that visitors are not only encouraged to touch, but may also scramble about on board many of the vessels.

Two other museums are a must: the Royal Albert Memorial Museum in Queen Street, the city museum with collections of archaeology, local history, Exeter silver and paintings; and Rougemont House, by the castle, a museum of costume and lace, opened in 1987.

AA recommends:
Hotels: Buckerell Lodge Crest, 3-star, *tel.* (0392) 52451
St Olaves Court, 3-star, *tel.* (0392) 217736
White Hart, 3-star, *tel.* (0392) 79897
Granada Lodge, *tel.* (0392) 74044
Restaurant: The Old Mill, Ide, *tel.* (0392) 74044
Self Catering: 72 Barrack Rd, 1 Denmark Rd, 18 Watermore Ct, *tel.* (0392) 71668
CC Ref 7098L, *tel.* (0392) 77001
Lafrowda, University of Exeter, *tel.* (0392) 3508
Guesthouses: Park View, 8 Howell Rd, *tel.* (0392) 71772
Sunnymede, 24 New North Rd, *tel.* (0392) 73844
Sylvania, Pennsylvania Rd, *tel.* (0392) 75583
Westholme, 85 Heavitree Rd, *tel.* (0392) 71878
Garages: Dunns Mtrs, Trusham Rd, *tel.* (0392) 77311 (day), (0392) 67293 (night)
Reid & Lee, Marsh Barton Rd, *tel.* (0392) 34851 (day), (0392) 34856 (night)
UBM Ford, Marsh Barton Rd, *tel.* (0392) 50141

This is a selection of establishments; see page 4.

The Mayor of Exeter presents prizes at the Craft Fair in the Cathedral Close; (bottom) the old bridge spanning the river at Exford

Exeter's Maritime Museum

From a modest collection of 23 vessels at its inception in the 1960s, the Maritime Museum at Exeter has grown into a splendid assembly of over 130 craft of all shapes, sizes and countries of origin. Housed among the ancient buildings that surround Exeter's quay, only a few minutes' walk from the city centre, the Museum is open all year, except for Christmas Day.

It is not only in the historic warehouses that the collection is to be found, although this is where the smaller craft can be seen, such as dug-out canoes from Africa and the flimsy craft from the Pacific. In the canal basin itself are moored fascinating examples of maritime craft, many of which can be boarded and explored by visitors. One of the best loved is the oldest working steam vessel in the world, *Bertha*. She was designed by Isambard Kingdom Brunel, built in Bristol in 1844 and spent her entire life until 1964 dredging mud from Bridgwater Docks. Another favourite is *St Canute*, a large Danish harbour tug, ice-breaker and fire float. An Arabian dhow, a Hong Kong junk, a Venetian gondola and the exotically named and coloured Portuguese Moliceiro and Xavega can all be seen. Small craft can be hired and there are trips by launch down the canal; hours can be spent here by all ages both learning from and enjoying the many exhibits. The warehouses once formed the backdrop for the television series *The Onedin Line* which was filmed here; now the whole quayside area is the subject of considerable improvement and sensitive development and is a delightful place that is one of Exeter's principal attractions.

Exford

Map Ref: 86SS8538

The geographical centre of the National Park establishes Exford's claim as the 'capital of Exmoor'. It is actually a pleasant village around an open triangular green.

It is at the hub of the Devon and Somerset hunting country; the staghounds are kennelled here and there are stables behind the Crown and White Horse hotels.

The church is set high on a hill, detached from the village. The base and shaft are all that are left of a Saxon cross in the churchyard. The church dates largely from the 16th century, when great improvements were made by the rector, George Elsworthy. The 15th-century rood screen was originally in St Audries Church near Watchet; it was installed here in 1929. The choir stalls were brought from Queens' College, Cambridge.

By the churchyard gate, a stone marks the grave of Amos Cann; he was caught in a snowstorm in the winter of 1891 walking home from Porlock to Exford and froze to death – it was three weeks before his body was found.

AA recommends:
Hotel: Crown Hotel & Restaurant, 2-star, *tel.* (064383) 554
Self Catering: Westermill Farm Cottages, *tel.* (064383) 238
Guesthouse: Exmoor House, *tel.* (064383) 304
Campsite: Westermill, 1-pennant, *tel.* (064383) 238

Exminster

Map Ref: 90SX9487

Situated on the west bank of the River Exe below Exeter, Exminster looks out over the flood plain of the river valley towards the reed-fringed canal and beyond, to the attractive river-side town of Topsham.

The church, as one of the county's early minsters, was possibly founded in the 8th century as a collegiate church and it is recorded that St Boniface received some of his education here. The peal of eight bells ringing out from the church tower is one of the finest in Devon.

Three miles south east, as the river breaks out into the estuary, the tree-speckled deer park of the **Powderham Castle** estate fringes the shore; the Castle has been the home of the Courtenays, the Earls of Devon, since 1390. The original building was a manor house, fortified by the addition of four angle-towers. In the 18th century the place was transformed; major reconstruction took place, including the insertion of the grand staircase. There are some interesting family portraits, notably of Lady Honeywood and her son by the noted Devon artist, Sir Joshua Reynolds.

Exmoor

The county boundary between Devon and Somerset splits the bare plateau of Exmoor just at the point where the wild Doones once rampaged at Badgworthy Water. The northern edge of the moor plunges sheer and steep to the sea, producing some of the most magnificent coastal scenery in the country. More than 30 miles across from east to west and nearly 20 miles at its widest point north–south, it is an area of smoothly-moulded hills, reaching a surprisingly constant height of about 1,400ft; only at Dunkery Beacon – at 1,705ft the highest point – does a significant peak mark the skyline.

Unlike the other high moorland masses of the south-west, Exmoor is not a granite intrusion, but is made up of layers of hard sedimentary rocks, sandstones, slates and limestones. The formations can best be seen at the coast between Baggy Point and Minehead.

The hilltops are bleak with coarse grass, heather, bracken and gorse, but the deep valleys, sheltered from the storms, are lush and richly wooded with tumbling streams rushing to the coast.

The prehistoric remains on the moor are many and intriguing, their interpretation frequently fogged by legend and folklore; round barrows are numerous, and there are stone circles, enclosures and hill-forts. A standing stone at Winsford,

Malmsmead, tucked away in Exmoor scenery close to the Doone Country

inscribed *CARACTACI NEPUS*, is thought to be a memorial. The mecca for visitors is the low clapper bridge of uncertain date over the River Barle, Tarr Steps.

The mineral wealth of Exmoor has been exploited since the 13th century, if not earlier. Veins of iron, copper and manganese ores traverse the belt of country between the Brendon Hills in the east and Simonsbath. Gold was found in small quantities and silver-lead deposits were worked at Combe Martin.

Although the central and most barren part of the moor is known as the Forest of Exmoor, it was never wooded, the word forest being used here in its medieval sense to mean an open hunting ground; but attempts have been made to tame the moors. In 1819 John Knight acquired 10,000 acres of the moor for £50,000 and together with his sons optimistically set about improvements. He built a boundary wall 52 miles long, and started to deep-plough the south-facing slopes. He bought 400 West Highland cattle at Falkirk Fair and brought them home to Exmoor where they caused quite a stir, his son Frederic reporting: 'When we tried to drive 20 of them to market they started off in different directions, tossed and gored everybody they met, and were shot in fields all over the country. I have a short summary giving a list of the wounded.'

Frederic inherited the estate in 1841 and doggedly continued the task; he lived at Simonsbath. He laid plans for a canal, and work actually began on a mineral railway.

Homesteads were built, like miniature model farms: Larkbarrow, Warren, Pinkery, Honeymead and Emmett's Grange. The Knight family's most dramatic contribution to the Exmoor landscape was the planting of beech trees as windbreaks and beech hedges in the top of double-skinned walls, as shelters for cattle.

The Exmoor pony is thought to be a direct descendant of the wild horse that survived the Iron Age.

Visitors are asked to remember that despite the title 'National Park', the 265 square miles of Exmoor are predominantly privately owned. This means that although visitors enjoy considerable freedom to explore the open countryside, that freedom is dependent upon the public respecting the life of the countryside and the rights of those that make a living from it. Advice and information about Exmoor National Park are available from the Information Centre, Exmoor House, Dulverton.

Exmouth

Map Ref: 90SY0081

A traditional seaside resort with two miles of golden sands, Exmouth stands at the mouth of the Exe estuary, where the sea sweeps in round Straight Point. Half-submerged sands stretch from the Warren at the river mouth along the front at Exmouth leaving a narrow channel to be negotiated by vessels heading upstream to Topsham and Exeter, and a similarly narrow access to Exmouth's busy port.

At the centre of the Esplanade, the Diamond Jubilee Memorial clock tower is surrounded by floral displays and sheltered gardens. Behind the sandy beach are numerous amusements for children and a large pleasant green sward known as the Maer.

The docks at the town end of the Esplanade present a contrasting picture of towering cranes, warehouses, oily quays and dockland pubs. All cargo vessels must enter and leave the dock basin by a narrow channel like a short stretch of high-walled canal.

On the northern outskirts of the town, a fairy-tale thatched house, A-la-Ronde, was built in 1795 by Jane and Mary Parminter. It is not in fact round, but 16-sided, containing 20 rooms around a central octagon, 45ft high and modelled on a Byzantine basilica, and a gallery decorated with shells.

AA recommends:
Hotels: Devoncourt, 3-star, *tel.* (0395) 272277
Imperial, 3-star, *tel.* (0395) 274761
Royal Beacon, 3-star, *tel.* (0395) 264886
Aliston House, 1-star, *tel.* (0395) 274119
Self Catering: 76 Elmfield Cres, *tel.* (03955) 77001

Hartland Point's lighthouse (left) rises 350ft, its light visible for 20 miles. Hartland's 15th-century church is one of the loveliest in Devon

27 Linden Close, *tel.* (0395) 264189
Lovering Farm Cott. *tel.* (0395) 271661
Guesthouses: Blenheim, *tel.* (0395) 264230
Carlton Lodge Hotel, *tel.* (0395) 263314
Clinton House, *tel.* (0395) 271969
Quentance, (farmhouse), *tel.* (03954) 2733
Garages: Derek Adams, Dinan Way, *tel.* (0395) day 270133, night 264821
Belvedere Mtrs, Belvedere Rd, *tel.* (0395) 276610
Highfield Coachworks, Dinan Way, *tel.* (0395) 263381
Richards & Son, Victoria Way, *tel.* (0395) 266375

Hartland and Hartland Point

Map Ref: 84SS2625

At Hartland Point, the sharp-nosed north-west corner of Devon, the rolling hills meet the roaring Atlantic. To the south, jagged saw-edged black rocks jut out into the ocean, a fearful sight made even more so by the broken wreck of a large boat which still litters the foreshore. To the west, the steep cliffs are marked by the folded beds of the rock strata, forming weird whirls like the grain around the knot of a tree trunk.

From this 'Promontory of Hercules', as Ptolemy is said to have called it, Lundy can usually be seen, about 10 miles offshore. There is a weekly helicopter service for visitors to the island in the summer. The lighthouse dates from 1874.

The little town of **Hartland** is sensibly sited inland, sheltered from the salt spray, if not from the gales. It is a pleasant place of low cottages lining the one main street leading to a small square. The Parish Church is a couple of miles west towards the coast, at the tiny hamlet of Stoke, and is well worth visiting;

the tower, 128ft high including the pinnacles, was tall enough to be seen over the surrounding hills and must have been a vital landmark to ships negotiating the Point before the lighthouse was built. The church is dedicated to St Nectan, a Welsh missionary, who was murdered here in the 6th century.

Hartland Quay is at the end of the road, a wild and bleak spot on a stormy day, but the Hartland Quay Hotel offers a warm welcome.

AA recommends:
Hotel: Hartland Quay, I-star, *tel.* (02374) 218
Self Catering: West Titchberry Farm (cottage), *tel.* (02374) 287
Guesthouse: Fosfelle, *tel.* (02734) 273
Garage: Heards, *tel.* (02734) 233

Holsworthy

Map Ref: 88SS3404

A busy market town serving a wide area of rural Devon in the north-west corner of the county. It stands at the centre of a remarkably undeveloped region, an ancient and

bleak landscape of tight lanes and rolling hills dotted with isolated farms and hamlets of cottages.

At the corner of Fry Street a plaque commemorates the Great Tree of Holsworthy, from which, by Royal Charter given in 1154, the annual proclamation of St Peter's Fair is made; the Fair is held in July. Another custom associated with Holsworthy is the Pretty Maid Ceremony: in 1841 a sum of money was left so that a single local woman, under the age of 30 and noted for her looks, quietness and attendance at church, could be given a small financial award.

The porch of the Parish Church of St Peter and St Paul has a Norman niche and a carving of a lamb with a cross. Inside, there is a particularly fine organ, built by Renatus Harris.

AA recommends:
Self Catering: Thorne Farm, *tel.* (0409) 253342
Guesthouses: Coles Mill, *tel.* (0409) 253313
Leworthy (farmhouse), *tel.* (0409) 253488

Holsworthy and its viaduct

Honiton

Map Ref: 91ST1600

Were it not for the bypass, the monstrous traffic of the 20th century might well have stifled Honiton; but today the broad main street, nearly 2 miles long, is a delight to explore with a pleasing variety of small shops, cafés, town houses and cottages.

Honiton was the first of the great serge manufacturing towns in Devon and there was a flourishing woollen industry in the 17th and 18th centuries. From Elizabethan times it was notable for the manufacture of fine lace, a technique introduced by Flemish refugees. Exquisite and delicate examples of old lace can be seen in the town's museum, and in the Museum of Costume and Lace at Rougemont House, Exeter. In the main street the Honiton Lace Shop has modern work for sale, together with bobbins, cottons and manuals on how to do-it-yourself.

Demonstrations of the centuries-old craft of Honiton lace-making take place in Allballows Museum; (below) bustling Ilfracombe harbour, a rare safe haven on Devon's dangerous north coast

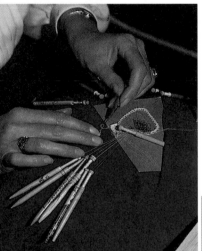

AA recommends:
Hotels: Deer Park, Weston, (2½m W off A30), 3-star, country-house hotel, *tel.* (0404) 2064
New Dolphin, High St, 2-star, *tel.* (0404) 2377
Guesthouses: Hill House Country Hotel, Combe Raleigh, (2m NE unclass rd), *tel.* (0404) 3371
Roebuck (farmhouse), *tel.* (0404) 2225
Monkton Court, Monkton (inn), (2m E A30), *tel.* (0404) 2309
Garages: Hillside, King St, *tel.* (0404) 2389
Honiton Auto Diagnostics, Exeter Auto Elec Ltd, Unit B3, Reme Drive, Heathpark Trad Est, *tel.* (0404) 41260
Reads, Monkton Rd, *tel.* (0404) 44291

Ilfracombe

Map Ref: 85SS5247

'Grandest old place in the world it be,
Dear old Ilfracombe by the sea.'

Between the great Iron Age cliff castle of Hillsborough and the seven hills of the Torrs, Ilfracombe is set in a basin with just two openings through the high cliffs to the sea; its growth has been controlled by this relief, with the old town sheltered in the bottom of the basin and terraces of guest-houses, hotels and cottages following the contours of the surrounding slopes.

St Nicholas Chapel on Lantern Hill above the harbour was built in the early 14th century as a landmark for mariners and a votive chapel for fishermen and sailors. Below on the pier the Lifeboat House, first opened in 1828, welcomes visitors; the boots and waterproofs of the crew are strung up like washing from the roof.

The town is well equipped with amenities – an indoor swimming pool, excellent golf course, the Pavilion Theatre and the usual variety of seaside entertainments – but it has not been overrun by tourism. It retains a style fitting its late Victorian and Edwardian growth. Characteristically, the museum, by Runnymede Gardens, includes exotic collections of ethnographic material carted back to Ilfracombe by retired colonials – a coiled cobra and alligator skin sit side-by-side with local carpentry tools and flat-irons.

AA recommends:
Hotels: Cliff Hydro, Hillsborough Rd, 3-star, *tel.* (0271) 63606
Langleigh Country, Langleigh Rd, 2-star, *tel.* (0271) 62629
Tracy House, Belmont Rd, 2-star, *tel.* (0271) 63933
Self Catering: High Gables, St Brannocks Rd, *tel.* (0271) 62861
Harbour Heights, 12 Hillsborough Terrace, *tel.* (0271) 64011
Guesthouses: Cresta, Torrs Park, *tel.* (0271) 63742
Merlin Court, Torrs Park, *tel.* (0271) 62697
Sunnyhill, Lincombe, *tel.* (0271) 62953
Westwell, Torrs Park, *tel.* (0271) 62792
Campsite: Big Meadow Camping Site, 1-pennant, *tel.* (0271) 62282
Garage: Robins, Northfield Rd; *tel.* day (0271) 62454; night (0271) 63414

This is a selection of establishments; see page 4.

Kingsbridge

Map Ref: 93SX7344

The capital of the South Hams, 'the frutefullest part of all Devonshire', Kingsbridge crests a spur of land at the head of a five-mile navigable inlet of the sea; Kingsbridge estuary, so-called, is properly a ria or drowned valley.

St Edmund's Church, towards the top of Fore Street, behind the Shambles, is largely 13th-century.

Just above the junction with Duncombe Street the Cookworthy Museum is housed in the old Grammar School endowed by Thomas Crispin; the school was opened in 1670 and admitted 12 boys 'in suits of grey frieze cloth'. The museum is named after William Cookworthy, a Quaker, who was born in Kingsbridge in 1705. He worked as an apothecary in Plymouth where he met traders from the Far East who brought back porcelain from China. He identified the china clays of Cornwall as 'kaolin', the basic ingredient of porcelain, and succeeded in making the first true English hard paste porcelain.

At Woodleigh, just off the B3196, the Woodland Trust manages a stretch of woods on the banks of the River Avon. It includes Woodleigh, Titcombe and part of Bedlime Woods, with the disused railway line from South Brent to Kingsbridge running alongside.

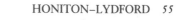

AA recommends:
Hotels: Buckland-Tout-Saints, Goveton, (2½m NE on unclass rd), 3-star, country house hotel, *tel.* (0548) 3055
King's Arms, Fore St, 2-star, *tel.* (0548) 2071
Rockwood, Embankment Rd, 2-star, *tel.* (0548) 2480
Saddlers, Embankment Rd, 2-star, *tel.* (0548) 2520
Self Catering: Little Melbury, 126 Church St (cottage), *tel.* (054884) 2883
Stanbrook Court, 114 Fore St (cottage), *tel.* (0548) 6959
Guesthouses: Ashleigh House, Ashleigh Rd, Westville, *tel.* (0548) 2893
Harbour Lights Hotel, Ebrington St, *tel.* (0548) 2418
Campsite: Island Lodge Farm, Slade Cross, Ledstone, (1½m N off A381), 1-pennant, *tel.* (0548) 2956
Garage: The Quay, *tel.* (0548) 2323

Lundy

Map Ref: 84SS1445

Twelve miles north of Hartland Point, 23 miles west of Ilfracombe, Lundy forms a breakwater in the teeth of the westerly winds which whip up the Bristol Channel. It is a lump of granite rock 3½ miles long and ½ mile across, with cliffs rising almost vertically from the shore to 400 or 500ft.

The name Lundy comes from the Norse word *Lunde* meaning puffin; the suffix *ey*, from the same language, means island.

The island was often used as a pirate hideaway. From here in the 12th century the Marisco family – who built the Keep – terrorised the neighbouring coasts until William de Marisco was caught with 16 of his followers and they were hanged, drawn and quartered. The island then became Crown property with various governors. In 1610 the self-styled King of Lundy was Captain Salkeld, a pirate who made daily attacks on merchants in the channel. The island was occupied by the Turks for 14 days in 1625, then raided by the French, who tricked the islanders by carrying their weapons ashore hidden in a coffin.

In the 19th century the quarries legitimately supplied granite for the construction of the Victoria Embankment and Charing Cross Hotel in London. Lundy was then owned by the Heaven family, and became known as 'the Kingdom of Heaven'.

Today the island boasts a hotel, Millcombe House, built by the Heavens in the 1830s, a pub, the Marisco Tavern, and the church of St Helena. There are a number of cottages, a small campsite and the lighthouses, one at each end of the island. Lundy is owned by the National Trust but leased to the Landmark Trust.

Apart from puffins, more than 400 different birds have been spotted on the island. Black rats live on Rat Island, next to the landing stage; deer, sheep, rabbits and Lundy ponies occupy the main island. The flora is equally rich, with wild flowers in abundance and the famous Lundy cabbage.

Day trips to Lundy can be taken from Ilfracombe and Bideford; those wishing to stay longer should be sure to book accommodation well in advance.

Lydford

Map Ref: 88SX5185

A quiet, unprepossessing village on the western edge of Dartmoor. This was the most westerly outpost and fortified burgh of the kingdom of Wessex under Alfred the Great. The town was never walled, but protected by a massive earth rampart across the neck of the promontory between the River Lyd and its tributary, forming a defensive site of great strategic importance.

Soon after the Norman Conquest the site was refortified by the building of a fort to the west of the church, but this was short-lived and the present castle dates from 1195. The great square stone keep was not built on a mound, as it appears, but had earth piled up against its walls at some later date. It was constructed for the custody of those who broke the strict forest and stannary laws. The Court was held on the second floor, while prisoners were kept below.

On either side of the castle are the pub and the church, dedicated to the Celtic missionary St Petroc, who may have built a timber church on this site in the 7th century. The font is Saxon or early Norman. Beside the porch the grave of the local watchmaker, George

Lydford: the path through the spectacular gorge passes some of Devon's loveliest woodland scenery; (top) its 12th-century castle and wheelwright's stone

Routleigh (died 1802) carries the epitaph that his life was 'wound up/in hope of being taken in hand/by his Maker/And of being thoroughlye cleaned repaired/And set agoing/in the World to come'.

The street pattern of the village follows the Saxon grid, with buildings in local grey slate, more reminiscent of a Cornish town. It was used as the film location for *The Hound of the Baskervilles* a few years ago, and the butcher has kept the antiqued film-set shop sign over his window. Outside the shop the inscribed granite slab housed a tap with the first piped drinking water supply, brought to the village by Daniel Radford in 1881.

South of the village, the River Lyd has cut dramatically into the rock to form a spectacular gorge, 1½ miles long. Access is from the stable block of Bridge House or further down the valley at the waterfall entrance. The bed of the stream has been potholed by swirling boulders carried by the flood waters and drilled into the channel, creating features like the Devil's Cauldron, just by Lydford Bridge. At the far end, the White Lady Waterfall illustrates the geographical process of river capture in a spray-showered 100ft drop.

AA recommends:
Hotel: Lydford House, 2-star, country-house hotel, *tel.* (082282) 347
Guesthouses: Castle (inn), *tel.* (082282) 242
Dartmoor (inn), *tel.* (082282) 221
Campsite: Pulborough Farm Caravan & Camping Park, The Croft, 2-pennant, *tel.* (082282) 275

Lynton and Lynmouth

Map Ref: 86SS7149/SS7249

Lynton crowns the brow of the great cliff, 600ft high, above its sister village of Lynmouth on the shore far below.

The two villages are linked by a zig-zag road and by the cliff railway, the gift of Sir George Newnes, the publisher and newspaper magnate. The railway, opened in 1890, is a hair-raising feat of engineering which allows two carriages, counterbalanced by watertanks, to ascend and descend over 900ft on a gradient of 1 in 1¾.

Lynton is a bright airy village, mainly Victorian, with terraces of boarding-houses and small hotels. The Exmoor Museum, housed in a restored 16th-century house, St Vincent's Cottage, displays the tools and products of former local craftsmen.

A mile west of Lynton in the Valley of Rocks, Jan Ridd in *Lorna Doone* visited Mother Meldrun, sheltering 'under eaves of lichened rock . . . within the Devil's Cheesering'. The valley is a natural gorge between two ridges of hills 'covered with huge stones and fragments of stone among the fern . . . the very bones and skeletons of the earth; rock reeling upon rock, stone piled upon stone, a huge terrific mass' (Robert Southey).

Lynmouth is picturesquely situated at the junction of the East and West Lyn where they meet the sea in a deep cleft between cliffs rising on either side to over 800ft. Gainsborough described it as 'the most delightful place for a landscape painter this country can boast' and the poet Southey enthused over the scenery – the 'English Switzerland'. Tragically, the position of the village was its undoing when on 16 August 1952 torrential rain on Exmoor choked the rivers and unleashed a fearful flood, carrying debris, boulders and tree trunks, that pounded the village through the hours of darkness, leaving a community shattered by the desolation and loss of life.

Another storm back in 1899 also caused Lynmouth to hit the headlines. On this occasion a full-

The charming village of Lynmouth has recovered from its 1952 disaster (right)

rigged ship, the *Forest Hall*, was in difficulties off Porlock, but the seas at Lynmouth did not allow the lifeboat to be launched from there. So the decision was taken to haul the lifeboat, *Louisa*, the 13 miles to Porlock. It took 10½ hours to negotiate the route, a party going ahead to widen the road; the 3½ ton boat had to be pushed and dragged and cursed up the 1 in 4 slope of Countisbury Hill, then down Porlock Hill on the other side. Thanks to the effort, the ship's crew was saved.

AA recommends:
LYNMOUTH
Hotels: Tors, 3-star, *tel.* (0598) 53236
Bath, 2-star, *tel.* (0598) 52238
Rising Sun, 2-star, *tel.* (0598) 53223
Rock House, 1-star, *tel.* (0598) 53508
Shelley's Cottage, 1-star, *tel.* (0598) 53219
Guesthouses: Countisbury Lodge Hotel, *tel.* (0598) 52388
East Lyn, *tel.* (0598) 52540
Glenville, *tel.* (0598) 52202
Heatherville, *tel.* (0598) 52327
LYNTON
Hotels: Hewitts, 2-star, *tel.* (0598) 52293
Castle Hill House, 1-star, *tel.* (0598) 52291
Neubia House, 1-star, *tel.* (0598) 52309
North Cliff Hotel, 1-star, *tel.* (0598) 52357
Self Catering: Oaklands, *tel.* (0598) 52344
Guesthouses: Gordon House Hotel, *tel.* (0598) 53203
Longmead House, *tel.* (0598) 52523
Lynhurst Hotel, *tel.* (0598) 52241
Southcliff, *tel.* (0598) 53328
Campsites: Channel View Caravan Park, 3-pennant, *tel.* (0598) 53349
Six Acre Caravan Park, 3-pennant, *tel.* (0598) 53384
Sunny Lyn Caravan Site, 2-pennant, *tel.* (0598) 53224
Garages: Granville, 41 Lee Rd, *tel.* (0598) 52513
Prideaux, Lee Rd, *tel.* day (0598) 3338; night (0598) 2587

This is a selection of establishments; see page 4

Moretonhampstead

Map Ref: 89SX7586

The gateway to Dartmoor from the east, Moretonhampstead is a hilltop town with the church tower marking the skyline. The cottages are close-packed around Fore Street and Cross Street and the heart of the town, and they fall away

quickly on all sides to reveal a patchwork of open fields and hedgerows, with the stark mass of the moors proper beyond.

In Cross Street, Mearsdon Manor was built in the early 14th century by Sir Philip Courtenay, Earl of Devon. The doorway and screens passage appear original and the interior bursts with beams; it is now a tea-room and gallery with local pictures, brassware and oriental ornaments. Beside the rector's short cut to the church, the 'Dancing Tree' grows out of a granite walled plinth. This tree is but a sapling, planted to replace an ancient elm, carefully pollarded to allow a platform for dancing to be fixed on high days and holidays. R D Blackmore describes in *Christowell* 'the most lively and dissipated' (of these festivities) 'being in the town of Moreton' and he pictured young people 'frisking among the verdure without dread of dewy feet or toes stuck in a mole-hill'. In fact it was probably the musicians who played on the platform, whilst the dancers frolicked in the street below.

At the end of the street the Almshouses, with mullioned windows and unusual granite arcade, are dated 1637.

AA recommends:
Hotels: Glebe House, North Bovey, 2-star country-house hotel, *tel.* (0647) 40544
White Hart, 2-star, *tel.* (0647) 40406
Guesthouses: Cookshayes, 33 Court Rd, *tel.* (0647) 40374
Elmfield, Station Rd, *tel.* (0647) 40327
Garage: Court Street, *tel.* (0647) 40225

Living history at Morwellham Quay

Mortehoe

Map Ref: 85SS4545

Sheltering just under the brow of the ridge that forms Morte Point, the northern horn of Morte Bay, the little village is scarcely protected from the fierce westerlies. Its character is derived from the grey rock on which it is built, Morte slate, and most of the older buildings are constructed from it.

The Church of St Mary's is largely unrestored. Its greatest treasures are the 16th-century carved bench ends depicting sea monsters, coats of arms, portraits and the instruments of the Passion.

The coast here is scattered with treacherous rocks.

AA recommends:
Hotel: Glenhaven, Chapel Hill, 1 star, *tel.* (0271) 870376
Self Catering: Priors Cottage, *tel.* (0271) 813885
Guesthouses: Baycliff Hotel, Chapel Hill, *tel.* (0271) 870393
Haven, *tel.* (0271) 870426
Sunnycliffe Hotel, *tel.* (0271) 870597
Campsites: Easewall Farm, 3-pennant, *tel.* (0271) 870225
Twitchen House & Mortehoe Caravan Park, 3-pennant, *tel.* (0271) 870476
Garage: Mortehoe, *tel.* (0271) 870354

Morwellham

Map Ref: 92SX4469

Only 20 years ago Morwellham was slowly disintegrating, overgrown by brambles and forgotten. Then in 1970 a Trust was founded with the purpose of restoring the quay and the buildings to their former glory,

and today the site is a fascinating example of living history.

Deep in the valley of the River Tamar, Morwellham was the nearest point to Tavistock which sea-going ships could reach; so a port developed for the export of tin and copper ore. In the early 19th century a canal was built to link the town with the port. Morwellham's boom-time came in 1844 when much larger quantities of copper were found five miles north at Blanchdown.

At that time, an investment of £1 in the Devonshire Great Consolidated Copper Mining Company rocketed to a value of £800 only two years later. But like all booms it eventually ended in loss and decay.

Today the place is brought to life by friendly staff in costumes of the 1860s who will chat at the fireside in the assayer's house, demonstrate the traditional crafts of the smith and cooper in their refurbished workshops or just take the part of a sailor for a posed photo on the water-front. There are pigs in the sty behind the miner's cottage, and a Victorian farm, complete with shire horses, just up the hill. A miniature railway carries visitors deep underground into the copper mine, last worked in 1868, where tableaux depict the grim realities of a miner's life.

Elsewhere there are traditional museum displays, an audio-visual show and horse and carriage rides along the Duke of Bedford's drive. The greatest copper port in Queen Victoria's empire has, most successfully, been brought back to life.

Newton Abbot

Map Ref: 93SX8671

At the head of the Teign Estuary, Newton Abbot straddles the River Lemon, which enters the Teign just below the town. Fishing has been both popular pastime and commercial activity:
'The Teign for Salmon, the Dart for Peel,
Fort Leat for Trout and the Lemon for Eel.'

The symbol and centre of the town, the ancient tower of St Leonard, is at the crossroads of Courtenay Street, East Street, Bank Street and Wolborough Street; the chapel that once adjoined it was demolished in 1836. Beside the tower, the first declaration of William III, Prince of Orange, 'the glorious defender of the Protestant religion and the liberties of England', was read in November 1688, as he made his way from Brixham to London. Prince William stayed at Forde House.

At the south-east corner of the town Forde House was built on an E-shaped plan by Sir Richard Reynell in 1610, adjoining an

earlier manorial house.

Bradley Manor, at the other end of the town in a secluded woodland setting, dates from the 13th century; it is now owned by the National Trust.

Newton Abbot has long been a route centre – first on the main road between Exeter and Dartmouth; later the Stover Canal brought granite from Haytor and ball clay from the Bovey Basin through the town; and in 1846, the railway arrived. Newton's position at the head of the estuary and at the meeting place of several valleys made it a natural junction, and branch lines were opened to Torbay (1848) and Moretonhampstead (1866–1959). The town became the centre of the GWR locomotive and carriage repair works, employing more than 600 people.

Much of the town was laid out at this time to house the railway workforce in neat terraces. More stylish Italianate villas were planned and built in Courtenay Park and Devon Square by the Courtenays who owned much of the site.

AA recommends:
Hotels: Globe, Courtenay St, 3-star, *tel.* (0626) 54106
Queens, Queens St, 2-star, *tel.* (0626) 63133
Hazelwood House, 33A Torquay Rd, 1-star, *tel.* (0626) 66130
Self Catering: CC Ref 460L, (cottage), *tel.* (03955) 77001
Guesthouse: Lamorna, Exeter Rd, Coombe Cross, Sandygate, (3m N A380), *tel.* (0626) 65627
Campsites: Dornafield, Two Mile Oak, 4-pennant, *tel.* (0803) 812732
Stover International Caravan Park, Lower Staple Hill, 4-pennant, *tel.* (0626) 82446
Garages: A J Blacker, Kingsteignton Rd, *tel.* (0626) 68322
Highweek, Ringslade Rd, *tel.* (0626) 4702
PCC Motor Bodies, 9 Milbur Trad Est, *tel.* (0626) 67555
Renwicks, The Avenue, *tel.* (0626) 2641
Station, Quay Ter, *tel.* (0626) 60504
Wadham Stringer, Wolborough St, *tel.* (0626) 4141

Newton Abbot: only the tower remains of the medieval Church of St Leonard

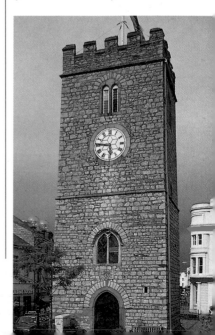

Oare

Map Ref: 86SS8047

A remote hamlet popularised by R D Blackmore in his great tale of Exmoor, *Lorna Doone*. Enthusiasts will search in vain for Plover Barrows Farm, the home of John Ridd, but the diminutive square-towered church attracts visitors as numerous as pilgrims to the shrine of a saint. Here, in the novel, Lorna, in her wedding dress of 'pure white, clouded with faint lavender', was shot by Carver Doone – just as poor John was about to kiss her 'as the bridegroom is allowed to do, and encouraged, if he needs it'. The church has a simple memorial to Blackmore, a portrait in a medallion.

Oare is surrounded by mile after mile of rolling moorland; a wild landscape in winter but a delight for walkers and naturalists at other times of the year. Doone Valley and Badgworthy Water, despite their ominous roles in the story, are gorgeous – rough grassland, a blaze of purple heather, bright yellow gorse and wind-twisted trees.

Okehampton

Map Ref: 88SX5895

The town is on the main road, the A30, between Exeter and Launceston, and eagerly awaits the bypass which will relieve the centre of memorable traffic jams. To the south Dartmoor rises abruptly to its two highest peaks, High Willhays and Yes Tor, both over 2,000ft. At Okehampton the wild moors break into tamed countryside.

Okehampton Castle, on the southern outskirts, commanded the road to Cornwall. The ruins are romantically placed on a high knoll in the steep, deep and wooded valley of the West Okement. The square keep towers over the remnants of the great hall and kitchen with its two ovens, the walls battered and broken.

In the main street the Chapel of St James was built by Sir Reginald Courtenay as a chantry chapel in the 12th century. The Town Hall, in Fore Street, is an impressive three-storey building erected in

A miniature water wheel at the Finch Foundry Museum near Okehampton

1685 as a town house for John Northmore; it was converted to its present use in 1821. On the opposite side of the road a pleasant cobbled courtyard and adjacent buildings are being restored as the Museum of Dartmoor Life with adjoining Tourist Information Centre; the museum is housed appropriately in an agricultural mill and warehouse, built in 1811. The exhibits include geology and archaeology, as well as relics of the tin and copper mines, quarrying and farming. One of the noted Dartmoor letter-boxes is here, for stamping souvenir postcards.

Three miles east, on the A30 at Sticklepath, the Finch Foundry Museum presents a fascinating glimpse of industrial life in Devon. From 1814 until 1960 the finest edged tools in the west of England were made here under the earth-shuddering blows of the trip hammers. All the machinery, restored to working order, is powered by three water wheels, through a Heath Robinson system of wheels, pulleys and belts.

AA recommends:
Guesthouse: Hughslade (farmhouse), *tel.* (0837) 2883
Garage: Yestor S/Sta (G McCullock & Sons), East St, *tel.* (0837) 2163

Ottery St Mary

Map Ref: 91SY1095

Surrounded by the gently rolling countryside of east Devon, Ottery St Mary is a charming unspoilt country town, prosperous and bustling but pleasantly off the main roads. It is sited on the east side of the broad valley of the River Otter. The town's streets are narrow and twisting and full of character, despite the usual saga of disastrous fires that swept away much of the medieval building in the 18th and 19th centuries.

Around the church, and especially opposite its east end at the top of Cornhill, are some of the finest Georgian houses – the Priory is a classic, in rich red brick with white paint-work.

The glory of Ottery, though, must remain the Church of St Mary, set up on a hill overlooking the town and the river valley. It began as an ordinary parish church in the 13th century, but was radically restructured by John de Grandisson, Bishop of Exeter, between 1338 and 1342. His work converted it into a cathedral in miniature, the focus of 'a sanctuary for piety and learning'; the college consisted of 40 members including eight choristers and a master of grammar.

Inside the church, the canopied tombs of Sir Otto and Lady Beatrix de Grandisson, who died in 1359 and 1374 respectively, are impressive, as are the altar screen,

Ottery St Mary's exquisite church

Lady Chapel and coloured carved bosses in the roof. An ancient clock mechanism ticks steadily in the south transept.

At the Dissolution much of Bishop Grandisson's creation was destroyed, but the school was refounded as The King's New Grammar School. In the mid-18th century the Rev John Coleridge was appointed Master of the School, later also becoming vicar; he produced 13 children by two wives, the youngest being Samuel Taylor (1772–1834), the poet and philosopher. The bronze plaque – with his profile and looming albatross – in the churchyard wall commemorates Samuel's childhood in the town.

AA recommends:
Hotel: Salston, 3-star, *tel.* (040481) 2310
Restaurant: Lodge, 17 Silver St, 2-fork, 1-rosette, *tel.* (040481) 2356
Self Catering: CC Ref 7667L (cottage), *tel.* (03955) 77001
Guesthouses: Fluxton Farm Hotel, Fluxton, *tel.* (040481) 2818
Pitt Farm, *tel.* (040481) 2439
Garages: Riverside Mtrs, Exeter Rd, *tel.* (040481) 3016
C H Salter & Son, 9-11 Alansway, Finnimore Trad Est, *tel.* (040481) 2054

Paignton

Map Ref: 93SX8960

The great sweep of Torbay stretches from Hope's Nose in the north to Berry Head in the south; Paignton lies at the centre of the bay, facing east, straight out to sea. It is sheltered on the landward side by the rich rolling countryside of south-east Devon with its fiery-red soil.

Saxon colonists founded a village here and by the Norman Conquest it was in the possession of the Bishop of Exeter, who had a palace here near the church. Surviving

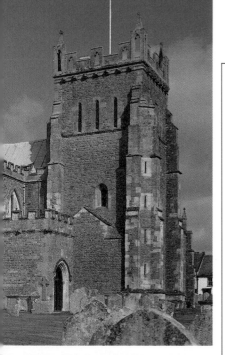

Steam Trains

Although British Rail ran its last steam train in 1968, south Devon is fortunate in having two completely separate lines where, during the summer months, travel by steam power need not be a thing of the past. The Dart Valley Railway, which runs from Buckfastleigh to Totnes, and the Torbay and Dartmouth Railway, between Paignton and Kingswear, have both been immaculately restored to recall the days of the famous Great Western Railway.

Opened originally in 1872 and 1864 respectively, they each cover approximately seven miles of track. The Dart Valley Railway was closed by the Beeching cuts in 1962 and ironically enough was reopened by the same Dr Beeching in 1969, after lengthy negotiations between the Dart Valley Light Railway Company and BR. In contrast, the Torbay and Dartmouth Railway never closed, simply transferring its ownership from BR to the DVLR, which runs both operations.

The coaches are painted in the famous GWR chocolate and cream livery, and so successfully has the period atmosphere been captured that several films and television series have featured the railways, among them *The French Lieutenant's Woman*, *The Hound of the Baskervilles*, *A Horseman Riding By* and *To Serve Them All My Days*. The two steam lines not only offer an opportunity for nostalgic travel, however, they also offer a practical means of transport since it is possible to connect with BR trains on both lines at Totnes and Paignton stations. What better way to enjoy some of south Devon's coastal scenery, or the wooded tranquillity of the Dart valley.

The harbour at Paignton, an oasis amid packed beaches and boarding houses

remnants of the medieval village can still be seen around the church, with 16th- and 17th-century cottages in Church Street and Kirkham Street. Kirkham House, open to the public, was the 15th-century home of a prosperous merchant or perhaps an official from the Bishop's palace.

A hundred years ago Paignton was described as 'a neat and improving village and bathing place' which had 'risen into notice as a place of resort for invalids during the last fifteen years, and is capable of being made a first-rate watering place . . .'. But it was still a farming parish, noted for its cider and its very large and sweet flatpole cabbages.

The railway reached the village in 1859, and from then on its success as a flourishing seaside resort was assured. New roads and new villas were built, not only for the summer visitors but also for an increasing number of permanent residents who chose to take advantage of Paignton's sheltered aspect and mild climate.

Paignton had one great asset over its popular and fashionable neighbour, Torquay, and that was (and is) its beach. In fact there are two beaches, separated by the appropriately named Redcliffe headland. The beaches provide safe, sandy bathing, ideal for families with young children; under the cliffs they are ruddy red, blending to gold in the flatter open stretches. A promenade, backed by lawns and gardens, borders the beaches, with the pier midway between Redcliffe and the harbour.

The little harbour at the southern end of the bay, tucked in under Roundham Head, was built in 1838. Although frequently packed with pleasure craft in the summer it remains a practical fishing harbour.

Not far from the centre of Paignton, Isaac Singer, founder of the Singer Sewing Machine empire, built the magnificent Oldway Mansion in 1874; it had 115 rooms and cost just £100,000. The mansion was originally a yellow brick villa, later extensively altered by Singer's son, Paris, in the style of Versailles. The marble staircase, incredible painted ceiling and gallery of mirrors date from this later period of reconstruction. At the same time neat formal gardens were laid out, with terraced lawns and box hedges to complete the grand design. Oldway is now used as council offices, but the best rooms and the gardens are open to the public.

At the top of Torbay Road, immediately opposite the Festival Theatre, a pair of old GWR iron gates mark the entrance to the Dart Valley Railway. From here the Torbay Express maintains a regular timetable of excursions, under steam, to Goodrington Sands, Churston and Kingswear.

AA recommends:
Hotels: Palace, Esplanade Rd, 3-star, *tel.* (0803) 555121
Redcliffe, Marine Dr, 3-star, *tel.* (0803) 526397
Seaford, 2-star, *tel.* (0803) 557341
Oldway Links, 1-star, *tel.* (0803) 559332
Self Catering: Barcombe Cottages, Old Torquay Rd, *tel.* (064722) 232
Casa Marina (flats), *tel.* (0803) 558334
Cranmore Lodge (flats), *tel.* (0803) 556278
South Eden Holiday Flats, Belle Vue Rd, *tel.* (0803) 558364
Guesthouses: Beresford, Adelphi Rd, *tel.* (0803) 551560
Clennon Valley, *tel.* (0803) 550304
Hotel Retreat, *tel.* (0803) 550596
Sea Verge, *tel.* (0803) 557795
Campsites: Beverley Parks Caravan & Camping Site, 5-pennant, *tel.* (0803) 843887
Byslades Camping Park, Totnes Rd, 3-pennant, *tel.* (0803) 555072
Lower Yalberton Farm & Caravan Camping Park, 3-pennant, *tel.* (0803) 558127
Widend Camping Park, Marldon, 3-pennant, *tel.* (0803) 550116
Garages: Perry's, Torquay Rd, *tel.* (0803) 522146
Rogers, Bishops Pl, *tel.* (0803) 556234
N. Snowden & Sons, Totnes Rd, *tel.* (0803) 559362

Plymouth in its incomparable setting; on the Hoe are the Armada Memorial and Smeaton's 1759 Lighthouse, while Drake (right) still scans the seas

Plymouth

Map Ref: 92SX4755

The largest conurbation in Devon, modern Plymouth is the amalgamation of three towns – Devonport, furthest west on the bank of the River Tamar, Stonehouse in the middle, and Plymouth itself in the east bordering Sutton Pool. Between the estuaries of the Tamar and the Plym, the Sound is one of the finest deepwater anchorages in Europe, and visually the most magnificent.

Unfortunately the Sound suffered from exposure to the prevailing south-westerly winds, and for many years Dartmouth harbour was favoured by the skippers of sailing vessels. The breakwater in Plymouth Sound was not completed until 1847. Nevertheless, from the 13th century the harbour was used increasingly as a place of assembly for military expeditions and for ships employed in the French wine trade.

In the 16th century the patronage of Plymouth by both Sir Francis Drake and Sir John Hawkins established the port's supremacy. It was from Plymouth that Drake sailed on 19 July 1588 to defeat the Spanish Armada, and it was on Plymouth Hoe, close to where his statue now stands, that he played his celebrated game of bowls.

New Street, in the area of the city known as the Barbican (after that part of the old castle) dates from this period; even the stone road surface is listed as being of historic importance. Timber-framed and jettied houses hang over the road on either side; one, the Elizabethan House, is open.

The Barbican is packed with historical associations, as listed on the quayside in a collection of commemorative plaques. Most famously, in 1620 the *Mayflower* departed to found New Plymouth after an evening's hospitality for the Pilgrims in the Island House at the quay-end of New Street, where a board lists the names of all who sailed in her.

Opposite the old Pannier Market in Southside Street visitors are welcome to tour the Plymouth Gin Distillery; the premises include the 15th-century Refectory of the Black Friars Monastery.

Towering over the old quay and dominating the seaward elevation of the Hoe is the Royal Citadel, built in 1666. It is a huge fortress with great angular walls forming bastions and gun positions. Its main gateway, dated 1670, is one of the best examples of baroque architecture in the country. Since 1962 the Citadel has been occupied by 29 Commando Royal Artillery, so access is restricted to officially-guided tours. There is a lot to see: the Royal Chapel of St Katherine, the 17th-century Governor's House.

From the breezy promenade of the Hoe, or better still from the top of Smeaton's Tower (an earlier Eddystone lighthouse re-erected here) the view to the south extends beyond the breakwater to the open sea between Penlee Point on the Cornish side, and Heybrook Bay in the east. Drake's Island, in the foreground, was fortified in the 16th century and has since been used as a prison; it is now an adventure-training centre.

To the north, the modern city is arranged in the rigid formality of a grid, the inspiration of post-war planners attempting to revive the commercial centre after the horrific destruction of the air raids in the spring of 1941. Two miraculous survivals amid the concrete and tarmac are Prysten House (15th-century) and the Merchant's House (16th-century), both open to the public, with exhibitions.

In Devonport a fascinating oasis in a desert of municipal housing centres on the Town Hall at the head of Ker Street. It was modelled on the Parthenon and built in 1823; a 100ft column commemorates the renaming of Plymouth Dock as Devonport on 1 January 1824; and the bizarre Egyptian House completes the group.

Modern Plymouth is very much a Navy town with walled enclosures surrounding many of the dockyards and supply stations; occasionally some of the ships can be visited.

Plympton, a couple of miles east of Plymouth, was the birthplace of Sir Joshua Reynolds. Several examples of his work can be seen at nearby Saltram House, just south of the A38, a mid 18th-century mansion embodying the remains of a Tudor house. The interior is rich in fine plasterwork and woodwork with two magnificent rooms by Robert Adam. In the great kitchen the brass pans sparkle like mirrors.

AA recommends:
Hotels: Mayflower Post House, Cliff Rd, The Hoe, 3-star, *tel.* (0752) 662828
Invicta, Osborne Pl, Lockyer St, 3-star, *tel.* (0752) 664997
New Continental, Millby Rd, 3-star, *tel.* (0752) 220782
Grosvenor, 2-star, *tel.* (0752) 260411
Restaurants: Chez Nous, 13 Frankfort Gate, 1-fork, *tel.* (0752) 266793
Clouds, 102 Tavistock Pl, 1-fork, *tel.* (0752) 262567
Self Catering: Breckon House, 20 Connaught Avenue, and Buckley Quarry, Plymstock, *tel.* (0752) 669066
Kobe House, 14a Alexandra Rd, Mutley, *tel.* (0752) 669066
Guesthouses: Chester, 54 Stuart Rd, Pennycomequick, *tel.* (0752) 663706
Georgian House, Citadel Rd, The Hoe, *tel.* (0752) 663237
Lockyer House, 2 Alfred St, The Hoe, *tel.* (0752) 665755
Trillium, 4 Alfred St, The Hoe, *tel.* (0752) 670452
Campsite: Riverside Caravan Park, Plympton, 4-pennant, *tel.* (0752) 344122
Garages: Allens, Coburg St, *tel.* (0752) 668886

Robert Adam's 1768 Salon at Saltram House

The famous medieval packhorse bridge at Postbridge, made of colossal granite slabs

Chaddlewood, Plympton, *tel.* (0752) 338481
Turnbulls, Bretonside, *tel.* (0752) 667111
Wadham Stringer, Union St, *tel.* (0752) 263355

This is a selection of establishments; see page 4.

Porlock and Porlock Weir

Map Ref: 86SS8846

Porlock is enclosed on three sides by towering hills; on the seaward side it is bounded by the Marsh, confined by a broad crescent of grey shingle. Saxon kings chose this site as a base from which to hunt on Exmoor, and nowadays it serves as an ideal touring centre. Its sheltered position and mild climate create a paradise of flowers.

Porlock retains its old world charm and character with narrow winding streets, thatched roofs and tall rounded chimneys on sturdy square bases. The Church of St Dubricius, in the centre of the village, dates from the 13th century; the spire lost its top in a thunderstorm 350 years ago. Sir Simon FitzRoger, who contributed to the building of the church, lies in full armour under a richly carved canopy, and John Harrington, chiselled in alabaster, fought at Agincourt; his wife has a mitred head-dress with fine lace.

Porlock once had a harbour of its own, at a place the Saxons called 'the enclosure by the harbour', but now the harbour is 1¼ miles west, at the little village of **Porlock Weir**. The harbour was formed out of a natural creek and a quay was built in the last century, with a wall and lock gates to the east. It is a picturesque place, with coarse pebbles on the beach and bracken-covered hillsides.

A cliff path through delightful woods leads to Culbone, less than 2 miles from Porlock Weir, where there is a smattering of cottages and the smallest complete parish church in England – 35ft by 12ft. Culbone is a corruption of *Kil Beun*, the church of St Beuno, a noted Welsh saint of the 6th century.

From Porlock the road to Lynton rises 1,350ft in less than 3 miles – a notorious hill, particularly for those towing caravans.

AA recommends:
Hotels: Oaks, Doverhay, 2-star, *tel.* (0643) 862265
Ship Inn, High St, 1-star, *tel.* (0643) 862507
Guesthouses: Gables, *tel.* (0643) 862552
Lorna Doone, High St, *tel.* (0643) 862404
Overstream, Parson St, *tel.* (0643) 862421
Campsite: Porlock Caravan Park, 3-pennant, *tel.* (0643) 862269

Postbridge

Map Ref: 92SX6579

At the very heart of Dartmoor, Postbridge comprises a scattering of farms, a few cottages, an inn and a chapel. The moorland here is wild and windswept with great vistas of tussocky grass and gorse grazed by weather-beaten sheep. Postbridge is the frequent starting point and thirst-quenching finish for some of the moor's most arduous walks. It is about the closest road point to the Dartmoor letter-box hunter's goal of Cranmere Pool, and convenient for the heads of the East and West Dart and Teign.

Beside the road bridge over the East Dart the clapper bridge looks like a giant's plaything; the huge slabs of granite measure 15ft by 7ft, resting on four piers of granite blocks. The earliest reference to the bridge is in Britain's first road atlas of 1675 where it is marked as 'Post Stone Bridge, 3 arches', although almost certainly it is 14th-century.

About a mile south-west, at Powder Mills, a gunpowder factory was built in 1844 by George Frean, a Plymouth man. The site was suitably isolated and the Cherry Brook provided plenty of water power for his machinery. There were plenty of customers nearby, too, as gunpowder was used to blast the stone in the granite quarries. The business prospered until the 1890s when gunpowder was superseded by the invention of dynamite. The old chimney and ground-level flue can be seen, together with the ruins of the cottages where the manager and foreman lived.

Two miles from Postbridge towards Moretonhampstead, the Warren House Inn, one of the most isolated pubs in the country, is a popular walkers' rest.

Devon's Gardens

The county is blessed with many glorious gardens open to the public, some of which are attached to National Trust properties. Others – some quite small and perhaps open only a few times each year – are privately owned under the National Gardens Scheme. This charitable trust donates the funds it receives from the opening of gardens to the public to a variety of causes. It is not possible to include here all the gardens open under this scheme, but a booklet listing them is obtainable from the National Gardens Scheme, 59 Lower Belgrave Street, London SW1W 0LR.

Gardens owned by the National Trust include those at Killerton, near Exeter, which boasts 15 acres of splendid walks; Knightshayes Court at Tiverton; Saltram House at Plymouth, with a total of 300 acres of landscaped garden; Castle Drogo at Drewsteignton, the last castle to be built in England, designed by Sir Edwin Lutyens; and the charming garden at Coleton Fishacre near Kingswear, which was planted with rare and exotic shrubs by Lady Dorothy D'Oyly Carte.

Other prominent gardens include those at Dartington Hall, with the splendid tiltyard and sculpture by Henry Moore; Bicton Park, with its fine orangery, woodland railway and countryside museum; and Tapeley Park at Instow which has a beautiful Italian garden.

Over two centuries, a great arboretum has been created at Killerton Garden

Rural Skills

The centuries-old country crafts which shaped and maintained Devon's landscape and rural buildings were largely taken for granted until the current trend towards conservation pinpointed a decline in these skills. For example, it was proving increasingly difficult for Dartmoor National Park to find craftsmen to assist in its programme of preservation of the countryside. As a result, the Devon Rural Skills Trust was set up in 1981 to draw attention to the plight of these crafts and to pass them on from practising craftsmen to anyone who is keen to learn.

Weekends are held to teach such skills as dry stone-walling, hedge laying, thatching, slating, cob wall-building, hay-rick making, leather-working, cane and wickerwork and wheel making. Some craftsmen have even been persuaded to come out of retirement to pass on their skills, such is the urgency of the situation perceived to be, and in the belief that it is far better to learn such a skill from the intimate knowledge of a practising craftsman of many years' standing, rather than try to pick it up from a sketchy outline described in a book. The teaching of these crafts is not a romantic notion, but an entirely practical one which has developed to meet a growing need.

The Trust produces a register which lists the skills of its members; it is a registered charity and is therefore always in need of donations. Anyone interested in finding out more should contact The Organiser, Devon Rural Skills Trust, c/o The Old Vestry, Lustleigh, Devon TQ13 9TD; tel. (06477) 455.

Dry stone-walling at Widecombe

Prawle Point

Map Ref: 93SX7735

From the little village of East Prawle a single track lane twists and turns through high-hedged fields to a convenient car park about half a mile from the Point; this is the southernmost extremity of Devon, flanked by some of the finest stretches of coastal scenery. From here the South-West Coastal Footpath heads east to Lannacombe and Start Point and west to Gara Rock and East Portlemouth, almost entirely under the auspices of the National Trust.

The Point, lashed by the full fury of the waves in stormy weather, has been chiselled and chipped into an almost vertical drop beneath the Coastguard look-out station.

A row of coastguard cottages follows the line of an earlier cliff, cut when the sea was several metres higher than its present level; the raised beach feature can clearly be seen towards the east where it has become a gently sloping green sward of close-cropped grass.

Princetown

Map Ref: 92SX5873

A bleak, grey, barren place, surrounded by wild, open moorland; an ideal spot for a prison, but even the warders' houses are laid out in a regimented and unfriendly way.

Princetown was named after the Prince of Wales (later George IV), because it and most of Dartmoor form part of the estates of the Duchy of Cornwall. In 1785, Thomas Tyrwhitt leased a large area of the moor from the Duchy hoping to convert it into good farmland. He encouraged settlement and in 1806 suggested that a prison

be built here to house the large number of French captured during the Napoleonic Wars.

The prison was completed in 1809 and soon incarcerated 9,000 French soldiers; later it was used for American prisoners taken during the war of 1812–14.

Prisoners built the parish church, a strange, drab building with square-cut pillars and extraordinarily narrow aisles. The Tricolor, Stars and Stripes and Union Jack at the west end serve to remind visitors of all those who have worshipped and suffered at Princetown. In the graveyard the tall granite cross is a memorial to all those prisoners whose bodies lie in unmarked graves; since about 1900 prisoners' graves have been marked with their initials and date of death on serried ranks of small stones.

After the war with America, the prison remained empty and the town was deserted until 1852, when the prison was revived for civil offenders.

Salcombe

Map Ref: 93SX7338

Devon's southernmost resort, boasting a superbly mild climate. The port shelters on the steep west bank of the Kingsbridge estuary, scarcely a mile from the open sea. In fact the river here is not an estuary, but a ria or drowned river valley.

For centuries Salcombe was a fishing town with a handful of shipwrights' yards and a scatter of cottages clinging to the valley slopes; the event of the year was the Whitsun fair. Towards the end of the 18th century visitors and those seeking quiet retirement sought out

Salcombe: fishermen's and yachtsmen's paradise

Salcombe, a development spurred on by the arrival of the railway at Kingsbridge in 1893.

A fishing fleet still works from the fish quay in Batson Creek, where the lobster pots are piled high, and the muddy reach between Island Street and the car park is lined with boat yards.

Salcombe's museum of maritime and local history at Custom House Quay illustrates local trades and industry and also contains mementoes from the Second World War battle training ground at Slapton. About a mile away at Sharpitor the National Trust has a museum of ships and shipbuilding within the exotic gardens at Overbecks.

Seaton's open-top trams are popular with visitors; (below) working exhibit at Alscott Farm Museum, Shebbear, a wonderful place for a family day out

AA recommends:
Hotels: Bolt Head, 3-star, *tel.* (054884) 3751
Soar Mill Cove, Malborough, 3-star, *tel.* (0548) 561566,
South Sands, 3-star, *tel.* (054884) 3741
Tides Reach, South Sands, 3-star, *tel.* (054884) 3466
Self Catering: Melbury Cottage, *tel.* (054884) 2883
Guesthouses: Bay View Hotel, Bennett Rd, *tel.* (054884) 2238
Charborough House Hotel, Devon Rd, *tel.* (054884) 2260
Devon Tor Private Hotel, Devon Rd, *tel.* (054884) 3106
Woodgrange Private Hotel, Devon Rd, *tel.* (054884) 2439
Campsite: Alston Farm Camping & Caravanning Site, Malborough, Kingsbridge, 3-pennant, *tel.* (0548) 561260

This is a selection of establishments; see page 4.

Seaton

Map Ref: 91SY2490

A port of some significance developed at the mouth of the estuary when the River Axe more or less filled the valley, but by the 16th century a bar of stones and pebbles had built up, narrowing the river to a channel on the east side of the valley. John Leland described the fruitless efforts of the 'Men of Seton' to divert the course of the Axe; they tried to dig away the pebble ridge in order to re-establish their safe harbour for trading and fishing vessels. By the 17th century it was realised that further work was useless so a bank was built beside the marshes on the estuary to reclaim the ground and create fresh pasture land; that bank was later used for a branch railway and now the Seaton trams, a popular visitor attraction, run along it for a couple of miles before crossing the river and rising to the terminus at Colyton.

The beach, off the ridge, slopes steadily and steeply into the sea: a wonderful south-facing crescent backed by tall cliffs of red stone on one side and white chalk on the

other. The gardens and parks make up for any lack of monuments or impressive buildings.

AA recommends:
Self Catering: West Ridge (bungalow), Harepath Hill, *tel.* (0297) 22398
Guesthouses: Eyre House, Queen St, *tel.* (0297) 21455
Harbourside, 2 Trevelyan Rd, *tel.* (0297) 20085
Mariners Homestead, Esplanade, *tel.* (0297) 20560
St Margarets, 5 Seafield Rd, *tel.* (0297) 20462
Garage: Swallowdale Motor Co Ltd, 56 Harbour Rd, *tel.* (0297) 20450

Selworthy

Map Ref: 87SS9146

A picture-book village of well-tended, whitewashed cottages preserved by the National Trust as part of the Holnicote Estate. The village lies in the shelter of Selworthy Beacon, which rises to over 1,000ft; near the Beacon and overlooking Selworthy Combe is the circular hill-fort of Bury Castle.

The cottages were built in 1810 by the 10th Holnicote baronet, Sir Thomas Acland (1787–1891), as retirement homes for faithful retainers from the estate workforce. They are grouped picturesquely around a communal green with interconnecting paths and attractive planting. The hillside behind the village was planted with blocks of trees by Sir Thomas, each block celebrating the birth of one of his nine children.

Holnicote House, used as a holiday home by the Aclands, has burnt down three times since the end of the 18th century. Most of the estate was given to the National Trust in 1944 by Sir Richard Dyke Acland and the house is now used as a holiday centre.

The 15th-century church has a square embattled west tower and

possesses one of Devon's finest wagon roofs, richly decorated with angels, bosses, shields and symbols.

Shebbear

Map Ref: 88SS4309

In the middle of the triangle of main roads between Great Torrington, Holsworthy and Hatherleigh, Shebbear is a scattered village, set in this quiet corner of north-west Devon.

The great stone (weighing over a ton) lying under the gnarled oak tree at the church lych-gate, is said to mark the site of the Saxon Moot; but there is also a local superstition that the stone was dropped by the devil, as he descended from Heaven to Hell. Whatever its origin, a highlight of the calendar is the ritual on Guy Fawkes' night when the bellringers create a discordant jangle on the church bells and the stone is overturned with crowbars.

The Alscott Farm Museum, in the parish, presents a wonderful exhibition of historical farming implements, from steam traction engines to butter pats, all in the environs of a working farm.

AA recommends:
Self Catering: JFH C6C (bungalow), *tel.* (0271) 66666

Sidmouth

Map Ref: 91SY1287

On Christmas Eve 1819, the Duke and Duchess of Kent arrived in Sidmouth with their infant daughter, the Princess Victoria, to seek seclusion from the Duke's creditors. They were suffering from what he himself described as 'gilded poverty' and where better to retreat than this quiet seaside hamlet. The Kents stayed at Woolbrook Cottage, now known as the Royal Glen. The Duke died here in 1820 and the family returned to London. Victoria never revisited Sidmouth, but in 1866 she presented a stained-glass window to the parish church, in memory of her father.

Although Sidmouth has grown considerably since those days, it has retained much of its Regency style as well as a pleasant air of tranquil gentility. The mile-long Esplanade is backed by York Terrace, a stately row of balconied Georgian houses with iron-work railings and sparkling brass door knobs. Beach House, also on the Esplanade, is a perfect example of sea-front architecture of that period, painted strawberry pink and white, with coloured glass in leaded panes and a decorative balcony over the bow window.

From the 1780s Sidmouth was increasingly patronised by the wealthy, who built cottages in every sheltered spot with views over the bay; many have since been converted into hotels. As the town became more popular, terraces of lodging houses were built, like Clifton Place and Elysian Fields.

Sidmouth Museum portrays the Victorian resort; note the gruesome barber-surgeon's signboard, and the poor albatross's swollen foot, used as a tobacco pouch. The museum has an interesting collection of local prints, a costume gallery and a good display of exquisite lace.

For more than 30 years Sidmouth has played host to the remarkable International Folklore Dance and Song Festival, usually held in early August; it has become a cosmopolitan extravaganza of music and dancing tradition from all over the world.

AA recommends:

Hotels: Riviera, The Esplanade, 3-star, *tel.* (03955) 5201
Salcombe Hill House, Beatland Rd, 3-star, *tel.* (03955) 4697
Westcliff, Manor Rd, 3-star, *tel.* (03955) 3252
Little Court, Seafield Rd, 2-star, *tel.* (03955) 5279
Self Catering: Character Cottages Ltd, 34 Fore St, *tel.* (03955) 77001
Guesthouses: Canterbury, Salcombe Rd, *tel.* (03955) 3373
Ryton House, Winslade Rd, *tel.* (03955) 3981
Campsites: Kings Down Tail, 3-pennant, *tel.* (029780) 313
Oakdown, 3-pennant, *tel.* (03955) 3731
Salcombe Regis, 2-pennant, *tel.* (03955) 4303
Garages: Stevens Cross, Sidford, *tel.* (03955) 2889
Woolbrook, *tel.* day (03955) 2931; night (03955) 77089

This is a selection of establishments; see page 4.

Simonsbath

Map Ref: 86SS7739

The site, chosen by James Boevey, the first commoner to acquire the freehold of the Royal Forest of Exmoor in 1652, was at the meeting point of several moorland tracks and reasonably sheltered in the valley of the River Barle. Boevey began by building a house

Still a popular resort, Sidmouth is surrounded by lovely countryside

for himself, now the Simonsbath House Hotel; the date 1654 is cut into an oak beam above the old kitchen fireplace. At the Restoration, the property was returned to the Crown, but Boevey remained as tenant. Following his death, the house was used by wardens of the forest.

In 1819 John Knight from Worcestershire, an optimistic agricultural improver, successfully bid for the forest at auction, paying £50,000 for 10,000 acres. He took up residence at Simonsbath House in 1827, but immediately set about building a 'handsome residence' on rising ground behind the old house – it was never completed and the blank shell was demolished in 1900.

John's heir, Frederic, continued to strive for the improvement of the moor. He built houses and farms for the shepherds and tenant farmers; he improved the roads and constructed miles of walls and hedges; he planted thousands of beech trees as windbreaks. After Sir Frederic's only son died at the age of 28 in 1879, the mortified father lost interest in further developments.

Sir Frederic and Dame Florence share their tomb with Frederic junior in the moorland churchyard by St Luke's, the little church they had built in 1856.

There are a handful of cottages, a pottery and another hotel in the village and a National Park Information Centre by the old village school. Simonsbath is a walkers' paradise, with wild moorland on all sides and fold after fold of heather-clad hills.

AA recommends:

Hotel: Simonsbath House, 2-star, country-house hotel, *tel.* (064383) 259

Slapton

Map Ref: 93SX8245

The little stone-built village of Slapton is about ½ mile inland from Slapton Sands, so called, although they are in fact a shingle ridge extending north from Torcross for more than 2 miles. The ridge encloses a remarkable freshwater lake, Slapton Ley.

Slapton itself is an attractive village, sheltered in a hollow of the South Hams hills and renowned for the early production of garden crops.

Inside the main (north) porch of the church the Sanctuary Ring allowed a criminal to elude justice by claiming sanctuary under the canon law; he had to make his confession and then leave the kingdom by the shortest route to the coast. The church spire is medieval, dating from the 14th century.

The great tower north of the church, 80ft high and built of Charleton slate, is the most impressive remains of a College of Chantry Priests founded in 1373 by Sir Guy de Brien, Lord of the Manor and Steward to Edward III.

Slapton Ley has been designated a Site of Special Scientific Interest. The reed beds are a rare habitat in the south-west and attract visiting wildfowl to roost in the winter.

AA recommends:
Self Catering: Gara Mill (cottage, chalets & flat), *tel.* (0803) 770295
Campsite: Camping & Caravanning Club Site, Middle Grounds, 2 pennant, *tel.* (0548) 580538

Slapton Ley is rich in wildfowl, pike, roach and perch; the reeds are used for thatching

South Molton

Map Ref: 86SS7125

The town is set on a south-facing slope between the raw hills of Exmoor and the rich rolling pasture country of central eastern Devon, a natural market centre.

The focus of the town is Broad Street, an elongated town square running east–west. On the south side of the street the Town Hall (1740) is carried on four pillars over the pavement. The interior is particularly fine, the Council Chamber and Mayor's Parlour decorated with moulded plaster friezes and panels, the pride of the town. The South Molton Museum on the ground floor includes an unusual collection of pewter, exhibits of mining on Exmoor and two of the town's old fire engines.

The Church of St Mary Magdalene is like a small cathedral. In the Middle Ages it was made a bishopric, but no bishop was ever appointed. The great 15th-century tower rises 140ft, its belfry windows laced in stone tracery.

An unusual attraction is the Quince Honey Farm, just off the A361 west of the town centre. Through glass screens visitors can closely observe the world of the honey bee and see an extraordinary selection of nests in odd places – a letter-box, for instance.

AA recommends:
Hotel: Marsh Hall Country House, 2-star, country-house hotel, *tel.* (07695) 2666
Restaurant: Stumbles, 134 East St, 1-fork, *tel.* (07695) 3683
Garages: Central Park, 135 East St, *tel.* (07695) 2135
Michael Tucker, Horsepond Meadow, *tel.* (07695) 2373

Start Point

Map Ref: 93SX8337

The cliffs here are over 100ft high, on the south side almost sheer and streaked by quartz veins running through the dark rock. The path follows the northern and more sheltered side of the ridge to the lighthouse at the very tip. There are two lights, a brilliant revolving one, flashing one second every 20 seconds, to guide ships heading up the Channel; and a fixed light to direct those running in-shore to avoid the Skerries, a dangerous bank off the coast.

The coastal footpath north of Start Point passes the dejected ruins of the village of Hallsands where there were once 37 houses on a rocky ledge beneath the cliff, protected by a shingle foreshore. In the early years of this century a contractor was given permission to dredge the shingle offshore. The beach level gradually dropped, leaving the fated village exposed to the sea. A severe storm, in the winter of 1917, destroyed all but one of the houses.

Standing securely above the cliff, Trouts Hotel is a symbol of stoicism and sheer hard work by two sisters, Ella and Patience Trout. They lost their home in the 1917 storm, and in the same year rescued an American seaman from a sinking ship. Ella was awarded an OBE, and the seaman's parents were so grateful that they sent a sum of money which the sisters used to start work on the hotel. It remains a good place to stop for cream teas, with wonderful views over the whole of Start Bay.

South Molton, with its flourishing market, serves a wide farming area

Tavistock

Map Ref: 92SX4774

An important market town on the west side of Dartmoor, 10 miles north of Plymouth.

The Saxons founded a *stoc* here beside the River Tavy, but it was the establishment of a Benedictine abbey in the 10th century that really set the town on its feet. Thanks to the wise choice of site and to generous endowments, the abbey became the richest and most influential in Devon, creating similar prosperity for the town.

In 1105 Abbot Osbert persuaded King Henry I to grant the abbey permission to hold a market outside its gates every Friday, and it has continued to the present day.

At the Dissolution the abbey was dismantled and extraordinarily little survives today: a remnant of decorated masonry in the Parish churchyard, Betsy Grimbal's tower beside the Bedford Hotel (no-one knows who she was), the Misericord and fragments of walls.

Bedford Square was built over the site of the abbey church, and Plymouth Road driven over the site of the cloisters and chapter house. Most of the abbey's land was granted to John Russell, a Dorset squire, as President of a Council of the West; he was later to become Earl of Bedford.

The Dukes of Bedford dominated Tavistock from the 16th to the 20th century, and gave it its present appearance and character. Copper mines in the vicinity brought great prosperity in the 19th century and most of the town buildings date from this time. The centre was remodelled in green Hurdwick stone by Francis, the 7th Duke, who surveys his handiwork from a plinth outside the police station.

AA recommends:
Hotel: Bedford, Plymouth Rd, 3-star, *tel.* (0822) 3221
Restaurant: Hidden Table, 67 West St, 1-fork, *tel.* (0822) 66520
Guesthouses: St Anne's, 31 Plymouth Rd, *tel.* (0822) 3280
Parswell Farm Bungalow, *tel.* (0822) 2789
Campsites: Harford Bridge Holiday Park, 3-pennant, *tel.* (082281) 239 (2 miles N on A386).
Higher Longford Farm Caravan Site, 3-pennant, *tel.* (0822) 3360

Remains of 10th-century Tavistock Abbey

Teignmouth, fishing village and small port for centuries, retains its involvement with the sea; a boat's hull frames the door of Salt Cottage (left)

Teignmouth

Map Ref: 93SX9473

A pleasant seaside town built on the north side of the mouth of the Teign estuary. The narrow channel, through which boats gain access to the shelter of the estuary or dock at the quayside, is scoured daily by the tide and the river. The currents are fast and strong and the sand bars so treacherous to shipping that all cargo vessels entering or leaving the port are navigated through by Trinity House pilots.

The west side of the bar, facing up the estuary, is full of the character of old Teignmouth; here were the boat building yards and rope walks. From the quays, international trade continues to flourish under the eye of the Customs House.

Dartmoor granite shipped from here was used for the building of London Bridge and the British Museum. Ball clay, from quarries in the Bovey Basin, has been shipped from Teignmouth since the 16th century.

In the late 18th and early 19th centuries Teignmouth became a fashionable seaside resort and the town retains a good deal of its late Georgian and early Victorian architecture, particularly the elegant terraces and crescents of Powderham Terrace and the Den, which was laid out with a carriageway and lawn.

The Esplanade, along the seafront, extends for nearly two miles. The pier, built in the 1860s, once marked the segregation point between male and female bathers.

AA recommends:
Hotels: Ness House, Ness Dr, Shaldon, 2-star, *tel.* (0625) 873480
Venn Farm Country House, Higher Exeter Rd, 2-star, *tel.* (06267) 2196
Drakes, 33 Northumberland Pl, 1-star, *tel.* (06267) 2777
Glenside, Ringmoor Rd, Shaldon, (1m S off A379), 1-star, *tel.* (0626) 872448
Restaurant: Minadab, 60 Dawlish Rd, 2-fork, *tel.* (06267) 2044
Self Catering: CC Ref ELP (house), CC Ref 4080 (cottage), *tel.* (03955) 77001
Redcliffe & Seascape, *tel.* (06267) 3574
Redsands, 24 Northumberland Pl (flats) *tel.* (06267) 5221
Guesthouses: Glen Devon, 3 Carlton Pl, *tel.* (06267) 2895
Hillrise, *tel.* (06267) 3108
Hillsley, *tel.* (06267) 3878
Knoll Hotel, *tel.* (06267) 4241
Garages: Bobetts, 21-29 Brunswick St, *tel.* (06267) 4220
Central, Northumberland Pl, *tel.* (06267) 2535

Tiverton

Map Ref: 87SS9512

Tiverton was referred to in King Alfred's will as *Twyfyrde*, 'double ford'; its strategic site was reached by fords over the rivers Exe and Loman, which join just below the town. It was probably founded as a Saxon settlement in the 7th century, and grew under the protection of the castle built by Richard de Redvers in the early years of the 12th century.

The earls of Devon occupied Tiverton Castle until the 16th century. By then the woollen industry was well established and particularly the manufacture of kersey – coarse ribbed cloth woven from long wool. One wool merchant, Peter Blundell, founded Blundell's School in 1599; the Old School, built in 1604, still stands near the Loman Bridge at the south-east end of town. R D Blackmore was educated here, and used the triangular lawn as the setting for a fight between John Ridd and Robin Snell in *Lorna Doone*.

A castle was first built in Tiverton at the command of Henry I in 1106 on a site dominating the River Exe. As a key Royalist stronghold during the Civil War, it fell in 1645 to the Roundheads, whose General, Sir Thomas Fairfax, destroyed the main fortifications to the west, thus ending its military importance.

In the 19th century Tiverton survived the demise of the woollen industry through the introduction of lace-making by John Heathcoat. As the inventor of the bobbinett lace machine, he was forced to leave his factory in Leicester after the Luddite riots. He and a handful of key workers settled in the town and opened a new factory in a disused woollen mill.

Tiverton Museum, in St Andrew Street, is one of the most comprehensive local museums in the county. Its collections and displays range from the *Tivvy Bumper*, a steam loco that ran the Exe valley line until its closure, to local wildlife; the museum is open throughout the year.

Since 1971, another local preservation society has been working on the restoration of the Grand Western Canal. From the terminus at Tiverton Basin, on Canal Hill, a horse-drawn passenger service follows a glorious route through unspoilt countryside.

AA recommends:
Hotels: Tiverton, Blundells Rd, 3-star, *tel.* (0884) 256120
Hartnoll Country House, Bolham, 2-star, *tel.* (0884) 252777
Restaurant: Henderson's, 18 Newport St, 2-fork, *tel.* (0884) 254256
Guesthouses: Bridge, 23 Angel Hill, *tel.* (0884) 252804
Lodge Hill, *tel.* (0884) 252907
Lower Collipriest, *tel.* (0884) 252321
Garage: Bolham Rd, *tel.* (0884) 254842

Topsham

Map Ref: 90SX9688

A fascinating and ancient port on the east side of the Exe at the point where the river broadens into the estuary.

There was a Roman port here from the middle of the 1st century, serving Isca Dumnoniorum (Exeter); then a Saxon settlement, the property of the monastery of St Mary and St Peter at Exeter. In 1282 the Countess of Devon built a weir across the river, cutting Exeter off from the sea and ensuring that all merchandise for the city had to be unloaded at Topsham – to the advantage of the Countess's coffers.

The canal to Exeter was not built until the second half of the 16th century, and even then Topsham continued to dominate as an outport of Exeter. There was considerable trade in woollen serges with Holland, and returning vessels brought back Dutch bricks as ballast and Dutch architectural styles. Along the Strand, facing the river, is a series of Dutch-gabled houses.

The ship-building yards are now derelict, and the ancient stone warehouses store pleasure yachts laid up for winter. The old ferry still plies to and fro across the river in front of the Passage House Inn, where a notice gives prices for people, prams, dogs and cycles.

Topsham Museum, towards the southern end of the Quay, is well worth a visit.

AA recommends:
Hotel: Ebford House, Exmouth Rd, Ebford, 2-star, *tel.* (039287) 7658

The entrance to a silver lead mine at Lydford, once a great mining centre

Mines and Quarries

It is strange to think that Devon once boasted one of the richest copper mines in the world: the Devon Great Consols Mine near Tavistock. So rich was the area in copper ore that a canal was constructed, the Tavistock Canal, to carry the ore to Morwellham Quay on the River Tamar. The canal is four miles long and runs from the centre of Tavistock; it was built in the early years of the 19th century using French prisoner-of-war labour, and its construction involved cutting a two-mile tunnel under Morwell Down. It was completed in 1817. Copper was discovered in vast quantities under the land of the Duke of Bedford, owner of Tavistock, which enjoyed the status of boom town while fortunes were made overnight in the 1850s and 60s. Many of the cottages in Tavistock were built at this time as homes for the miners. The copper finally ran out, however, and for a time arsenic was mined. The quay at Morwellham can now be visited and you can take a trip into one of the old mine workings. Other evidence of mining on Dartmoor includes the ruined engine-house and stack at Wheal Betsy, near Mary Tavy, and the chimney which stands on the copper mine at South Zeal, near Okehampton; this too was once a mining community.

Dartmoor was also valued for its granite, as can be seen in the quarries at Haytor, where granite trackways were built to carry heavy wagons; these can still be followed. Granite from Haytor – just one of 400 varieties found on the moor – was used to build London Bridge.

Torquay

Map Ref: 93SX9164

Torquay claims to be the sophisticated playground of the English Riviera, comparable with Monte Carlo or Cannes; certainly its palm trees are real enough and the night life as exciting and varied as anywhere. An historical travel writer said of Torquay: 'It is not England, but a bit of sunny Italy taken bodily from its rugged coast and placed here amid the green lanes and the pleasant pastoral lands of beautiful Devon.'

The terraces and villas of the town follow the contours of the hills that ring the harbour bobbing with pleasure boats; it is sheltered on all sides except due south and that faces the pleasant sweep of Torbay, with Paignton and Brixham on the adjacent shores. Its balmy climate has attracted summer sun-seekers and winter patients since the early 19th century, but before that there was little here besides a sprinkling of fishermen's cottages around the quay.

Torre Abbey was founded near the shore in 1196. Considerable remains are preserved within the brightly blooming municipal gardens behind Tor Abbey Sands, including the 12th-century entrance to the chapter house, the 14th-century gatehouse, the guest hall and, most impressive of all, the Great Barn – locally it is known as the Spanish barn, because about 400 prisoners from the Armada

Torquay: Victorian, marine and modern

were brought here from a captured Spanish ship. The present house at Torre Abbey is 17th- and 18th-century in date and was the home of the Cary family; it now serves as the town's art gallery.

During the Napoleonic Wars, the fleet anchored in Torbay for long periods, so it was convenient for the officers to find accommodation ashore for their wives and families. Continental trips were out during wartime so civilian visitors also began to enjoy the town as a summer resort.

In 1848, a branch line of the railway from Newton Abbot reached Torquay, ensuring continued growth; by 1850 the town was advertising itself as 'the Queen of Watering Places'.

East of the harbour the cliffs rise up to Daddy Hole Plain; the great chasm in the cliff where the plain meets the sea was attributed to 'Daddy', the Devil. The views over the bay are superb, and further east through Lincombe Gardens, at Meadfoot, the way continues past Thatcher Stone, an isolated craggy rock ¼ mile off shore, to the point at Hope's Nose.

In Wellswood, off the Ilsham Road, Kent's Cavern has attracted visitors to its caves since the 16th century; at that time they marvelled at the stalactites and stalagmites. It was not until 1824 that some fossil bones were found, and excavations beneath the stalagmites revealed a world of cave-dwellers, in an untamed landscape populated by sabre-toothed tigers, mammoths and bears; many of the finds are now housed in the Torquay Museum.

AA recommends:

Hotels: Grand, Sea Front, 4-star, *tel.* (0803) 25234
Homers, Warren Rd, 3-star, *tel.* (0803) 213456
Orestone House, Rockhouse Ln, Maidencombe, 2-star, *tel.* (0803) 38098
Fairmont House, Herbert Rd, Chelston, 1-star, *tel.* (0803) 605446
Restaurants: Green Mantle, 135 Babbacombe Rd, 2-fork, *tel.* (0803) 34292
Old Vienna, 6 Lisburne Sq, 1-fork, *tel.* (0803) 25861
Self Catering: Hesketh Apartments, Meadfoot Beach, *tel.* (0803) 26530
Marina Court, Warren Rd, *tel.* (0803) 27612
Overmead Cottages, Daddyhole Rd, *tel.* (0803) 212944
Villa Capri, Daddyhole Rd, *tel.* (0803) 27959
Guesthouses: Crewe Lodge, 83 Avenue Rd, *tel.* (0803) 28772
Glenorleigh Hotel, 26 Cleveland Rd, *tel.* (0803) 22135
Mapleton Hotel, St Lukes Rd North, *tel.* (0803) 22389
Tregontle Hotel, 64 Bampfylde Rd, *tel.* (0803) 27494
Garages: Babbacombe Garage, 55-57 Babbacombe Rd, *tel.* day (0803) 313377; night (0803) 314167
Chelston, Walnut Rd, Chelston, *tel.* (0803) 605858
Dutton Forshaw, Lawes Bridge, *tel.* day (0803) 62781; night (0803) 34129
Moores Mtrs, 230 Lymington Rd, *tel.* (0803) 37369
Reed, Lawes Bridge, Newton Rd, *tel.* (0803) 62021
Westhill, Chatto Rd, *tel.* day (0803) 38351; night (0803) 552406

This is a selection of establishments; see page 4.

Totnes: the 11th-century castle commanded the navigable reaches of the River Dart where three valleys meet; (right) the view up Fore Street, heart of the Saxon town

Torrington (Great)

Map Ref: 85SS4919

This town is extraordinarily sited on a cliff top with precipitous drops to the River Torridge. From the ramparts of the former castle the landscape to the south is laid out in a patchwork of hedges and fields to the hills beyond.

During the Civil War, General Fairfax took the town in a surprise attack and captured the Royalist garrison; the prisoners were locked up in the tower of the parish church. By some terrible accident there was an explosion of gunpowder in the church which killed 200 men and destroyed most of the building; the long mound by the churchyard path is thought to be the mass grave. An inscription commemorating the event is outside the porch, on the wall to the left. The church was rebuilt in 1651 and has a fine 17th-century pulpit.

The town's commercial fortune rested on the fate of the woollen and gloving industries. Knitted wool gloves were a speciality and glove-making has continued to the present day. In 1874 the Torridge Vale Butter factory was established, processing dairy produce from the surrounding farms; much expanded and highly mechanised, this has become the Milk Marketing Board's Dairy Crest plant. An extremely successful industrial venture and visitor attraction, on the north side of the town down School Lane, is the Dartington Glass factory. Here bubbles in glowing gobs of molten glass are skilfully blown into fine crystal glass forms of great variety: decanters, goblets, vases and ornaments.

AA recommends:
Hotel: Castle Hill, South St, 2-star, *tel.* (0805) 22339
Restaurant: Rebecca's, 8 Potacre St, 1-fork, *tel.* (0805) 22113
Self Catering: Greenways Valley Holiday Park (chalets), *tel.* (0805) 22153
Guesthouses: Smytham Manor, *tel.* (0805) 22110
Lower Hollam (farmhouse), *tel.* (0805) 23253
Campsite: Greenways Valley Holiday Park, 3-pennant, *tel.* (0805) 22153

Totnes

Map Ref: 93SX8060

A fascinating town, rich in history, on a hill rising from the west bank of the river up to the keep of the castle on its mound at the top of the High Street.

The quayside is bustling with the activity of renovation – many of the old warehouses have been converted into new shops, restaurants and houses – but it is a working port too, with sizeable cargo boats from Finland and Sweden arriving regularly with timber, and cruises to and from Dartmouth. The first bridge over the river was built by the 13th century, when the Pomeroys founded a separate borough on the east bank; Bridgetown is now part of Totnes proper.

The main shopping street, Fore Street, leads up the hill towards the broad arch over the road at the East Gate. Set in the pavement, the Brutus stone is where, according to legend, Brutus stood to survey the area before founding Totnes and the British race. Opposite, Atherton Lane is adorned with flowers and cottages painted the colours of Neapolitan ice-cream.

Under the arch a footpath follows the ramparts of the old town walls round to the medieval Guildhall, behind the church; it was built in 1553 on the foundations of the refectory of Totnes Priory.

The Parish and Priory Church of St Mary dates from the 15th century. Its glory is the stone rood-screen of delicate tracery carved out of Beer stone. Notice the corporation pews, cushioned in velvet plush.

At the top of the High Street the pillared arcades, the Butterwalk and Poultry Walk, once sheltered the market stalls on the pavement's edge. The new Market Place features an Elizabethan costumed market every Tuesday in the summer.

The castle, a classic example of Norman motte and bailey design, dates from the 11th century. The motte rises some 50ft and is crowned by a small circular castellated keep. The views from the ramparts, over the roof tops of the town and beyond to the Dart valley, are superb.

Many of the town's buildings are 16th- and 17th-century, notably the Elizabethan House, now the Totnes Museum, where a number of internal features can be seen. Slate-hanging, a characteristic local form of weather-proofing in the 18th and 19th centuries, has disguised several buildings of much earlier date.

The Dart Valley Railway runs steam trains from Totnes to Buckfastleigh; there is an excellent Motor Museum beside the Steamer Quay.

AA recommends:
Hotels: Bourton Hall, Newtown Rd, 2-star, 1-rosette, *tel.* (0803) 862608
Royal Seven Stars, 2-star, *tel.* (0803) 862125
Restaurant: Elbow Room, 2-fork, *tel.* (0803) 863480
Guesthouses: Four Seasons, 13 Bridgetown, *tel.* (0803) 862091
Old Forge, Seymour Pl, Bridgetown, *tel.* (0803) 862174
Broomborough House, Broomborough Dr (farmhouse), *tel.* (0803) 863134
Garage: Harrisons, The Plains, *tel.* (0803) 862247

Uffculme

Map Ref: 87ST0612

A large village on the River Culm, which was an important centre for the wool trade, exporting serges to Holland. Its surviving woollen mill at Coldharbour, to the west of the village, closed down in 1981, but was then converted into a Working Wool Museum. Visitors can watch the whole process of woollen and worsted manufacture. The wool and cloth made up on the machines can be bought in lengths and in garments. Other attractions include a weaver's cottage, dye and carpenters' workshop, the water-wheel and steam engine and a picnic area beside the mill leat.

The parish church, St Mary's, is mainly 15th-century, but the tower and spire were rebuilt in the 19th century. The church is noted for having the longest rood-screen in Devon; it is also one of the earliest, dated *c*1400.

Westward Ho!

Map Ref: 85SS4329

Following the publication of Charles Kingsley's novel in 1855, a company was set up to develop the site. The Countess of Portsmouth laid the foundation stone of what is now the Golden Bay Hotel, a church was built and two or three rows of cottages. Unfortunately things did not work to plan – the pier and some houses were washed away in a storm and the place was left prey to speculators.

The site is spectacular, the great rounded bracken-covered hillside

The Church of St Pancras, Widecombe, etched against the moor beyond it

rises behind, with terraced rows and detached villas looking out over two miles or so of sand stretching to the mouth of the Torridge and Taw estuary. The sands are backed by a pebble ridge, 2 miles long, 50ft wide and 20ft high.

Today Westward Ho! is a self-catering holiday resort of beachside chalets, caravans and flatlets. The Burrows are a highlight: 650 acres of sand dunes, salt marsh and pasture, a first class golf course and a country park.

AA recommends:

Hotels: Buckleigh Grange, Buckleigh Rd, 2-star, *tel.* (02372) 74468
Culloden House, Fosketh Hill, 2-star, *tel.* (02372) 79421

Self Catering: Buckleigh Pines, Buckleigh Cross, *tel.* (02372) 74783

Guesthouse: Buckleigh Lodge, 135 Bayview Rd, *tel.* (02372) 75988

Widecombe in the Moor

Map Ref: 93SX7176

Nobody knows quite when Widecombe Fair began, but the song was first published in 1880. Ever since, people have wanted to visit the village to discover more about the folk-heroes 'Old Uncle Tom Cobley and all'.

The village, sheltering in the broad valley of the East Webburn River, is surrounded by high granite-strewn ridges reaching 1,500ft. From the valley floor, cultivated fields extend up the hillsides to peter out into grass and bracken. The moors here are dotted with Bronze Age sites – hut-circles, barrows and burial chambers. At Foales Arrishes, archaeological excavations have revealed that the hut-circles were occupied into the Iron Age.

The church tower, topped by four striking pinnacles, is 120ft high. In the 13th century the population around Widecombe was given permission to attend church here rather than at the 'parish church of the Moor' at Lydford. Tin miners contributed much of the money for the building, which dates from the 14th century and is known as 'the Cathedral of the Moor'. Even then, many outlying farming families had to travel a considerable distance to reach Widecombe, so the Church House was built in about 1500 as a resting place for them; later it was divided into almshouses and it has been used as a Poor House and a school. It is now owned by the National Trust.

The village, for all its coach tours and cream teas, is remarkably unaffected; it surrounds the Green, or Butte Park, where medieval archers set up their targets. The Old Inn dates back to the 14th century but has been much altered; the last occasion was after a fire in 1977 which destroyed the roof and most of the first floor. The Glebe House, built in the 1500s on land rented from the vicar, is now a gift shop, retaining a huge open fireplace and oven for baking bread.

The smithy continued in use until 1950 when it was preserved as a small museum, and just beyond is the old Saxon well, said never to run dry.

Winkleigh

Map Ref: 89SS6308

Winkleigh boasts two castle sites, at opposite ends of the village. Court Castle, beside the main road, forms a wooded knoll, with ivy-covered trees and jackdaws cawing in the ruins of the old tower. At the south-west end of Castle Street, behind the old Castle School, there is a smaller mound, known as Croft Castle. In fact they were probably both moated manor houses, rather than castles proper; the mounds date from the Norman period.

Fore Street has all the characteristics of an old market place, with a stone-mounted pump, 'erected by permission of the Lord of the Manor'. Winkleigh was a borough, with a market and fair; the borough court sat until 1848. The cottages, stone and rough-cast, knobbly and rounded, thatched and slated, are on either side of Queen Street, High Street and Vine Street.

From Dial Street, steep steps lead up to the south porch of the parish church which is mainly 15th-century; the wagon roof is richly carved and painted.

Sheep enthusiasts will appreciate the Ashley Countryside Collection, on the B3220, where 48 breeds of rare and unusual British sheep are kept; there is an exhibition of fleeces and items of farm livestock.

Along the Coast

In 1965 the Duke of Edinburgh launched 'Enterprise Neptune', an appeal by the National Trust to save Britain's unspoilt coastline, after it was realised that only 900 miles out of a total of 3000 miles remained unspoilt. To date, the Trust has managed to acquire about half of this, and Devon is the county with the second largest number of miles of coastline under the Trust's protection, around 70 in all.

Much of Devon's coast offers spectacular scenery, and one of the best ways to enjoy it is by walking. Both of Devon's coastlines are taken in by the South West Peninsula Coast Path, also known as the South West Way, which starts at Minehead in Somerset and follows the coast for over 600 miles, via Land's End, to Shell Bay in Dorset.

This makes it the longest path in Britain, twice as long as the Pennine Way and in places just as tough walking. Since 1973 the South West Way Association has worked in co-operation with the Ramblers' Association to secure completion of the path; it produces an annual guide which is updated each spring.

The aim of 'Enterprise Neptune' is to own the wild coast and the open country behind it; farm rents provide revenue while redundant buildings can make houses for the wardens who watch over the coast, or holiday cottages. Several stretches of Devon's coast are designated as areas of outstanding natural beauty, and there is no lack of variety, from north Devon's 'hogsback' cliffs to the vast dunes of Braunton Burrows; from the spectacular climb to Beer Head to the fascinating Slapton Ley, Devon's largest natural freshwater lake.

The unspoilt cliffs of Bolt Tail near Salcombe

A West Country tradition – crabbing at Woolacombe

Woolacombe

Map Ref: 85SS4543

'Where the sands are long and golden, and pools of sea water are mirrors of the sky's perfect blue, where there are miniature ravines and carpets of heather ablaze on the moors, close-clipped grass for the tired limb . . . and, at one's feet, a million dancing, quivering waves.' (From the Ward Lock *Guide to Ilfracombe*, 1938.)

The beach has become a mecca for surfers, riding their boards out to sea and patiently waiting for that big wave to sweep in from the Atlantic; the U-shaped bay faces due west. The sands are a paradise for children, with rock pools under the craggy cliffs, gleaming in places with veins of white quartz.

Woolacombe was developed tastefully from the 1820s by the Fortesques and Chichesters (of Arlington Court), who owned most of the land. The handful of original cottages and a farm gave way to rest-homes, villas and hotels. Up the combe a rash of caravan and camping sites now covers the grassy slopes, but the style and character of the earlier development has not been compromised. The grounds of West Bay Hotel have prevented growth to the south, and the Downs behind the sands are now owned and protected by the National Trust.

AA recommends:
Hotels: Woolacombe Bay, South St, 3-star, *tel.* (0271) 870368
Atlantic, Sunnyside Rd, 2-star, *tel.* (0271) 870469
Devon Beach, The Esplanade, 2-star, *tel.* (0271) 870449
Crossways, The Esplanade, 1-star, *tel.* (0271) 870395
Self Catering: Golden Coast Holiday Village, *tel.* (0271) 870343
Quarry Dene, Bay View Rd, *tel.* (0271) 870690
Woolacombe Bay Hotel Mews, *tel.* (0271) 870388
Woolacombe Court Apartments & Flats, *tel.* (0271) 870388
Guesthouses: Castle, The Esplanade, *tel.* (0271) 870788
Combe Ridge Hotel, The Esplanade, *tel.* (0271) 870321
Holmesdale Hotel, Bay View Rd, *tel.* (0271) 870335
Campsite: Golden Coast Holiday Village, Station Rd, 5-pennant, *tel.* (0271) 870343
Garage: Cowlers Central, Arlington Rd, *tel.* (0271) 870428

Woolfardisworthy

Map Ref: 84SS3321

This mouthful of a name is locally abbreviated to Woolsery, even on the signposts, so it is as well to know before attempting to find the place. It is a tucked-away village, in a nook sheltered from the worst of the Atlantic storms that sweep over this corner of north-west Devon.

The settlement is scattered, but in front of the church there is a triangle of pretty cottages, a village shop, primary school and a thatched and whitewashed pub, the Farmers' Arms. The church architecture is plain, no fripperies to be knocked off by the westerly gales, but the entrance porch is decorated with zig-zag designs and carved heads typical of Norman work. The pillars of the nave are monolithic slabs of granite shipped from Lundy, each shaped from a single block. The 16th-century carved bench ends illustrate the occupations of the parish inhabitants with symbols of their trades: carpentry tools and farming implements.

A couple of miles north east, on the precipitous coast, the attractive little hamlet of **Bucks Mills** has lived for centuries by fishing. It is similar to Clovelly, with a steep cottage-lined road in a valley leading to a final plunge to the beach.

AA recommends:
Hotel: Manor House, 2-star, *tel.* (02373) 380
Guesthouses: Stroxworthy (farmhouse), *tel.* (02373) 333
Westvilla (farmhouse), *tel.* (02373) 309

Yealmpton

Map Ref: 92SX5751

On the main road, the A379, between Plymouth and Kingsbridge, Yealmpton – pronounced 'Yampton' – is a seldom-explored village. From the road the village follows the south-facing slope down to the pretty River Yealm, just above the head of the estuary.

In the churchyard of St Bartholomew's there is a stone pillar inscribed with the name Toreus, thought to be the monument of a Roman chieftain. The font inside the church is Saxon, but the rest of the church was totally rebuilt in 1850. Nevertheless Sir John Betjeman described it as 'the most amazing' Victorian church in Devon. Highly polished marble from quarries at Kitley has been inset in the walls and carved to make the low chancel screen and altar table. Some of the earlier monuments have been preserved, notably that to Isobel Copelston (1580), with a double-sided brass.

At the east end of the village Old Mother Hubbard's restaurant creaks with blackened oak beams under a thatched roof; Mother Hubbard is thought to have been the housekeeper at Kitley, where the rhyme was written by Sarah Martin in 1805.

Buckland Abbey, converted to an Elizabethan mansion after the Dissolution, has a splendid early 14th-century monastic tithe barn

About a mile east, at Modbury, the National Shire Horse Centre is based at a traditional Devon livestock farm, with buildings dating back to 1772, and worked in the old way by heavy horses. There are exhibitions of harness and carts as well as demonstration activities.

AA recommends:
Guesthouse: Broadmoor (farmhouse), *tel.* (0752) 880407

Yelverton

Map Ref: 92SX5267

The moor probes into the heart of Yelverton with a great wedge of open grassland. On the south side the row of shops provides all the village amenities; on the north a terrace of tall town houses appears oddly suburban against the backdrop of gorse, heather and tussocky grass grazed by shaggy sheep and Dartmoor ponies.

Yelverton and the nearby village of Crapstone have become attractive for retirement homes and are within convenient commuting distance of Plymouth. A new and rather grand church was completed in Yelverton in 1912 by the architect Sir Charles Nicholson; the interior is finished in Ham Hill stone, giving a honey-coloured glow in pleasant contrast to the grey exterior.

The rocky crag of Sheepstor crowns the skyline to the east, and just below it is the Burrator Reservoir, which supplies Plymouth. It is said that Sir Francis Drake constructed the first leat to provide drinking-water for Plymouth. The Mayor's toast at the annual *Fishinge Feaste* at Burrator pleads: 'May the descendants of him who brought us water never want wine.'

Buckland Abbey shelters in the valley of the River Tavy, two miles west; the founder in 1278, Amicia, Countess of Devon, is portrayed in stone over a doorway behind the main building. At the Dissolution the abbey was sold to Sir Richard Grenville; he or his successors converted the abbey church into a mansion which later became Drake's home. Drake's drum, rescued by his brother Thomas who was with him when he died of dysentery on the Spanish Main in 1596, is a much-prized exhibit.

The adjacent medieval tithe barn is magnificent, and is used by Plymouth City Museum to house a collection of carts and carriages.

The Broughton Collection of over 800 antique and modern glass paperweights can be seen at Leg O'Mutton, Yelverton.

AA recommends:
Hotels: Moorland Links, 3-star, *tel.* (0822) 852245
Saddlers Retreat Country House, Tavistock Rd, 1-star, *tel.* (0822) 852099
Guesthouses: Harrabeer Country House Hotel, Harrowbeer Ln, *tel.* (0822) 853302
Waverley, 5 Greenbank Ter, *tel.* (0822) 854617
Garage: Roundabout and Moxham, The Parade, *tel.* (0822) 852931

Directory

This directory of places to visit and things to see and do in Devon and Exmoor introduces you to some of the best-known attractions in the area. It is not an exhaustive list and you can use the tourist information centres to find additional and more detailed information.

CRAFTS

The fat-bellied and simply decorated harvest jug is a traditional Devon product, as is the style of scraffito, using the red Devon clay and a white slip. It can be seen at Brannam Potteries in Barnstaple (open all year, Mon to Fri. *Tel* Barnstaple (0271) 43035). The development of pottery in the area owes much to the late Bernard Leach, who brought to it influences from Japan, where he had worked.

Smocking and weaving are widely practised, and also particularly notable is the making of Honiton lace, as displayed in Allhallows Museum (see under Museums).

A wide range of craft work is on view in the galleries and shop of Riverside Mill in Bovey Tracey (see also under Museums). The Mill is also the headquarters of the Devon Guild of Craftsmen and a source of further information about local crafts.

ACTIVITIES

Fishing

The fast-flowing rivers of Devon and Exmoor have long been revered by the salmon and sea trout fisherman, drawn to the area by names like Taw, Torridge, Tamar, Dart, Tavy, Lyn and Teign. These streams also hold large stocks of brown trout and, in East Devon, the Otter and Axe provide dry fishing of the chalk stream type. Fishing on the moorland streams is cheaply available and the wild 'brownies' provide exciting sport on light fly tackle.

The rivers mostly flow too fast for coarse fish, but many reservoirs, lakes, ponds and canals have been stocked, both by the South West Water Authority and by private enterprises.

The sea fisherman will find countless opportunities along both coastlines for boat fishing out of the ports of Plymouth and Brixham and elsewhere, and for shore fishing for bass.

For details of game and coarse fishing in the area write to South West Water, Peninsula House, Rydon Lane, Exeter EX2 7HR. *Fishing in England's West Country* is available free from West Country Tourist Board, Trinity Court, Southernhay East, Exeter EX1 1QS.

Devon crafts: Brannam Potteries, Barnstaple, is an attractive Victorian building much influenced by William Morris; embroidery demonstration at Morwellham Quay (above); exhibitions of work at Bovey Tracey (below)

Golf

The picture of golf played in Devon is dominated by the great links courses of Saunton and the Royal North Devon Club at Westward Ho! At Saunton there are two courses, both shaped by the ridges and valleys of the links land and the dunes. Westward Ho!, the first seaside links in England, is a most testing course, characterised by natural hazards of sandhills, rushes and the wind. Wind is also a hazard of the flat, seaside links of the Minehead and West Somerset Club.

Superb views and fairly easy walking are features of the clifftop downland of the Ilfracombe course. Likewise, there are fine views from the downland turf of the course at Thurlestone, views of Tor Bay and Brixham Harbour from Churston, and views of Lyme Bay from the East Devon Club's course at Budleigh Salterton.

Inland, on Dartmoor, the undulating downland of the Tavistock course, the parkland of the Manor House Hotel at Moretonhampstead, and the springy moorland turf at Yelverton offer considerable variety for all golfers.

The AA Guide to Golf in Great Britain is an annual publication which gives descriptions, telephone numbers and local arrangements for courses in the area.

Walking

The South West Peninsula Coast Path
This footpath, the longest of all long-distance paths in England, is unbroken along the contrasting north and south coasts of the Devon and Exmoor area.

After a gentle start in Minehead the path follows the coastline of the National Park, with spectacular views, and continues through an Area of Outstanding Natural Beauty. It passes Hartland Point, where rugged cliffs provide a foretaste of the walk down the west-facing coasts of north Devon and Cornwall.

The south Devon section of the path follows the undulating South Hams coastline before entering the busy resort of Torbay. As it continues eastwards the walker enjoys the calmer airs and scenery from Exmouth to the Dorset border.

A descriptive leaflet covering the path is available from the

From signposted guided tours to hidden paths and stiles, Devon offers superb walking country

Countryside Commission, John Dower House, Crescent Place, Cheltenham GL50 3RA. *The South West Way*, published by Devon Books, is a complete guide to the path and includes details of transport, ferry services and tide tables for river crossings.

The National Parks
It is not only the coast of Exmoor which attracts the serious and casual walker. The wild heather moorland and deep wooded valleys of the inland moor offer a considerable traditional freedom of access and the National Park Authority, which maintains and signs over 600 miles of footpaths, administers a programme of guided walks. Write to Exmoor National Park, Exmoor House, Dulverton, Somerset.

The Two Moors Way is not officially designated a long-distance footpath, but it runs from the north Devon coast and Exmoor to Dartmoor and south Devon, passing through the varying mid-Devon landscape of farmland, wooded valleys and traditional rural communities.

The rugged grandeur and natural beauty of Dartmoor is most often associated with the area of high moor, where even the most experienced walker must beware of rapidly changing weather conditions. More gentle walking is offered by the valleys, villages and small towns around the edge of the National Park. On open moorland there is traditional freedom of access, but on enclosed farmland the marked rights of way must be followed. The National Park Authority administers a programme of guided walks; apply to Dartmoor National Park, Parke, Haytor Road, Bovey Tracey, Devon.

Country Parks
There are officially recognised country parks on the limestone headland of Berry Head, near Brixham, on the heath and meadowland at Farway, near Honiton, and along the wooded parkland of the River Dart valley near Ashburton. There are further opportunities for walks and circular routes on the 11 miles of restored towpath of the Grand Western Canal in mid-Devon.

For information about woodland walking write to the Forestry Commission, 231 Corstorphine Road, Edinburgh. *Walking in England's West Country* is available free from West Country Tourist Board, Trinity Court, Southernhay East, Exeter EX1 1QS. Tourist Information Centres will advise on local nature trails and urban walks.

Watersports

The north and south coastlines of Devon and Exmoor offer contrasting opportunities for a wide variety of watersports. The Atlantic-facing beaches of Saunton and Woolacombe have always attracted surfers from all over the world, as well as the less energetic holidaymaker. To the south, river estuaries, harbours and the marina at Torquay, with all its modern facilities, cater for yachtsmen with craft of any size. There are open bays for water-skiing and windsurfing, and Paignton has hosted the World Board Sailing Championship. Coastal Tourist Information Centres will advise on moorings, local conditions and other information for watersports enthusiasts.

Inland, there are several reservoirs with facilities for sailing, board-sailing, canoeing and rowing. These activities are usually controlled by the local club, and full details of these are given in the *Reservoir Recreation* leaflet available from South West Water, Peninsula House, Rydon Lane, Exeter EX2 7HR.

PLACES TO VISIT

Many of these places have fuller descriptions within the gazetteer section of this book.
BH = Bank Holiday

Castles

Dartmouth
Dartmouth Castle is a small 15th-century fort, built for coastal defence and largely added to in the late 16th century. A massive chain links it to Kingswear Castle on the opposite shore. Open all year, daily. *Tel* Dartmouth (08043) 3588

Castle Drogo
Sir Edwin Lutyens built **Castle Drogo** from the local granite between 1910 and 1930. It enjoys beautiful views over Dartmoor and the valley of the River Teign. Open Apr to Oct, daily. *Tel* Chagford (06473) 3306

Dunster
Standing over the attractive market town, **Dunster Castle** has been the fortified home of the Luttrells for 600 years and is noted for its 17th-century staircase, plaster ceilings and terrace gardens. Open Apr to Oct, Sat to Wed. *Tel* Dunster (064382) 314

Okehampton
Okehampton Castle was founded in the 11th century and largely reconstructed in the 14th century. A series of courts leads to a rectangular keep. Open all year, daily. *Tel* Okehampton (0837) 2844

Totnes
The stone keep of **Totnes Castle** remains quite complete and is a fine example of a Norman fortification, built originally by Judhael, leader of William the Conqueror's West Country campaign. Open all year, daily. *Tel* Totnes (0803) 864406

Gardens

Budleigh Salterton
At **Bicton Park**, 2 miles inland from Budleigh Salterton, there is an Italian garden laid out in 1735. There is a changing programme of exhibitions and family attractions. Open Easter to Oct, daily. *Tel* Colaton Raleigh (0395) 68465

Kingswear
Coleton Fishacre is a delightful 18-acre garden, now in the care of the National Trust, with views of the spectacular heritage coastline. Open Apr to Oct, Wed, Fri & Sun. *Tel* Kingswear (080425) 617

Taunton
At **Hestercombe House** the gardens, designed by Gertrude Jekyll and Sir Edwin Lutyens, are now restored to their original planting. Open all year, Tue to Thu. *Tel* Taunton (0823) 87222

Torrington
Rosemoor Gardens, in the valley of the River Torridge, provide a number of sheltered walks with trees, shrubs, roses and alpines of botanical interest. Open Apr to Oct, daily. *Tel* Torrington (0805) 22256

Historic Houses

Barnstaple
Some 6 miles north-east of Barnstaple is **Arlington Court**, housing an interesting collection of *objets d'art* and a carriage museum. There are nature trails in the wooded gardens. Open Apr to Oct, Sun to Fri & BH Sat. *Tel* Shirwell (027182) 296

Buckland
Buckland Abbey was once a Cistercian monastery and was then converted to become the home of Sir Francis Drake. Open Easter to Sep, daily. *Tel* Yelverton (0822) 853607

Chudleigh
Robert Adam designed **Ugbrooke House** and Capability Brown its park and grounds. Fine furniture and paintings are on display. Open May to Aug, Sat, Sun & BHs. *Tel* Chudleigh (0626) 852179

Combe Sydenham
The Elizabethan **Combe Sydenham Hall** stands on the ruins of monastic buildings and is surrounded by gardens, a deer park, waymarked woodland walks and trout ponds. Open Apr to Oct, Mon to Fri. *Tel* Stogumber (0984) 56284

Exeter
The city's **Guildhall** is the oldest municipal building in the country. Behind its Tudor frontage is a medieval main hall and displays of paintings and silver. Open all year, Mon to Sat. *Tel* Exeter (0392) 72979

About 8 miles south of Exeter is **Powderham Castle**, a family home for 600 years and restored in the 18th century with Georgian interiors and fine furnishings. Open Spring BH to Sep, Sun to Thu. *Tel* Starcross (0626) 890243

Killerton House, 7 miles north of the city, is an 18th-century house which contains an extensive collection of costumes displayed in room settings. Open Apr to Oct, daily. *Tel* Exeter (0392) 881345

Exmouth
À la Ronde is a unique 16-sided house with gothic grottoes, a shell gallery and a feather frieze and dado. It is set in 12 acres of parkland with views of the estuary of the River Exe. Open Apr to Oct, daily. *Tel* Exmouth (0395) 265514

Lydeard St Lawrence
On the eastern edge of Exmoor is **Gaulden Moor**, a small country house whose hall has a magnificent plaster ceiling, an oak screen to its chapel, and fine antique furniture. Open Easter & May to Sep, Sun, Thu & BHs; Jul to Sep, also Wed. *Tel* Lydeard St Lawrence (09847) 213

The Victorian watering-place of Ilfracombe is a good base for exploring the treasures of the north Devon coast

Ottery St Mary
Cadhay is an Elizabethan manor house built around a central courtyard. Its Great Hall has a fine timber roof. Open Spring BH Sun & Mon; Jul to Aug, Tue to Thu & BH Sun & Mon. *Tel* Ottery St Mary (040481) 2432

Plymouth
The Elizabethan House is a 16th-century house furnished with Elizabethan and Jacobean furniture. There are gardens and a courtyard. Open Easter to Sep, daily; Oct to Easter, Mon to Sat. *Tel* Plymouth (0752) 668000 ext 4380

On the outskirts of the city is **Saltram House**, a George II mansion with magnificent interior plasterwork and decoration, two rooms by Robert Adam and portraits by Sir Joshua Reynolds. Open Apr to Oct, Sun to Thu & Fri & Sat of BH weekends. *Tel* Plymouth (0752) 336546

Tiverton
Knightshayes Court is a Victorian house with a richly decorated interior. Its fine gardens are mainly of woodland, rare shrubs and formal terraces.
Open Apr to Oct, Sat to Thu. *Tel* Tiverton (0884) 254665

Totnes
The oldest house in Totnes is **Bowden House**, a Tudor mansion with a Queen Anne façade. Open Apr to Sep, Tue to Thu & BH Sun & Mon. *Tel* Totnes (0803) 863664

Museums and Galleries

Bideford
The Burton Art Gallery houses a collection of oils and water-colours, pewter and ceramics, and a changing programme of visiting exhibitions. Open all year, Mon to Sat. *Tel* Bideford (02372) 76711 ext 315

Bovey Tracey
The Devon Guild of Craftsmen has its own craft centre with exhibitions, a museum of craftsmanship and a retail shop. Open all year, daily. *Tel* Bovey Tracey (0626) 832223

Brixham
The continuing story of the fishing industry is recorded with models of ships and photographs at the *British Fisheries Museum*. Open Jun to Sep, daily; Oct to May, Tue to Sat. *Tel* Brixham (08045) 2861

Chittlehampton
The Cobbaton Combat Vehicles Museum houses a private collection of World War II tanks, trucks, armoured cars and allied equipment. Open Apr to Oct, daily. *Tel* Chittlehampton (07694) 414

Cullompton
4 miles north of the town is *Coldharbour Mill*, a working museum of the Devon wool textiles industry. Open Easter, Apr to Oct, daily; Nov to Easter, Mon to Fri. *Tel* Craddock (0884) 40960

Exeter
The Royal Albert Memorial Museum is the largest museum in the West Country and houses major collections of silver, glass, paintings and natural history exhibits. Open all year, Tue to Sat. *Tel* Exeter (0392) 56724
In the *Exeter Maritime Museum* there are more than 100 boats from all over the world, including Brunel's steam dredger. Open all year, daily. *Tel* Exeter (0392) 58075

Honiton
There are fine displays of Honiton lace and other local history exhibits in the *Allhallows Museum*. Craft demonstrations are held in the summer.
Open Easter, May to Oct, Mon to Sat. *Tel* Farway (040487) 307

Kingsbridge
The Cookworthy Museum of Rural Life houses a wide variety of local history displays, a farm gallery and a Victorian pharmacy in a 17th-century panelled school.
Open Easter to Sep, Mon to Sat; Oct, Mon to Fri.
Tel Kingsbridge (0548) 3235

Plymouth
In the *City Museum and Art Gallery* there are extensive displays of Plymouth porcelain and silver, and fine and decorative arts.
Open all year, Mon to Sat.
Tel Plymouth (0752) 264878
The Merchant's House Museum is a newly-restored Tudor town house with a museum of the city's social history. Open Easter to Sep, daily; Oct to Easter, Mon to Sat. *Tel* Plymouth (0752) 668000 ext 4381

Tavistock
Morwellham Quay is an open air museum which recreates many aspects of Victorian life and where a riverside tramway journeys underground into a copper mine. Open all year, daily.
Tel Tavistock (0822) 832766

Wembworthy
40 rare breeds of sheep and more than 1,000 antiquities of the ox, horse and open fireplace era are features of the *Ashley Countryside Collection*.
Open Easter to Oct, Mon, Wed, Sun & BHs; Aug, Fri to Wed. *Tel* Ashreigney (07693) 226

Wildlife Attractions

Bovey Tracey
The Parke Rare Breeds Farm is set in beautiful parkland at the gateway to Dartmoor. There are woodland and riverside walks and the estate houses the offices of the National Park Authority.
Open Apr to Oct, daily.
Tel Bovey Tracey (0626) 833909

Buckfastleigh
At **Buckfast Butterflies** exotic butterflies and moths fly freely in an undercover landscaped garden with a waterfall and large pond.
Open Easter to Oct, daily.
Tel Buckfastleigh (0364) 42916

Clovelly
160 cows are milked in a space age parlour at the **Milky Way**, and visitors can hand-milk a cow and bottle-feed lambs, kids and calves.
Open Easter to Sep, Sun to Fri.
Tel Clovelly (02373) 255

Combe Martin
Bodstone Barton is a working dairy farm in spectacular surroundings. The hand and machine milking of cows and goats can be seen in the traditional farm buildings.
Open Easter to Sep, Sun to Fri; Apr & Oct, Wed, Thu & Sun.
Tel Combe Martin (027188) 3654

Paignton
The 75 acres of botanical gardens are the home of a large collection of exotic animals at **Paignton Zoo**. **The Ark** is a family activity centre with nature trails and miniature train rides.
Open all year, daily.
Tel Paignton (0803) 557479

Plymouth
To the east of the city are two wildlife attractions. At the **Dartmoor Wild Life Park** there are over 100 species of animals, including the big cats, bears, wolves and seals, in 25 acres of countryside. Open all year, daily. *Tel* Cornwood (075537) 209

Saltram: 'one of the most magnificent houses in the Kingdom' – Fanny Burney

The National Shire Horse Centre
is the venue for regular daily parades
of the shire horses, and new foals
can be seen. There are craftsmen's
workshops, a saddlery and a
children's adventure playground.
Open all year, daily.
Tel Plymouth (0752) 880268

Porlock
At Bossington, near Porlock, there
is the **Saxon Farm Park** with old
English farm animals and birds, and
the National Exmoor Pony
Exhibition.
Open Easter to Sep, Mon to Fri.
Tel Porlock (0643) 862816

South Molton
Quince Honey Farm is a working
honey farm where the live bees are
exhibited in specially-constructed
cases, and honey and beeswax
products are on sale.
Open all year, daily.
Tel South Molton (07695) 2401

**Railways, Parks, Gnomes
and more**

Ashburton
The River Dart Country Park has
children's adventure playgrounds, a
bathing lake, pony rides and nature
trails. Open Apr to Sep, daily.
Tel Ashburton (0364) 52511

Buckfastleigh
Buckfastleigh is one terminus for
the **Dart Valley Steam Railway**,
along which carefully restored trains
run to and from Totnes.
Open Easter & May BH; Jun to
Sep, daily.
Tel Buckfastleigh (0364) 42338

Lynton
The Exmoor Brass Rubbing Centre
offers the materials and friendly
guidance needed to have a go at
making brass rubbings.
Open Apr to Sep, Mon to Fri; Aug,
also Sat & Sun.
Tel Lynton (0598) 52529

Torquay
The **Model Village** in Babbacombe
is a scale model of an English
countryside scene, set in 4 acres,
and inhabited by models and figures
in towns and villages.
Open all year, daily.
Tel Torquay (0803) 38669

Torrington
The factory of **Dartington Glass**
manufactures its famous hand-made
lead crystal glassware and gifts.
Guided factory tours may be taken
to see craftsmen at work.
Open all year, Mon to Fri.
Tel Torrington (0805) 23797

West Putford
The world's first **Gnome Reserve**
is 8 miles north of Holsworthy,
where more than 1,000 gnomes and
pixies live in a wooded garden with
a stream running through.
Open Apr to Oct, Sun to Fri & BH
Sat. *Tel* Bradworthy (040924) 435

TOURIST INFORMATION CENTRES

Listed below are the tourist
information centres in Devon
and Exmoor. All can provide
further information about local
accommodation, the opening times
and admission charges of tourist
attractions, and ideas for places to
visit and things to do. The
National Park Authorities also
operate several National Park
Information Centres on Dartmoor
and Exmoor.

*****Axminster:** Old Courthouse,
Church Street. *Tel* (0297) 34386

Barnstaple: 20 Holland Street.
Tel (0271) 72742/78950

*****Bideford:** The Quay.
Tel (02372) 77676

*****Bovey Tracey:** Lower Car Park.
Tel (0626) 832047

*****Braunton:** The Car Park.
Tel (0271) 816400

*****Bridgwater:** Town Hall, High
Street.
Tel (0278) 427652/424391

Brixham: The Old Market House,
The Quay.
Tel (08045) 2861

*****Budleigh Salterton:** Fore Street.
Tel (03954) 5275

*****Combe Martin:** Sea Cottage,
Cross Street.
Tel (027188) 3319/2692

*****Dartmouth:** Royal Avenue
Gardens. *Tel* (08043) 4224

Dawlish: The Lawn.
Tel (0626) 863589

Exeter: Civic Centre.
Tel (0392) 265297
*****Granada Service Area, M5.
Tel (0392) 37581

*****Exmouth:** Manor Grounds,
Alexandra Terrace.
Tel (0395) 263744

*****Honiton:** Angel Hotel Car Park,
High Street. *Tel* (0404) 3716

Ilfracombe: The Promenade.
Tel (0271) 63001

Kingsbridge: The Quay.
Tel (0548) 3195

Lynton: Town Hall, Lee Road.
Tel (0598) 52225

Minehead: Market House, The
Parade. *Tel* (0643) 2624

*****Modbury:** 31 Church Street.
Tel (0548) 830159

Newton Abbot: 8 Sherborne Road.
Tel (0626) 67494

*No need to get your feet wet: use the
island's unique sea-tractor*

*****Okehampton:** Museum
Courtyard, 3 West Street.
Tel (0837) 3020

*****Ottery St Mary:** Hill House,
Silver Street. *Tel* (040481) 3964

Paignton: Festival Hall, Esplanade
Road. *Tel* (0803) 558383

Plymouth: Civic Centre, Royal
Parade. *Tel* (0752) 264849/264851
*12 The Barbican.
Tel (0752) 223806

Salcombe: Main Road.
Tel (054884) 2736

*****Sampford Peverell:** Junction 27,
M5. *Tel* (0884) 821242

*****Seaton:** 18 The Esplanade.
Tel (0297) 21660

*****Sidmouth:** The Esplanade.
Tel (03955) 6441

*****South Molton:** 1 East Street.
Tel (07695) 4122/2378

Taunton: The Library, Corporation
Street. *Tel* (0823) 274785/270479

*****Tavistock:** The Guildhall, Bedford
Square. *Tel* (0822) 2938

Teignmouth: The Den, Sea Front.
Tel (06267) 6271 ext 207/258

Tiverton: Phoenix Lane.
Tel (0884) 255827

Torquay: Vaughan Parade.
Tel (0803) 27428

*****Torrington:** Town Hall, High
Street. *Tel* (0805) 24324

*****Totnes:** The Plains.
Tel (0803) 863168

*****Wellington:** The Museum,
28 Fore Street. *Tel* (082347) 4747

*****Woolacombe:** Hall 70, Beach
Road. *Tel* (0271) 870553

* denotes summer opening

CALENDAR OF EVENTS

This calendar of major annual events gives you an idea of how much there is going on in the Devon and Exmoor area. Actual dates and times may vary from year to year, so phone or call in at any tourist information centre for current details and information about other local events.

May
Devon County Show, Exeter
English Riviera Dance Festival, Torbay
Torrington May Fair
Head of the Dart Rowing Race, Dartmouth
Exeter Festival
Minehead Hobby Horse Celebrations

June
Brixham Trawler Race
Babbacombe Regatta
Drake Naval Base Fair, Plymouth
Sidmouth Arts Festival

Plymouth & District Horse Show, Bickham House, Roborough
Medieval Fayre, National Shire Horse Centre, Yealmpton
Devonport Field Gun Public Races
Britannia Royal Naval College Open Day, Dartmouth

July
Torbay Carnival
Saltram Fayre
Ancient Ceremony of Ale Tasting and Bread Weighing, Ashburton
RAF Chivenor Air Day
Ottery St Mary Jazz Festival
Minehead and Exmoor Festival
Historic Vehicle Gathering, Powderham Castle
Dunster Fair
Royal Marines Open Day, Lympstone

August
Brixham Regatta
Sidmouth Folk Festival
Exeter Air Days, Exeter Airport
Honiton Exhibition of Lace
Paignton Regatta
Dartmoor Folk Festival
Festival of Transport, South Molton
Port of Dartmouth Royal Regatta

Plymouth Navy Days
Torbay Sea Angling Festival
Devon Traction Engine, Veteran and Vintage Car Club Steam Rally, Umberleigh
Torbay Royal Regatta
Paignton Children's Week

September
Widecombe Fair
South Western Show Jumping Club Championships, East Budleigh
British Bike Show, Plymouth
Colyford Medieval Michaelmas Goose Fayre
River Exe Struggle, Tiverton

October
Tavistock Goose Fair

November
Ottery St Mary Carnival and Tar Barrel Rolling
Hatherleigh Carnival and Tar Barrel Rolling

December
Devon & Cornwall Winter Wonderland Floral Festival, Plymouth

DEVON
AND
EXMOOR

Atlas

The following pages contain a legend, key map and atlas of the area, four circular motor tours and sixteen planned walks in the Devon and Exmoor countryside.

Above: near Clovelly

Devon Legend

TOURIST INFORMATION

⚊	Camp Site	⚊	Nature reserve
⚊	Caravan Site	☆	Other tourist feature
ⓘ	Information Centre	⚊	Preserved railway
P	Parking Facilities	⚊	Racecourse
⚊	Viewpoint	⚊	Wildlife park
✕	Picnic site	⚊	Museum
⚊	Golf course or links	⚊	Nature or forest trail
⚊	Castle	⚊	Ancient monument
⚊	Cave	((	Telephones : public or motoring organisations
⚊	Country park	PC	Public Convenience
⚊	Garden	▲	Youth Hostel
⚊	Historic house		

◆ ◆ ▬▬ ▬ ·▬· Waymarked Path / Long Distance Path / Recreational Path

ORIENTATION

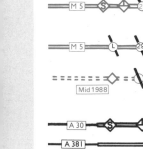

True North
At the centre of the area is 1° 25′ E of Grid North

Magnetic North
At the centre of the area is about 5°W of Grid North in 1987 decreasing by about ½ ° in three years

Diagrammatic Only

GRID REFERENCE SYSTEM

The map references used in this book are based on the Ordnance Survey National Grid, correct to within 1000 Metres They comprise two letters and four figures, and are preceded by the atlas page number.

Thus the reference for Exeter appears 90 SX 9292

90 is the atlas page number

SX identifies the major (100km) grid square concerned (see diag)

9292 locates the lower left-hand corner of the kilometre grid square in which Exeter appears

Take the first figure of the reference 9, this refers to the numbered grid running along the bottom of the page.
Having found this line, the second figure 2, tells you the distance to move in tenths to the right of this line. A vertical line through this point is the first half of the reference.

The third figure 9, refers to the numbered grid lines on the right hand side of the page, finally the fourth figure 2, indicates the distance to move in tenths above this line. A horizontal line drawn through this point to intersect with the first line gives the precise location of the places in question.

KEY-MAP 1:625,000 or 10 MILES to 1″

ROAD INFORMATION

─⚊M 5⚊S⚊A⚊27─	Motorway with service area, service area (limited access) and junction with junction number
─⚊M 5⚊L⚊29─	Motorway junction with limited interchange
═══◇═══ Mid 1988	Motorway, service area and junction under construction with proposed opening date
─A 30─S─	Primary routes } Single and dual carriageway with service area
─A 381─	Main Road }
▬ ▬ ▬ ▬	Main Road under construction
─ ─ ─ ─	Narrow Road with passing places
─── B 3357 ───	Other roads { B roads (majority numbered) Unclassified (selected)
──┃TOLL──	Gradient : 14% (1 in 7) and steeper, and toll
⚲24 ⚑15	Primary routes and main roads
⚲24 ⚑15	Motorways

Primary Routes
These form a national network of recommended through routes which complement the motorway system. Selected places of major traffic importance are known as Primary Route Destinations and are shown on these maps thus **EXETER** This relates to the directions on road signs which on Primary Routes have a green background. To travel on a Primary Route, follow the direction to the next Primary Destination shown on the greenbacked road signs. On these maps Primary Route road numbers and mileages are shown in green.

Motorways
A similar situation occurs with motorway routes where numbers and mileages, shown in blue on these maps correspond to the blue background of motorway road signs.

Mileages are shown on the map between large markers and between small markers in large and small type

1 mile = 1·61 kilometres

GENERAL FEATURES

══════	Passenger railways (selected in conurbations)
AA··A RAC··R PO··T	Telephone call box
+─+─+─+─+─+─+─+─+	National Boundary
─ ─ ─ ─ ─ ─ ─ ─	County or Region Boundary
✈ o	Large Town Town / Village
⊕	Airport
427.	Height (metres)

WATER FEATURES

By Sea { Internal ferry route / External ferry route

Ferry.............. Short ferry routes for vehicles are annotated Ferry

────── Canal

  Coastline, river and lake

ATLAS 1:200,000 or 3 MILES to 1"
TOURS 1:250,000 or 4 MILES to 1"

ROADS   Not necessarily rights of way

M 5

Motorway with service area and junction with junction number

A 38(T)   Dual Carriageway   Trunk road

A 3022   Dual Carriageway   Main road

A 38(T)   Dual Carriageway   Roundabout or multiple level junction

B 3357   Dual Carriageway   Secondary road

Other tarred road

Other minor road

Gradient: 14% (1 in 7) and steeper

RAILWAYS

Road crossing under or over standard gauge track

Level crossing

Station

Narrow gauge track

WATER FEATURES

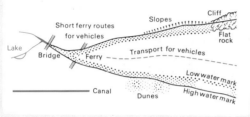

Cliff
Slopes
Flat rock
Short ferry routes for vehicles
Lake
Bridge   Ferry
Transport for vehicles
Low water mark
Canal
Dunes   High water mark

ANTIQUITIES

Native fortress

Roman road (course of)

Castle •   Other antiquities

CANOVIVM •   Roman antiquity

GENERAL FEATURES

Buildings

Civil aerodrome (with custom facilities)

Wood

Radio or TV mast

Lighthouse

Telephones : public or motoring organisations

RELIEF

Feet	Metres	
		274
		Heights in feet above mean sea level
3000	914	
2000	610	
1400	427	
1000	305	Contours at 200 ft intervals
600	183	
200	61	
0	0	To convert feet to metres multiply by 0.3048

WALKS 1:25,000 or 2½" to 1 MILE
ROADS AND PATHS Not necessarily rights of way

M 5	M 5	Motorway	Path
A 38(T)	A 38(T)	Trunk road	
A 381	A 381	Main road	Narrow roads with passing places are annotated
B 3357	B 3357	Secondary road	
A 3022	A 3022	Dual carriageway	

Road generally over 4m wide

Road generally under 4m wide

Other road, drive or track

RAILWAYS

Multiple track   Level crossing

Single track   Cutting

Narrow Gauge   Embankment

Road over & under

Siding   Tunnel

GENERAL FEATURES

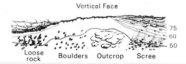

Church   { with tower
or   { with spire
Chapel   { without tower or spire

Electricity transmission line
pylon   pole

Gravel pit   NT National Trust always open

Sand pit   NT National Trust opening restricted

Chalk pit, clay pit or quarry   FC Forestry Commission pedestrians only (observe local signs)

Refuse or slag heap   National Park

HEIGHTS AND ROCK FEATURES

Contours are at various metres / feet vertical intervals

50 } Determined { ground survey
285 · } by { air survey

Surface heights are to the nearest metre / foot above mean sea level. Heights shown close to a triangulation pillar refer to the station height at ground level and not necessarily to the summit .

Vertical Face

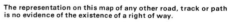

75
60
50

Loose rock   Boulders   Outcrop   Scree

PUBLIC RIGHTS OF WAY

Public rights of way shown in this guide may not be evident on the ground

Public Paths { Footpath
{ Bridleway

+ + + + + By-way open to all traffic

Road used as a public path

Public rights of way indicated by these symbols have been derived from Definitive Maps as amended by later enactments or instruments held by Ordnance Survey between 1st March 1968 and 1st January 1984 and are shown subject to the limitations imposed by the scale of mapping. (Note: some walk maps do not show rights of way symbols) Later information may be obtained from the appropriate County Council .

The representation on this map of any other road, track or path is no evidence of the existence of a right of way.

WALKS AND TOURS (All Scales)

7   Start point of walk

Route of walk

Line of walk

Alternative route

3   Start point of tour

Route of tour

Featured tour

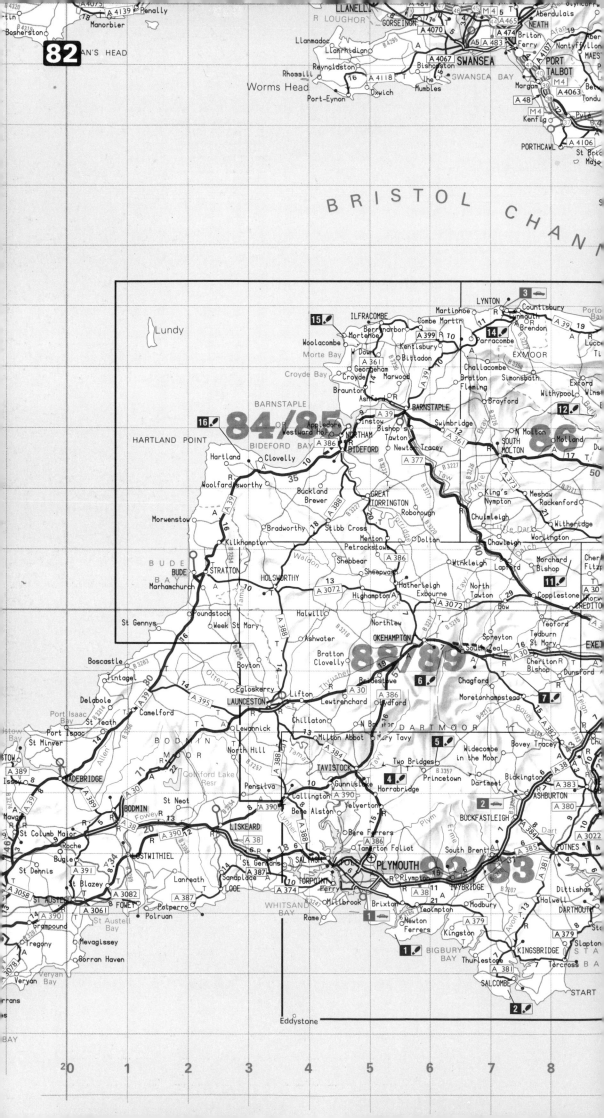

83

Key to Atlas pages

Distances in miles to EXETER
Map Ref: 90 SX 9292

Birmingham	158	London	170
Bournemouth	82	Manchester	239
Bristol	80	Oxford	152
Cardiff	119	Penzance	112
Leeds	288	Southampton	114

DEVON

North West Point

LUNDY

466

South West Point — Rat Island

0 Kilometres 5 10
0 Miles 5

B A R N S T A P L E

O R

B I D E F O R D   B A Y

W

HARTLAND POINT — Titchberry — Windbury Point

Stoke — Hartland — Clovelly

Hartland Quay — 564 — Clovelly Dykes — Buck's Mill — 10

B 3248

16 — Dyke

Millford — Philham — 710 — Buck's Cross

Elmscott — Woolfardisworthy — Parkham Ash — 709

South Hole — Melbury

Knaps Longpeak — Welcome — 771 — Ashmansworthy

Gooseham — Eastcott — East Putford

Morwenstow — 512 — 734 — Dinworthy — 708 — West Putford

Higher Sharpnose Point — Shop — Youlstone — Bradworthy — Abb Bick

Woodford — 656 — Upper Tamar Lake

Lower Sharpnose Point — Sutcombe

Coombe — Kilkhampton — Alfardisworthy — Soldon Cross — Milton

88 — Waldon

Stibb — B 3254 — Lower Tamar Lake

A 39 — 571

B U D E — Poughill — Holsworthy Beacon — 635

Flexbury — **STRATTON** — Grimscott — Chilsworthy — Coo

Bude Haven

BUDE — Launcells — Pancrasweek — **10** — A 3072 — **HOLSWORTHY**

B A Y — 216 — Marhamchurch — Bridgerule — Pyworthy — 531 — Hollacombe

Widemouth Bay — 440

Dizzard Point — Coppathorne — 449

Poundstock — Whitstone — North Tamerton — Clawton

Tregole — 544 — Week St Mary

Cambeak — St Gennys — Trewint — 3 — Tetcott — Lana — Ashwater

Crackington — Wainhouse Corner — Jacobstow — **18**

Heddon's Mouth
Woody Bay
Trentishoe
Martinhoe
Combe Martin Bay
ILFRACOMBE
Lee
Slade
Hele
Berrynarbor
Combe Martin
Kemacott
A 39
Shallowford
Bull Point
Rockham Bay
Mortehoe
Morte Point
Pickwell
North Buckland
Georgeham
Croyde Bay
Croyde
Saunton
Braunton
Braunton Burrows
Bideford Bar
Trimstone
West Down
Bittadon
Milltown
Muddiford
Halsinger
Pippacott
Marwood
Prixford
Heanton Punchardon
Ashford
Chivenor
Fremington
Yelland
Bickington
Instow
Bickleton
Appledore
NORTHAM
Westleigh
Bideford
East-the-Water
Horwood
Newton Tracey
Hiscott
Ensis
Woodtown
Alverdiscott
Landcross
Littleham
Weare Giffard
Yarnscombe
Monkleigh
Frithelstock
Great Torrington
Little Torrington
Langtree
Peters Marland
Winswell
Beaford
Merton
Huish
Dolton
Dowland
Shebbear
Buckland Filleigh
Petrockstowe
Meeth
Iddesleigh
Winkleigh
Bradford
Sheepwash
Black Torrington
Highampton
Monkokehampton
Hatherleigh
Holemoor
Graddon Moor
Halwill Junction
Halwill
Beaworthy
Northlew
Ashbury
Exbourne
Jacobstowe
Sampford Courtenay
Folly Gate
OKEHAMPTON
East Down
Patchole
Arlington
Loxhore
Wistlandpound Resr
Blackmoor Gate
Knightacott
Bratton Fleming
Shirwell
Stoke Rivers
Goodleigh
Gunn
BARNSTAPLE
Newport
Bishop's Tawton
Landkey
Swimbridge
Tawstock
West Buckland
Herner
Chapleton
Cobbaton
Chittlehampton
Umberleigh
Atherington
Warkleigh
Satterleigh
Chittlehamholt
High Bickington
Sherwood Green
Northcote Manor
Portsmouth Arms Sta
King's Nympton
King's Nympton Sta
Elstone
Chulmleigh
Romansleigh
George Nympton
Alswear
Clapworthy
Challacombe
Shoulsbarrow Common
Lydcott
Brayford
Charles
East Buckland
Heasley
Parracombe
Kentisbury
Pinkworthy Pond
Leworthy
Wembworthy
Eggesford Sta
Coldridge
Nymet Rowland
Brushford
Ashreigney
Riddlecombe
Roborough
Burrington
Kingscott
St Giles in the Wood
Ashley
Hollacombe
Broadwoodkelly
Bondleigh
East Leigh
Honeychurch
North Tawton
Taw Green
Spreyton
Inwardleigh
Nymet Tracey

B 3343
B 3230
A 39
A 399
A 361 (T)
A 39 (T)
B 3226
B 3227
B 3232
B 3217
B 3220
B 3216
A 3072
A 386
A 388
A 3072
B 3215
B 3219

Morte Bay

15

88
89

Due to open Mid 1987

TOUR 1 *57 MILES*

Western Dartmoor

Open moorland dotted with sheep and ponies is the theme for the first part of this tour. Later, it follows lovely Devon lanes to reach the reconstructed quay at Morwellham, and Buckland Abbey, once home of Sir Francis Drake.

From Plymouth City Centre *(see page 60) or the Tamar Bridge road A38, follow signs Exeter to reach March Mills roundabout. Here take the exit signed Plympton on to the B3416.* Shortly pass a road on the left leading to the Marsh Mills, headquarters of the Plym Valley Railway, which is re-opening the former Great Western line through the valley.

In ½ mile on the right is a road leading past the entrance to Saltram House. This 18th-century National Trust property is set in attractive grounds.

Nearly ¾ mile farther at the mini-roundabout turn left, signed Exeter. Alternatively turn right to visit Plympton (see page 60). It has two interesting old churches, one being Plympton St Mary, the other at Plympton St Maurice, where there is also a 16th-century guildhall, a 17th-century grammar school and the keep of a Norman castle.

In ½ mile turn left, signed Sparkwell, Cornwood, and in ¼ mile at a mini-roundabout turn right. Proceed through pleasant countryside to Sparkwell, beyond which is the entrance (on the left) to the Dartmoor Wildlife Park. More than 100 different kinds of animals and birds can be seen here.

Continue to Lutton before reaching Cornwood. At the crossroads in Cornwood turn left, signposted Tavistock, and start a long, gradual ascent onto Lee Moor, situated beneath Penn Beacon (1,402ft) and Shell Top (1,546ft). Pass some of the pits and spoil-heaps of Devon's only moorland china-clay area and proceed to the edge of Lee Moor village.

Continue with wide views over the whole of the Plymouth area and after 2½ miles at crossroads turn on to the Cadover Bridge road. Alternatively keep forward and pass through the village of Shaugh Prior to Shaugh Bridge – the meeting point of the rivers Meavy and Plym at the entrance to the National Trust's Goodameavy Estate.

The main route continues northwards to reach Cadover Bridge, spanning the infant River Plym. Bear left across the bridge and ascend, and at the top turn right, signed Sheepstor, Meavy. In 1 mile descend (1 in 6) into the Meavy Valley and in ½ mile cross the river to reach the edge of Meavy. Here keep forward, signed Princetown, and in ½ mile turn sharp right, signposted Burrator. In ¾ mile turn right, signed Sheepstor, across the dam wall of the Burrator Reservoir. A circular tour of the reservoir is then made – it is attractively situated between Sharpitor (1,312ft) and Sheeps Tor (1,150ft).

In almost ¾ mile turn left (no sign) along a narrow road, and continue the drive round the reservoir's wooded bank. After 3 miles turn sharp right, signed Princetown, and ascend, and in ¾ mile at crossroads turn right on to the B3212 signed Princetown. The drive then climbs on to open moorland with extensive views on the left into east and north Cornwall. The BBC television transmitter on North Hessary Tor (1,695ft) is seen to the left on the approach to Princetown (see page 62), situated at a height of 1,400ft.

Turn left on to the Tavistock road, B3357 and shortly pass the prison, then in 1 mile at a T-junction turn left again. With Great Mis Tor (1,768ft) on the right and extensive views ahead stretching from the Tamar estuary to Bodmin Moor, the drive gradually descends from Dartmoor, past Merrivale quarry in the Walkham valley, to reach Tavistock (see page 66). This pleasant town, situated on the River Tavy, has remains of an abbey and an imposing town hall.

Leave by the Liskeard road, A390, and in 2½ miles, at the Harvest Home PH, branch left onto an unclassified road signed Morwellham. In 1 mile at crossroads go forward and start a long descent to reach Morwellham (see page 57). A former copper loading port on the River Tamar, it is now a major industrial museum of the port and the local copper mines.

Return to the crossroads and turn sharp right, signed Bere Alston, to proceed along a high ridge between the Tamar and Tavy valleys. After 2¾ miles turn sharp left, signed Denham Bridge, Plymouth, and start a long descent (1 in 4 at the end) along a narrow road to cross the River Tavy at the secluded Denham Bridge. Immediately turn right, signposted Plymouth, to ascend out of the valley, and in ¾ mile at a T-junction turn right, signed Buckland Abbey. In ½ mile at crossroads turn right then left, signed Roborough, Plymouth, passing the entrance immediately on the right to Buckland Abbey. Once owned by Sir Francis Drake, it now contains the Drake Museum.

In 1¼ miles the drive starts to cross Roborough Down and at crossroads bear left to reach a T-junction with the A386. Here turn right (no sign) on to the main road and later pass the edge of Roborough. Plymouth Airport is then skirted before the long gradual descent to Plymouth city centre.

Grave stones in the prisoners' burial ground at Princetown

Prehistoric stone row and circle at Merrivale

On Plymouth Hoe: Smeaton's revolutionary lighthouse, built between 1756 and 1759, was moved here in 1882 from Eddystone Rock when a new lighthouse replaced it

TOUR 2 44 MILES
The Tors of South-east Dartmoor

The famous Dartmoor tors are important features of this drive, which also visits some of the moor's prettiest villages.

The tour starts at Ashburton (see page 36), one of Devon's four stannary towns, with many old and attractive buildings including a 15th-century church with a magnificent Devonshire tower.

From the town centre follow Buckland signs along an unclassified road, shortly turning left across the River Ashburn before starting a long ascent through well-wooded country. The drive later keeps forward to pass beneath the slopes of Buckland Beacon (1,282ft). On the summit stands the Ten Commandments Stone, carved by a local stonemason. To the left are occasional views over the deep and thickly wooded Dart valley.

Continue along a narrow, winding road through Buckland in the Moor. This is a scattered hamlet with a picturesque group of thatched granite cottages.

One mile farther at a T-junction turn left, signed Widecombe, and descend into the attractive East Webburn valley. Cross the river and ascend to another T-junction and turn right. In 1 mile enter Widecombe in the Moor (see page 70). The village is dominated by the 120ft-high tower of its fine 14th-century church. Adjacent are the 13th-century Church House (NT) and the village green, whose connection with the well-known song 'Widecombe Fair' is celebrated by the carved sign.

Leave by the Bovey Tracey road, bearing right past the green, and ascend steeply onto open moorland. The drive passes Rippon Tor (1,506ft) on the right, then reveals a magnificent view – from 1,250ft – over south Devon to Torbay. On the left are Saddle Tor (1,350ft) and the famous Haytor Rocks, which rise to 1,490ft and make a fine viewpoint.

Start the long descent to the Bovey valley and, after 3 miles, at the crossroads by the Edgemoor Hotel, turn left (no sign). From this point a short detour can be made to visit the Parke & Rare Breeds Farm and Dartmoor National Park Centre near Bovey Tracey by keeping forward at the crossroads and in ½ mile turning right. The entrance is ¼ mile farther on the left. On leaving, turn right and rejoin the main route near Yarner Wood.

The main tour turns left again after ½ mile, signed Manaton, Becky Falls. In a further ¾ mile pass on the left an entrance to the Yarner Wood National Nature Reserve (guided walks available). Continue the winding climb across the slopes of Trendlebere Down, with excellent views of the thickly wooded Bovey valley to the right, before entering dense woodland surrounding the picturesque Becky Falls (entrance on right). Continue past the hamlet of Manaton (once the home of the novelist John Galsworthy) and at the T-junction ¼ mile beyond Manaton's 15th-century church turn right onto the North Bovey road. Descend steeply along a narrow, winding road and after 1½ miles cross the River Bovey and ascend into North Bovey. One of Dartmoor's most attractive villages, North Bovey is set round a pleasant green.

Leave by following signs for Postbridge and in ½ mile at crossroads turn left. Three-quarters of a mile farther at a T-junction turn left onto the B3212, signed Princetown. Ascend, with good views to the right, on to open moorland; to the left rises high ground leading to Hameldown Tor (1,737ft). Near the Warren House Inn, where a peat fire is always burning, the road reaches its highest point, at 1,426ft. Go through Postbridge (see page 61). A medieval stone clapper bridge can be seen to the left as the drive crosses the East Dart River.

The next turning on the left can be taken along an unclassified road past Bellever Wood to Bellever picnic site and nature trail. This relatively new coniferous woodland has a reasonable cross-section of birds. Its setting beside the East Dart River is extremely attractive.

At the edge of Two Bridges turn left onto the Dartmeet, Ashburton road B3357, following the line of the West Dart. After 4¼ miles the drive descends steeply to reach the picturesque Dartmeet Bridge, where the East and West Dart rivers converge, before starting a long winding ascent (1 in 5) on the Ashburton road, unclassified, to the vicinity of Sharp Tor (1,250ft) from where there are fine views down the valley. From Poundsgate a steep, winding descent (maximum 1 in 4) leads to a crossing of the River Dart at New Bridge, adjacent to which is a picnic site. After entering the woods of Holne Chase (where an unclassified road on the right leads to Holne, birthplace of the author Charles Kingsley) the River Dart is crossed for the second time, at the 15th-century Holne Bridge. One mile farther the drive passes the entrance (on right) to the River Dart Country Park and in a further ¾ mile turns left to re-enter Ashburton.

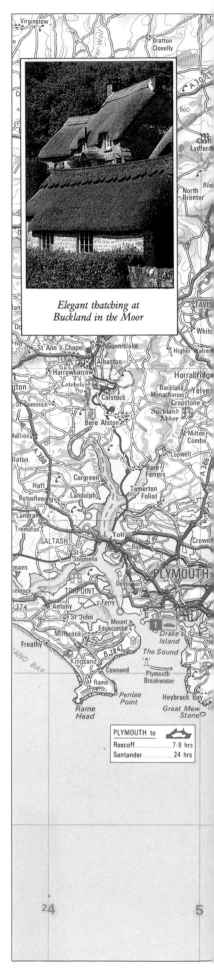

Elegant thatching at Buckland in the Moor

PLYMOUTH to	⛴
Roscoff	7-9 hrs
Santander	24 hrs

Widecombe in the Moor, a lovely village in a perfect setting. The church was struck by lightning in 1638, killing four and injuring 62

TOUR 3
58¾ MILES

Exmoor – combes and cliffs

The rolling uplands of Exmoor are a dominant feature of this tour, which also makes its way along the coastline with its steep hills and dramatic sea views.

The drive starts from the large hill-top village of Lynton *(see page 56)*. *Leave by the Lynmouth road and on the descent turn sharp left with the B3234. Continue the steep descent of Lynmouth Hill (25%) to the small resort of Lynmouth – attractively situated at the mouth of the East and West Lyn rivers. Follow signs Minehead A39 and ascend Countisbury Hill (1 in 4).* This is one of the most famous hills in the West Country. It has good seascape views over the Bristol Channel to the Welsh coast.

After the long climb to the hamlet of Countisbury the road emerges on to the northern extremity of Exmoor. Three miles farther the drive enters Somerset and shortly passes the turning to Oare (on the right). A short detour from here leads down to Oare Church (see page 58), famous as the location of the wedding ceremony in Blackmore's *Lorna Doone*. The nearby village of Malmsmead provides access to the legendary 'Doone Country'.

The main tour continues along the A39 for almost 6 miles and then makes the notorious twisting descent of Porlock Hill (1 in 4) to reach the village of Porlock (see page 61). A diversion to the left along the B3223 leads to the coast at Porlock Weir (1½ miles), with its small harbour.

At Porlock go forward through the village with the Minehead road and at the end keep left then turn right with the one-way system. Half a mile farther turn right on to an unclassified road, signed Horner and Luccombe, and proceed through the attractive Horner Valley.

In 1½ miles, at the crossroads, turn right, signed Dunkery Beacon. (Alternatively keep forward to visit the delightful village of Luccombe – ½ mile – with its thatched cottages.) The main tour immediately ascends (1 in 5) and after ¾ mile it bears left in order to continue the long climb over the shoulder of Dunkery Hill. At the 1,453ft summit a footpath on the right leads to the AA Viewpoint on Dunkery Beacon. Dunkery is Exmoor's highest point and is a popular destination for many. Walkers to the viewpoint will be rewarded by extensive views on clear days. Some may be lucky enough to see the red deer which live on the moor. They spend most of their time hidden in the deep combes, but are sometimes to be seen in the open, most often in early morning or at twilight.

There is an easy descent for 2¾ miles after which turn right on to the Simonsbath road, B3224. Continue through undulating countryside for 3¾ miles before turning left on to an unclassified road, signed Winsford. This pleasant byroad later enters the valley of the River Exe to reach Winsford. At the telephone kiosk turn right (signed Molton) then bear left. After another 1½ miles meet the crossroads junction with the B3223. The road ahead leads to Tarr Steps, a medieval clapper bridge and well known Exmoor beauty spot on the River Barle.

The main route turns right onto the Lynton, Simonsbath road, B3223, and crosses Winsford Hill (1,405ft summit). Proceed through more open countryside and in 4 miles at the crossroads turn left. At the small Exmoor village of Simonsbath (see page 64) *branch left with the B3358, signed Blackmoor Gate and Ilfracombe. Follow this moorland road to Challacombe and after a further 2¼ miles at the T-junction turn right on to the B3226. At Blackmoor Gate turn left then immediately right, A399, signed Combe Martin. Two miles farther turn right on to an unclassified road, signed Trentishoe and Hunter's Inn. In another 1¼ miles turn right again and later pass the car park for Holdstone Down (on the left)* from where there are fine views. *Almost a mile farther bear right (still signed Hunter's Inn) and descend into the wooded valley of the River Heddon to the beautifully situated Hunter's Inn.* Heddon's Mouth, where the River Heddon reaches the sea, is a particularly attractive spot made all the more pleasing by the fact that it can only be reached on foot along paths that are a delight in themselves.

Here turn left, signed Martinhoe, and ascend along a narrow byroad. At the top turn left again and continue to the hamlet of Martinhoe. Pass the church and in almost ½ mile branch left, signed Woody Bay Hotel then take the next turning left. After the descent continue with signs Lynton via Toll Road, passing the Woody Bay Hotel – with impressive views across the Bristol Channel.

Follow the narrow coast road and in 1¼ miles pass through a tollgate. Later go forward at the roundabout, entering the spectacular Valley of the Rocks with its many jagged tors and rocky outcrops, before the return to Lynton.

Oare Church, where Lorna Doone was married

Lynton's extraordinary cliff railway, built in 1890

Lynmouth: The superb countryside and cliff scenery surrounding the town ensure its popularity and make it an ideal base for walkers

TOUR 4 64 MILES
East Devon resorts

As well as seaside places such as Exmouth and Sidmouth, this tour explores the countryside of east Devon, passing many a pretty village and several notable churches.

The drive starts at Exeter (see page 50). *From the city centre follow signs Exmouth (A376) to leave by the B3182 Topsham Road. In 2 miles, at a roundabout, take the second exit, unclassified, signed Topsham. Later pass under the M5 viaduct and enter Topsham.* This former port has a number of old houses – including several attractive 17th- and 18th-century examples in the Strand built by Dutch merchants.

Pass the Lord Nelson Public House then turn left, signed Exmouth (for town centre keep forward). Go over the level crossing then bear right. On the descent pass the 16th-century Bridge Inn before crossing the River Clyst. In ¾ mile at the roundabout turn right on to the A376. This road runs parallel, but inland, to the estuary of the River Exe, skirting Exton and Lympstone before continuing to the resort and residential town of Exmouth (see page 52). The good sandy beach offers fine views across the estuary to Dawlish Warren and Torbay.

Leave by the Budleigh Salterton road, A376. Budleigh (see page 41) is a small resort with a shingle beach at the mouth of the River Otter. Keep forward through the town, passing (on the left) the thatched Fairlynch Arts Centre and Museum. At the end of the seafront ascend and turn sharp left, then leave by following the main A376 northwards through the Otter Valley.

After another ¾ mile is the Brick Cross, a curious obelisk at a crossroads with directions in biblical phrases. At this point a short detour across the valley to the right can be made to visit Otterton. The village contains attractive houses with a craft centre and old mill.

The main drive then skirts Bicton Park. Within the extensive grounds there are magnificent gardens, a woodland railway, theme halls and a countryside museum.

Continue through Colaton Raleigh and in 1½ miles turn right on to the A3052, signed Sidmouth, entering Newton Poppleford. At the end cross the River Otter and ascend (1 in 8). Shortly beyond the summit turn right on to the B3176 and later descend to the edge of Sidmouth town centre (see page 64). This Regency and Victorian resort has a mainly shingle beach and is bounded by fine red cliff scenery to both the east and west.

At the mini-roundabout turn left signed Honiton, Lyme Regis, into All Saints Road. (For the seafront and car parks go forward.) At the end turn left and leave by the B3175 to reach Sidford. Here turn right on to the Lyme Regis road, A3052. Shortly pass an old packhorse bridge over the River Sid (on the left) then ascend (1 in 7) on to higher ground. Three miles farther turn left on to the B3174, signed Ottery and Honiton. After 2½ miles a detour to the right leads to Farway Countryside Park. Here rare breeds and present-day farm animals can be seen in a picturesque farm setting.

Continue with the B3174 and in ¾ mile branch right, unclassified, signed Farway. Keep forward along the top of the forested Farway Hill and in 2¾ miles at the T-junction turn left, signed Honiton. A 1 in 5 descent is then made to reach Honiton (see page 54).

Turn left into the main street and in ¾ mile turn left again on to the Sidmouth road, A375. An ascent is then made of Gittisham Hill to cross Bittisham Common. After a further 1½ miles, at the Hare and Hounds Public House, turn right on to the B3174, signed Ottery. One mile farther a diversion to the left, signed Sidbury, may be taken to the White Cross Picnic Site (2¾ miles) from where there are magnificent views.

The main drive descends Chineway Hill (1 in 5) to reach Ottery St Mary (see page 58). This small town has literary associations with Thackeray and Coleridge, and was the birthplace of the latter. The 14th-century church, with its twin towers, is one of the most notable in Devon.

Turn right, signed Exeter, then bear left (one-way) through the square. At the end turn right on to the B3176, signed Fairmile and Talaton. Later cross the River Otter and pass the entrance to the fine Tudor and Georgian building of Cadhay House. At Fairmile cross the A30, signed Talaton and Clyst Hydon. Continue along this secondary road through Talaton to Clyst Hydon. At the end of the village turn right signed Cullompton, then in ¾ mile turn left on to the unclassified Hele road. Follow this byroad round to the broad Culm Valley. At the junction with the B3181 turn left on to the Exeter road and 2 miles farther pass the junction with the B3185. From here a detour to the right leads to the National Trust property of Killerton House. Remain on the B3181 past Broad Clyst and later enter the suburbs of Exeter at Pinhoe. Go forward at the mini-roundabouts (signed Ring Road) then in 1 mile at the traffic signals turn right, B3212, for the return to Exeter city centre.

Moll's Coffee House in Exeter's Cathedral Close

Ottery St Mary has one of Devon's best churches

Sidmouth. Despite the car parks and modern buildings, the centre of the town is an unspoilt delight

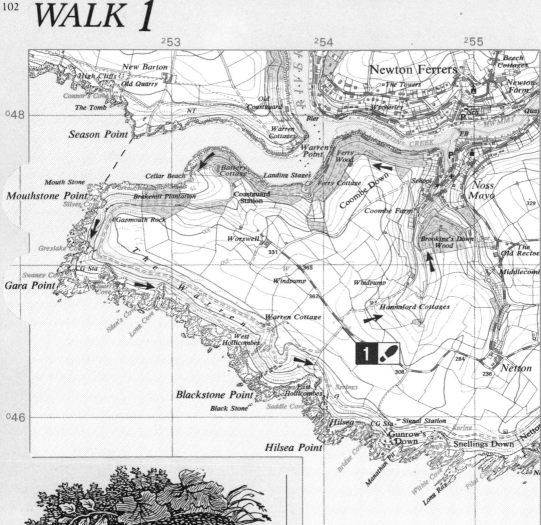

Rabbit – always at the mercy of men

Southern Cliffs

Allow 2½ hours

A simple, level walk, suitable for elderly people or families with small children and worth doing at any time of the year. The route is largely through National Trust property – farmland, woods and open cliff land – with constantly-changing views.

From the Trust's Warren Cliffs car park (SX541466), leave by the way you entered, turn left and then right after 35yds down a gravel track. You pass down a small valley to the delightful village of Noss Mayo clustered round Noss Creek. Across this creek of the River Yealm is the prosperous yachting resort of Newton Ferrers.

Turn left opposite Noss Mayo car park, and then right along a narrow road with a 7ft width restriction. After the last cottage on the left mount a few steps on the left into Fordhill Plantation. This National Trust path takes the walker off the road, which is never busy, but is narrow. This is the Revelstoke Drive, or the Ten Mile Drive, built as a carriage drive in the last century by Lord Revelstoke. The family seat was at Membland, to the east of Noss Mayo, and Lord Revelstoke laid out the drive to enable him to circumnavigate his property from the comfort of a carriage and show off his estate to his guests at the same time. The path undulates through beech, sycamore and sweet chestnuts. Soon the mouth of the River Yealm (pronounced 'Yam') is seen coming in from the north.

Where the path rejoins the drive, back-track for about 25yds, turn sharp left and take the track leading to the (summer only) ferry slip. The path continues to rejoin the Revelstoke Drive. Battery Cottage is passed, a sprawling country house on the site of a one-time defensive position. After passing through Brakehill Plantation the path reaches open cliff land. The Great Mew Stone is seen ahead, and Eddystone lighthouse may be spotted to the south-west if the day is clear. At Gara Point the path bears left above the coastguard look-out. About 50yds east of the point cormorants or shags may be seen resting on a waterline rock. These gently sloping cliffs, Warren Cliffs, are so called as rabbits were positively encouraged to breed here for their meat and skins. Warren Cottage is where the warrener lived. Sheep graze the sidelands, so dogs should be kept on leads.

Having rounded the corner beyond Warren Cottage, the path turns inland through a gate and returns to the car park.

Around Bolt Head

Allow 3 hours

A not too energetic walk around the rocky headland guarding the entrance to Salcombe Harbour and the cliffs on either side.

From the car park serving Overbecks Museum and Garden (National Trust) (SX728374) return down the approach road and turn right along a track signposted Bolt Head via Starehole Bay. This is the Courtenay Walk, and is named after the family who built the path. It is cut through Sharpitor, the craggy outcrop of mica schist forming the northern approach to Starehole Bay. As you look down into the bay, provided the tide is low and the water unruffled, you may be able to spot the shadow of the four-masted Finnish barque *Herzogin Cecilie,* which struck a rock to the west in 1936 and was abandoned here after attempts at salvage had failed.

Follow the path round the back of the bay and out to Bolt Head and up some steps to a World War II look-out. The structure is windowless and rather ugly, but of historic interest. A catwalk leads round to a lavatory cubicle and the actual look-out – a tiny structure – facing the sea.

The path now continues westwards up a grassy gulch, bears left and passes over a stile. The path is level and pleasingly open, and soon bears right to go round Off Cove. After two more stiles, follow the wall dividing the open cliff land from farm land. Turn right off this open land along a path leading inland past the unoccupied farm of Middle Soar to a road. Turn left here, and right just beyond a gravel depot along a straight track. To your left is a Ministry of Defence installation on the site of a World War II airfield where Spitfires once took off for raids against the German-occupied Channel Islands.

At the end of the straight track, turn right and then left over a stile signposted YHA and Salcombe. This is a National Trust permissive path. Follow the path straight across several fields and stiles, then left at a path signposted Overbecks. From this high ground the landlocked waters of Salcombe Harbour are visible. Across the bay are Pig's Nose, Ham Stone and Gammon Head!

Walk along the grassy strip between a fence and hedge to one last stile which is at the top of the lane leading down to Overbecks car park. (If it is open, a visit to Overbecks is well worthwhile. The southernmost garden in Devon, it contains many exotic plants and is especially noted for its glorious springtime displays of magnolias.)

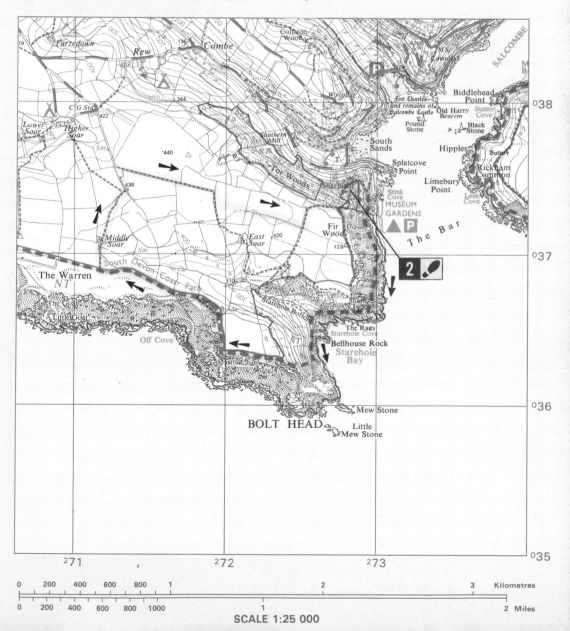

WALK 3
The D'Oyly Carte Cliffs

Allow 3 hours, but with the possibility of an extension

A strenuous circuit of the Coleton Fishacre estate on the south Devon coast, entirely on National Trust land.

From the Trust's car park (SX904510) near Higher Brownstone Farm, walk along the so-called Military Road towards the coast. The route passes a stone tower called the Daymark, an 80ft hollow daytime-only navigational aid built in 1864 by the Dart Harbour Commissioners.

Enter a gate into a grove of Monterey pines and follow the road to the remains of a World War II harbour defence battery. This is one of the few wartime coastal defences to survive. Further down the cliff, connected by steps and paths, are two gun sites, two sea-level searchlight positions and shell magazines, which can be visited.

Turn away from the headquarters area, and walk east along the signposted path through the trees. After you leave the woods, take the right-hand path option which loops steeply down, giving good views of the Mew Stone. The raucous clamour of gulls and other sea birds announces its importance as a sea bird breeding station.

The path switchbacks along the coast, eventually crossing the mouth of the Coleton Fishacre valley above Pudcombe Cove. It is difficult to realise that 60 years ago this valley was treeless. The D'Oyly Carte family – of Gilbert and Sullivan fame – cruising in their yacht, anchored in Pudcombe Cove and were captivated by its beauty and remoteness. Rupert D'Oyly Carte built Coleton Fishacre House in 1925–6, and the gardens were laid out between 1926 and 1940 by Lady Dorothy D'Oyly Carte behind the shelter-belts which were the first plantings. The 18 acres of Coleton Fishacre may be visited at the times advertised. A fascinating collection of uncommon trees and rare shrubs thrives here.

Climb steeply up and follow the coast path along to the back of Ivy Cove. (The walk may be extended by 1½ miles by carrying on along the coast path to Downend Point, then taking the higher path at a fork and heading inland along a line of hedges. Coleton Camp will be met as in the main route.) Now turn away from the coast using a link path through the fields provided by the National Trust. This leads to the remains of Coleton Camp. Coleton Camp was a World War II radar installation, but it has a longer history – Trinity Chapel stood here in the 16th and 17th centuries, and the Admiralty had a flag signal station here in 1800.

Pass through the camp area to the road which should then be followed back to the car park.

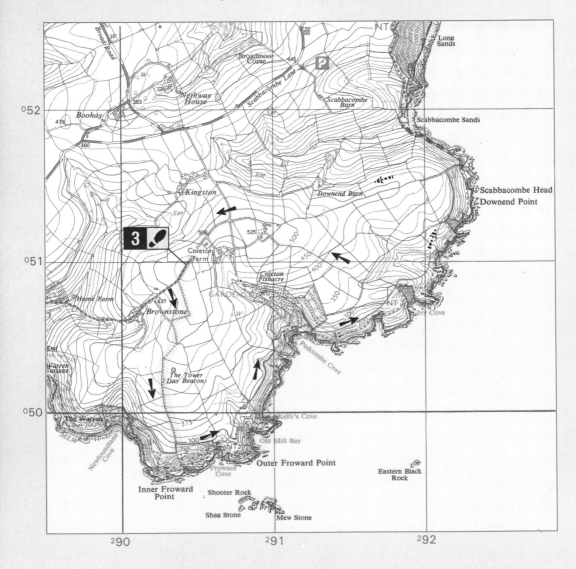

Dartmoor's Archaeology

Allow 3 hours

A varied walk with little climbing through the beautiful scenery of the Walkham Valley, returning along the line of the defunct Princetown railway past once-busy quarries, and visiting at the end an impressive group of Bronze Age antiquities.

From the car parking area (SX550751) near the old bridge over the River Walkham at Merrivale, cross the 'new' road and enter the signposted farm track next to Hillside Cottages. This will be the route for the next 2½ miles. A disused quarry is passed on the left, then Longash Farm which is no longer actively farmed. Across the valley is Vixen Tor, one of Dartmoor's finest granite outcrops. The Longash Brook (or the Pila Brook: some Dartmoor streams have alternative names) is crossed, and the track passes through Hucken Tor, a charming little tor where a gate is hung between the rocks. A fine view now opens up, the track becomes a road and several farms are passed.

At the first crossroads turn up left signposted Criptor, and after crossing a cattle grid bear off right towards the prominent pile of Ingra Tor where the track of the

old Princetown railway is met. Follow it left. The line began as a horse-drawn tramway in the 1820s, was converted to a railway, and closed in 1956. There was a halt here from 1936 which displayed a sign warning of the danger of snakes to dogs. As you walk, the track of the 1820s tramway will be seen taking a longer route round Yes Tor Bottom, the name of this shallow valley. Soon the waste tips of Swelltor quarry will be seen with the grass-covered Royal Oak siding beyond.

As the railway bends tightly round to the right (east) keep an eye open for the bold face of Yellowmeade Farm, and when it comes in sight bear down left off the track and make for the wall corner, following it round left and crossing the upper reaches of the Longash Brook which was crossed earlier. Head for a prominent stone on the immediate skyline ahead. This is one of a number of guidestones erected about 1700 to assist travellers in finding their way between Ashburton and Tavistock. An A and a T are incised on the sides of the stone facing these towns.

By aiming north-west from the stone towards Merrivale quarry you will pass through the most interesting, comprehensive and convenient group of prehistoric antiquities on Dartmoor, dating from somewhere between 750BC and 2500BC. These are groups of hut circles (the stone foundations of circular dwellings), burials in the form of stone cairns or stone chests, menhirs (prominent standing stones), a stone circle (presumably a temple of some kind), and most enigmatic of all, lines of upright stones, usually called stone rows.

Return to Merrivale Bridge in the dip beneath Merrivale quarry.

WALK 5
Wistman's Wood and Crockern Tor

Allow 2½ hours

An easy walk over open moorland to the curious grove of gnarled oaks known as Wistman's Wood, visiting several typical tors on the return route, one of which was the meeting place of the Stannary Parliament.

From the quarry car park (SX609751) at Two Bridges pass through the gate and walk north along the track past Crockern, and bear up right following the signpost directions and yellow waymarks to a stile. Once over the stile Wistman's Wood comes into view ahead. Crowning the hill to your left (west) are the Beardown Tors, one of which carries a flagpole from which a red flag flies when firing is taking place on the Merrivale field firing range, but this walk does not enter the firing area. The Devonport Leat follows the hillslope beneath the Beardown Tors, taking water from the West Dart River to Plymouth, via Burrator reservoir.

Climb a ladder stile to reach Wistman's Wood. Wistman's Wood is growing at between 1300ft and 1400ft. This is high and very exposed for an oak wood. Lichen, ferns and moss add to its interest. The granite boulders from which it appears to grow provide shelter for the younger trees which manage to attain maturity despite the nibbling sheep. Visitors are asked not to venture into the wood as it is a National Nature Reserve. In any case it is easy to twist an ankle or break a leg on the mossy rocks. Outside the top edge are some pillow mounds or buries, artificial warrens where rabbits were encouraged to breed for their flesh and fur.

At the northern limit of the wood, head uphill to Longaford Tor, from which a splendid view unfolds.

To the north, on a clear day, Cut Hill can be seen, the most remote summit on Dartmoor, and in the nearby valley to the south-east are the ruined buildings of the 19th-century Powder Mills, where gunpowder was made.

Now walk south along the ridge. Some of the blocks comprising Littaford Tors look like masonry, but are entirely natural. Dartmoor's tors have not been satisfactorily explained, and even geologists disagree as to their origin.

Carry on to a gap in the wall ahead where three walls meet and pass through, still heading south. Soon the summit of Crockern Tor comes into view, the assembly point for the Stannary Parliament from 1494 to 1703. This was the Great Court of the Dartmoor tinners, and Crockern Tor was chosen as it was about equidistant from the Stannary towns of Ashburton, Chagford, Tavistock and Plympton, which all sent representatives.

Now head west and downhill to the first stile climbed on the outward walk, and return to the car park.

Meadow pipit – in wild and lonely places its 'peet-peet' call is often the only bird voice to be heard

Dartmoor's Northern Tors

Allow 2 hours

**After visiting the lively East Okement River in its delightfully wooded valley, the walk returns along the lofty crest of the Belstone Tors. This route is best followed in good visibility.
NB: although this walk does not cross Ministry of Defence ranges, walkers are advised to check that firing is not in progress, either by 'phoning Plymouth (0752) 772312 ext 249 or by ensuring that the red flag is not flying on Belstone Tor.**

After parking beside the village green in Belstone (SX619935), leave the village by the road near the Post Office signposted Okehampton Indirect. Follow this lane for about ½ mile to a turning left just past Cleave House. This brings the walker to a splendid viewpoint overlooking the East Okement valley at Cleave Tor. Cleave Tor is not a granite tor, but is composed of metamorphic rock, a type of rock found round the edge of the moor. Across the valley the Moor Brook descends from the high land to the west to join the East Okement.

Turn left and follow the track which descends the hillside diagonally to Chapel Ford. This is a good place for a picnic. All three ways of crossing a river

are found here – a ford, stepping stones and a footbridge.

Continue upstream with the river on your right, and having passed through a hedge head due south for Winter Tor on the rocky hillside ahead. There are more tracks than are shown on the map, and these can be followed so long as the general direction is maintained. Once at Winter Tor carry on to the top of the ridge. An enormous panorama now unfolds. The two highest points of Dartmoor, Yes Tor and High Willhays, are about 3 miles to the south-west, and the great bowl to the east is Taw Marsh. The rounded hill beyond is Cawsand (or Cosdon). To the south is the blanket bogland of high Dartmoor. Much of this is used by the Army for live firing, but may be visited when the red flags are not flying on high points.

Now turn north along the rock-strewn ridge past Higher Tor and the various summits of the Belstone Tors. Crossing the ridge is a tumbledown wall called Irishman's Wall. This represents the efforts of an Irishman and some of his countrymen to enclose part of the moor against the will of the local people who waited until he had nearly finished before they gathered in strength and pushed much of it over.

Where the ridge falls away steeply to the north descend to the Nine Stones on Belstone Common. The Nine Stones – or Nine Maidens – are in fact twelve stones (they were once called the Seventeen Brothers), and in folklore are an example of petrifaction, or being turned to stone for dancing on a Sunday. In reality they are likely to have formed the retaining circle of a Bronze Age burial, the hollow of which can still be seen in the centre.

Now walk north along the nearby track to return to Belstone.

| 0 | 200 | 400 | 600 | 800 | 1 | | 2 | | 3 | Kilometres |

| 0 | 200 | 400 | 600 | 800 | 1000 | | 1 | | | 2 Miles |

SCALE 1:25 000

WALK 7

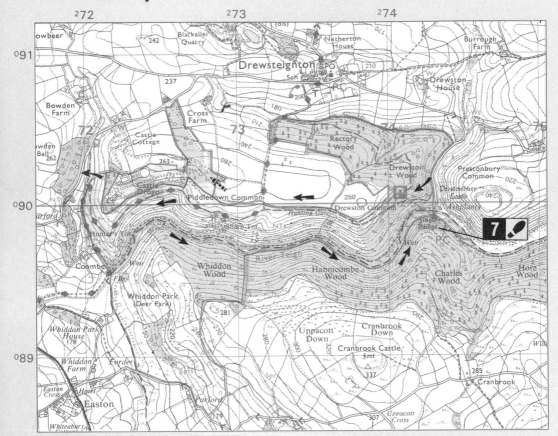

Valleys and Slopes around Castle Drogo

Allow 3 hours

A gentle but long climb early in the walk leads to a panoramic high-level track. The return route is along a riverside path with one short, stepped ascent over a rocky buttress. There is an opportunity – between April and October – to visit a 20th-century castle, Castle Drogo, owned by the National Trust.

From the car park (SX743898) on the south side of Fingle Bridge (next to the lavatories) walk back over the bridge and away from it for 170yds, then take the signposted path going through the woods up the flank of the Teign Gorge. Initially the trees are oaks, but silver birch becomes dominant further up. Large domed wood ants' nests punctuate the path verges. Where the trees are left behind the view ahead tempts the walker on. This is the Hunters' Path, and high Dartmoor forms the western skyline; Castle Drogo stands four-square behind its shelter-belt of pines – looking rather like an enormous packing case.

At a rocky promontory – Sharp Tor – a path leads off right to the castle, which is well worth visiting if it is open. This striking neo-medieval mock fortress was built for Julius Drewe between 1910 and 1930 by Sir Edwin Lutyens. Fallow deer are sometimes seen along here.

Castle Drogo – built between 1910 and 1913 for Sir Julius Drew by architect Sir Edwin Lutyens

If a detour is made to Castle Drogo, the Hunters' Path can be rejoined further on. The Hunters' Path reaches the western end of the Teign Gorge at Hunts Tor (not Hunters Tor as shown on OS maps). Across the valley is Whiddon (deer) Park, surrounded by a lofty stone wall 8ft 6in high in places.

Follow the path as it turns away from the valley, then doubles back on itself at a lower level to reach the River Teign at a metal anglers' bridge. Turn left, downstream, and follow this Fisherman's Path back to the car park. The deep pool in the Teign is formed by a weir which diverts some of the flow to a turbine house on the south bank which provides DC electricity to Castle Drogo. Built into the weir is a fish ladder. As you walk down-river a scree of frost-shattered shale is crossed, and where Sharp Tor's lower buttresses meet the river a steep climb up and down has to be negotiated. A short distance before Fingle Bridge there is another weir which took water to the waterwheel of Fingle Mill, destroyed by fire in 1894. Its ruins are visible at the far end of the car park.

Raleigh's Childhood Playground

Allow 3 hours

A long but easy walk, mostly along heathland tracks, over the commons of east Devon.

From the car park near Woodbury Castle (SY032872) cross the road and take the right-hand track which leads down to a farm access track running along the hedge at the bottom. Follow this left to the road near Four Firs. The sea-smoothed pebbles in the track show that this area was under the sea millions of years ago. The overlay is agriculturally unproductive so it is largely left to heather and the growing of conifers.

Cross the road and walk on the grass verge into the car park beyond Four Firs. Now take the left-hand track making for the isolated clump of fir trees to the left of the young shelter-belt. Notice a high seat positioned in front of the trees with good visibility down the valley. Here marksmen cull roe deer. Their numbers have to be controlled, or they would damage crops and trees to an unacceptable extent.

Follow the wide, pebbly firebreak downhill and then up to the far corner of Thorn Tree Plantation. Turn right, and left at the top to meet a minor road at Fryingpans where there is a brick building left over from World War II. The Royal Marines had a camp near here, and they still use the commons for training purposes, coming from Lympstone on the Exe Estuary.

Turn left down the road, and take the second turning on the right signposted East Budleigh. The first house you pass is Hayes Barton, Walter Raleigh's birthplace in 1552.

About 150yds beyond Hayes Barton, turn left and follow the hedge through three fields to Yettington. Turn right into the village, then left. At the end of the fields enter a track to the right. The fields end where the good land ends, the woods and heath marking the poor soil.

At the end of a long banana-shaped field, take the valley path which climbs to a broad track. The landscape opens up to heathland once more. If it is a weekend, over to your left you may hear and see radio-controlled model aircraft flying. Look back, and the prominent tower in Baker's Brake, 2 miles away, is the China Tower, built as a surprise birthday present for her husband by Lady Rolle about 1837 as a repository for their collection of porcelain.

Carry on up the broad track heading for the large clump of trees beside which the car park is situated, though a slight detour is necessary when you get near. The trees, mostly beech, mark an Iron Age earthwork – Woodbury Castle. Enormous ditches and banks would have presented a considerable obstacle to potential attackers.

East Devon's Deep Combes

Allow 3 hours

A walk along the east Devon coast between Weston Combe and the village of Branscombe. There is likely to be mud where the path passes through cattle pastures. One steep climb follows a visit to Branscombe Church which is one of Devon's most interesting parish churches.

Leave Weston car park (SY166889) by the bottom track and bear round left, leaving the track for a footpath where a signpost reads Weston Cliff. Notice how the track is surfaced with flint, and once on the narrow footpath see how the steeper valley sides are uncultivated, while the valley bottoms provide pasture. This is typical east Devon scenery: deep combes breaking up a flat plateau. Weston Cliff is reached at the edge of a 500ft-plus declivity, and **walkers are warned not to go near** the cliff-edge as the subsoil is unstable. The view extends from Portland in Dorset to Scabbacombe Head beyond Torbay. A few chalets mark Weston Mouth, but the beach cannot be reached by cars, so is always quiet.

Take the coast path heading east, following the signposts, waymarks and stiles. One field after the National Trust sign, the path bears left away from the cliff and meets a hedged track at the point where another track comes in from the left. Carry on eastwards, looking out for Branscombe Church through the trees to the left. When nearly level with the church, turn left down a steep path through the woods at a waymark post. This leads to the churchyard. The church is a Norman building, somewhat altered in medieval times, but unspoilt. Notice the three-decker pulpit, the pews and the gallery, only accessible by outside stairs. Much of the furniture is Jacobean, but the splendid pulpit dates from the 18th century. The village of Branscombe extends for well over a mile down this beautiful winding valley. About 200 yards down from the church is a thatched forge and a traditional country bakery whose oven is still heated by ashen faggots.

Leave the churchyard by the main gate, walk left up the road and turn down and immediately up across a steep field just before the old chapel. Climb a stile into the woods and follow the path to rejoin the outward route. Turn right here, and right again where the track comes in from the right. Badgers find these steep scrub-covered hillsides very much to their liking.

At Berry Barton Farm turn left and return along a relatively quiet road to Weston, about 1¼ miles away.

Herring gull – partial to holidaymakers' sandwiches

Among Devon's Redlands

Allow 2½ hours

A steep climb to a wonderful viewpoint in rolling farmland not far from Exeter. This is a walk best done in summer on a clear day. Stout shoes or boots essential. Allow time to have a look at Silverton. There are several pubs and shops and, surprisingly, a health club.

From the car park near the Health Centre in Silverton (SS957030) walk to Fore Street and turn up right. This is an attractive large village with many thatched houses in the older part.

Turn right up Parsonage Lane beside the Methodist Chapel. Note how the cob (dried mud) walls of the cottages on the right are built on stone plinths. Cob is a good building material provided it has a good hat (roof) and a stout pair of shoes (stone footings).

Carry straight on up passing the school on your right. Where the track deteriorates enter a hunting gate on the left and continue up the field with the hedge on your right. The views are now expansive with Dartmoor and the sea both visible. Super-tankers can be picked out beyond Exmouth. Beneath your feet is the red soil for which Devon is famous.

At the end of the third field, join the road, turn right and climb steeply to Christ Cross (locally Criss Cross). This is about 850ft high, and the views now extend to Somerset, with the Wellington Monument prominent on the northern shoulder of the Blackdown Hills on a clear day.

Turn right along a gently-falling road, and right again down a steep rough track just as the ridge road begins to ascend, and follow it helter-skelter down and through Greenslinch Farm. This rough lane is how all Devon's roads were once. A water-splash a short distance down may call for desperate measures. The badger runs through the hedges are very noticeable, and rabbits also inhabit this lane.

At Greenslinch, take the slightly climbing track behind the cottages, and turn left over a stile where the track turns sharp right. Aim for the stile at the top of the field – Silverton is now spread out in the foreground. *Having crossed the stile, descend the field with the hedge on your right.* Dolbury Hill, on the Killerton estate (National Trust) is the wooded hill 2½ miles away. The park is open to the public, as is the house between April and October.

Pass through the gate, turn half right and follow the track to the road. Silverton is now ½ mile to the west. Before returning to your car, have a look at the church. The best feature is the west gallery.

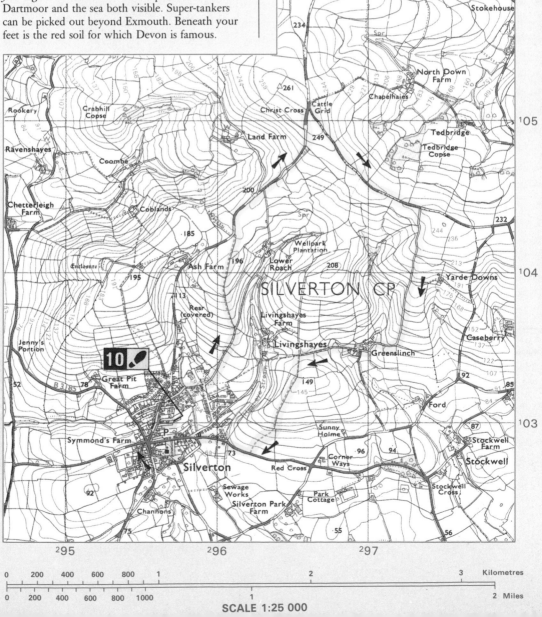

SCALE 1:25 000

WALK 11

In Deepest Devon

Allow 1½ hours

A gentle but possibly muddy walk in a remote parish where the charm lies in the ordinariness of the scenery and the lack of moorland drama or coastal theatricality. The drive to the starting point is part of the experience, and the view across mid-Devon deserves a clear day and time to lean on field gates.

From the church car park at Woolfardisworthy (SS828086) enter the church. Woolfardisworthy is a Saxon name meaning the farm of *Wolfeard*, but the church was rebuilt in the 19th century. The churchyard is best seen when the snowdrops or daffodils are in bloom.

Leave the churchyard by the gate at the west end and turn right towards the road near a new house. Turn left up the quiet, gently-rising road, taking time to appreciate the views as the road ascends. Nearly at the top, turn right along a track past a new house. This is good sheep-grazing land, with most of the woodlands confined to the valleys. You may hear a buzzard mewing overhead. Buzzards are relatively common throughout Devon and Exmoor, their numbers having recovered from the days when birds of prey were persecuted by farmers and gamekeepers. They are opportunist feeders, taking whatever is available, including carrion such as dead lambs. Buzzards can sometimes be mistaken for eagles – but there are no wild eagles in the West Country!

Follow the track down to East Densham. Passing through the yard and leaving the farmhouse on your right, descend a track to the valley beyond. Cross a small stream and take the left-hand track which follows the stream to a bridge. A comparison with the map will show that Densham Plantation has been felled and converted to farmland.

At the bridge turn right up the road, turn right again and then left. Woolfardisworthy Church tower is now visible to the right. Take the first right and the car park is soon reached. Woolfardisworthy is usually abbreviated to Woolsery, and an identically-named parish in north-west Devon means that this one is sometimes referred to as East Woolfardisworthy. The gothic, barge-boarded house near the church used to be the parish school.

Buzzard – quite likely to be seen perching on fence posts or telegraph poles

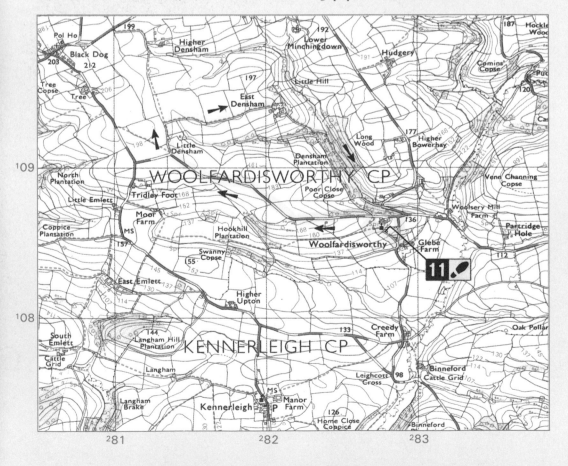

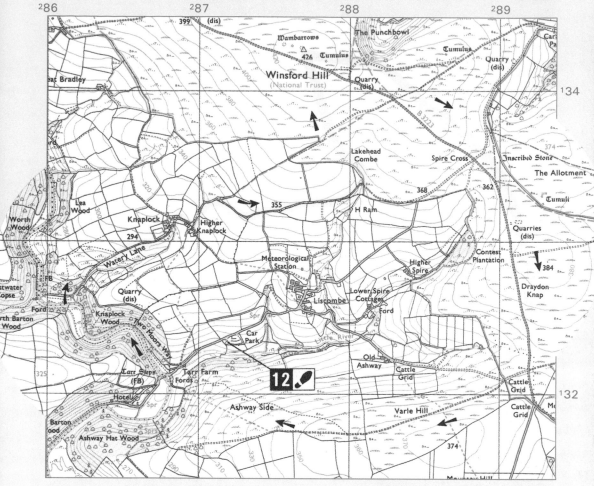

113

River Bank and Breezy Hilltop

Allow 4 hours

A varied walk along the River Barle and over the open moorland of Winsford Hill. A fine, dry, clear day is recommended.

Skylark – few birds can match the joy of its song

Walk downhill from the car park (SS872323) to Tarr Steps which crosses the Barle. Tarr Steps is a 17-span clapper bridge, 55yds long, dating from medieval times. Alongside is a wide ford. The bridge has been damaged several times by floods, so a cable debris-arrester is now sited upstream to intercept floating logs.

Follow the permissive path upstream. It is soon joined by a bridleway, and this should be traced to the point where the first side valley comes in from the right. Notice the prolific growth of ferns and mosses on the older trees on this stretch.

Turn up Watery Lane, a rocky track which degenerates into a muddy lane near Knaplock Farm. Pass both the Knaplock farms and stay with the approach track until the open moor is reached at a cattle grid. The beech hedges on the farm track are noted features of the Exmoor landscape.

At the cattle grid turn left, cross a small stream and make for the top of Winsford Hill, out of sight until you are nearly there. After initially passing through bracken, heather takes over. In spring and summer the area is alive with the song of skylarks and meadow pipits, and the buzz of insects when the heather is in flower adds to the assaults on one's senses. There are Bronze Age barrows on the summit of Winsford Hill (1399ft) and comprehensive views in every direction.

Head due east to the rim of the Punchbowl. This is a deep, steep combe in the northern flank of Winsford Hill, where trees have managed to gain a hold. Few of the thousands of visitors to Winsford Hill suspect its presence.

Keeping a short distance east of the B3223, make for the small building which protects the Caratacus Stone. It probably dates from between AD450 and 650.

Continue walking south a short distance east of the road, cross it and pass over the cattle grid on the Tarr Steps side road. Now follow the footpath to Tarr Steps. Ashway Farm, the birthplace of Sir George Williams, the founder of the YMCA, is out of sight to the south as the path descends to the river.

At Tarr Steps, walk back up the road to the car park.

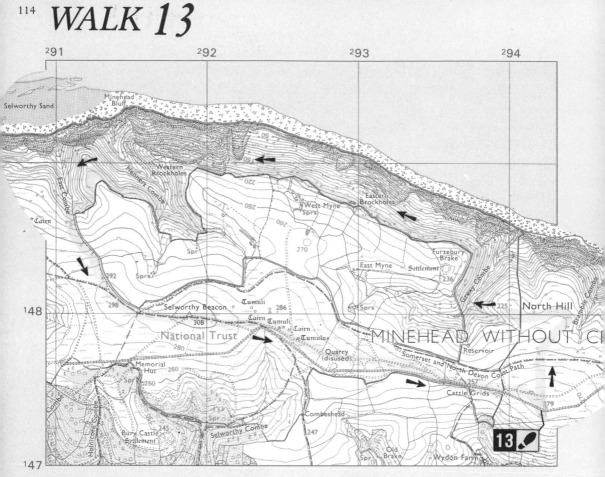

Exmoor's Coast and Combes

Allow 4 hours

Advertised at each end by the National Trust as a 'rugged path', the outward leg of this walk has several steep pitches but is not dangerous. The return leg traces the ridge of this detached lump of Exmoor with spectacular views across to Wales and inland to Dunkery Beacon, Exmoor's highest point. Choose a clear day to do this walk, and take your time over it. No dogs are allowed.

The car park (SS942474) is handy to the viewpoint indicator on the summit of North Hill (842ft) which gives a wonderful panorama of the Bristol Channel and the north Somerset and Welsh coasts. The prominent islands are Flatholm and Steepholm. Turn your back on the indicator and walk north down the track towards the sea. Where another wider track is met, carry on down a narrow footpath which soon joins another track near a seat. Bear round left and the path soon meets the enclosures at a prominent stile and notice. The route is now continuously waymarked to the far end of the enclosures, 1 mile short of Hurlstone Point. Once committed there is no opportunity to opt out (short of retracing your steps) as agricultural land intervenes.

The National Trust has performed a notable service in opening this exciting path. It is much nearer the sea than the designated coast path, and there are constant surprises as it undulates beguilingly along this elevated promenade. The loops on the map and crushed-together contours betray deep and secretive combes. Red deer may be seen, and the place-names Eastern and Western Brockholes indicate a medieval badger population. Badgers still live in this area, but only quiet and patient watchers are likely to see them, since they are extremely shy. They live in setts which may be the selfsame setts excavated by their ancestors hundreds of years ago. Usually, they emerge a little before dusk, their first priority being to visit the latrines, which are carefully dug. They then go off in search of a drink and food. Play is an important part of their lives, especially when there are young cubs. It is these signs of activity – setts, latrines, tracks, holes scratched in search of insects or bulbs, grass or bracken flattened during play – that are far more likely to be seen than the badgers themselves.

At the end stile the enclosure wall retreats uphill and inland. Follow it up and around to Selworthy Beacon (1012ft) and back along the ridge to the start. Several tracks can be traced along this breezy upland. Selworthy Beacon was one of the links in the chain of warning fires during times of national emergency. Bronze Age cairns stand both on its summit and nearby. The whole area was used for tank training during World War II and some of the tracks date back to this use. The views inland are now particularly fine.

Badger – secretive West Country resident

Watersmeet

Allow 2 hours

A beautiful easy walk through oak woodlands in the steep valleys of the East Lyn and the Hoar Oak Water.

Leave Hillsford Bridge car park (SS740477) and picnic site past Combe Park Lodge and walk up the grass verge of the A39 behind the AA box. Where it tapers, head for the National Trust sign ahead. Pass through the gate and walk up the track. The track levels out as it emerges from these delightful woodlands, and fine views of hills and valleys interfolded in fascinating complexity open out.

At a signpost by a seat take the path marked Watersmeet. It re-enters the woods and goes downhill, reaching open ground again and meeting a path from the left. Turn right here. Lynton is visible on its hillside platform towards the sea, and the scree-sloped dry valley ahead is Chisel Combe. The path crosses an Iron Age earthwork, but it is masked by bracken in the summer.

The path reaches the road, which must be crossed with care to a small lay-by. Steps from here are signposted Watersmeet. Go down and cross two footbridges to Watersmeet House. Watersmeet is where the East Lyn river and Hoar Oak Water come together, and Watersmeet House is an 1832 fishing lodge now

Blue tit – familiar woodland companion

owned by the National Trust and open from April to October as a café and shop.

Return from the house over the first (the East Lyn) footbridge, and opposite the National Trust money box turn steeply up left signposted Hillsford Bridge, bearing right at the top. (These steep steps do not last long.) After ¼ mile, opposite a seat on the left, a short path goes down right to an attractive waterfall. Along this valley it is still possible to see scars caused by the great flood disaster of August 1952. Some 9in of rain fell on Exmoor in 24 hours, and 90,000,000 tons of water surged down the valleys converging on Lynmouth. Thirty-four people lost their lives.

By carrying on up the river bank path, Hillsford Bridge is easily reached.

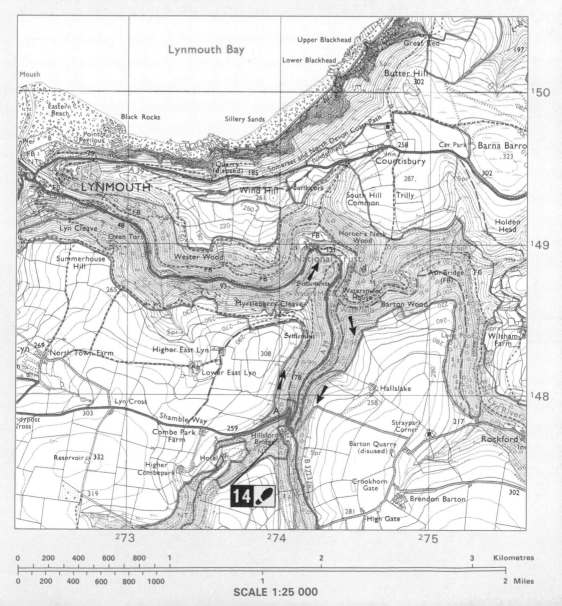

SCALE 1:25 000

WALK 15
Bull Point and Morte Point

Allow 2¾ hours

An energetic coastal walk on National Trust property. There are wide-ranging views to Wales, Lundy and along the north Devon coast.

From Mortehoe car park (SS458452) cross the road and take the road opposite signposted to Lighthouse and Lee. At the end of the public road pass through the Trinity House gate and walk along the lighthouse road. Go down the steps on the right signposted Lee, and at the footbridge follow the path beside Bennett's Water, the small stream flowing down the valley. This is a pleasant sheltered combe with trees, and of local importance for breeding and wintering birds. In spring the wild daffodils and primroses are followed by a sweep of bluebells.

Where the stream meets the sea at Bennett's Mouth, turn steeply up left and stay on the coast path right round Morte Point. Bennett's Mouth is hardly a beach, simply an exposure of jagged slaty rock of a kind called morte slate. Bull Point lighthouse is soon reached. This structure replaces an earlier lighthouse which became unsafe in 1972.

The path passes on the landward side and switchbacks along behind Rockham Beach, a good place for a bathe at low tide. Visitors will notice that the Trust's stiles are provided with dog gates, a sliding guillotine-type trap. These were devised by Tony Ash, the warden for this stretch of coast. The arrowhead of Morte Point, aimed at the island of Lundy to the west, has been Trust property since 1910, and is a tumbled rocky landscape of grassy straths, gorse thickets and heather. Seals are sometimes seen in the sea, and adders are common. The tip of the point was used as a bombing range during World War II. Once round the point the view changes: the great arc of Woolacombe Bay is enclosed by Baggy Point in the south, and the distant headland is Hartland Point.

When nearly at the houses, turn up left to reach the road through a gate beside the chapel with the stumpy spire. Turn left and return to the car park at Mortehoe.

Shipwreck – once a constant danger on this coast

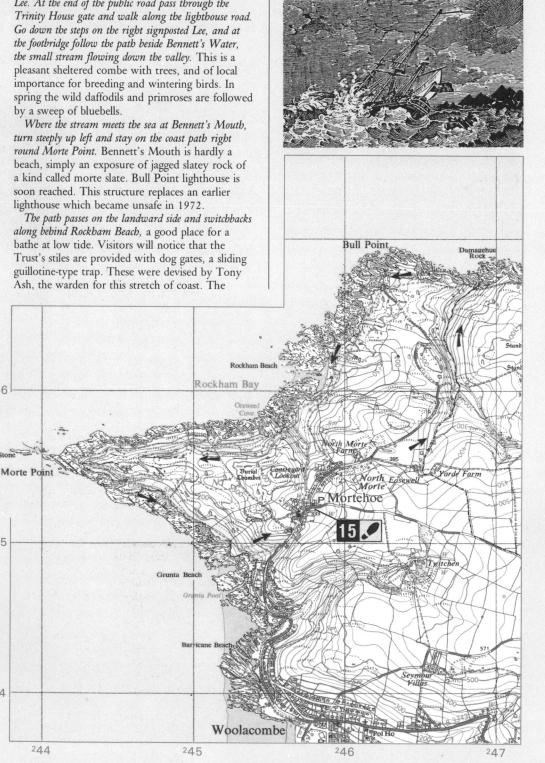

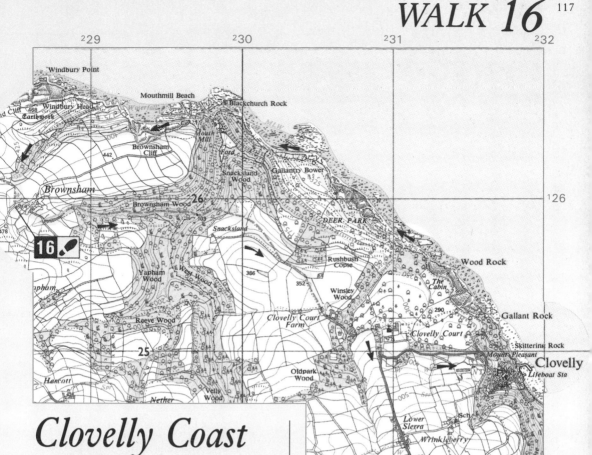

Clovelly Coast

Allow 3½ hours
(plus 45 minutes for the optional extension)

A walk which is full of surprises and packed
with variety. There is one very steep climb – up
from Mouth Mill – and another if the optional
walk down Clovelly's tortuous cobbled street is
undertaken. There is a chance of mud,
particularly on the outward leg.

*Leave Brownsham car park (SS285259) and walk
down the track through an attractive wooded side valley.*
The metallic note of wrens – tit-tit-tit –
accompanies the walker, while the occasional
strident alarm call of a cock pheasant is
unmistakable as, lower down, the track passes
through conifer plantations. Roe deer are
sometimes seen here.

*Cross the stream at the bottom, turn left and almost
immediately up to the right. From here to Clovelly
Church the route is signposted and waymarked and
passes through woods, fields and a farmyard.* The
architecture of the buildings beyond the farm is a
little curious, and owes its eccentricity to Mrs
Christine Hamlyn whose initials occur throughout
the Clovelly Court estate. The Court itself is not
open to the public and is tucked away behind the
church which is of interest for the array of family
monuments. The lodge, where the road is reached,
bears the inscription 'Go east, go west, home's the
best'.

*Turn left here, and keep on the pavement where there
is one, bearing left where a large sign commands 'All
Vehicles To Clovelly→'. Where the road bears steeply
down left, note a gate to Clovelly Court Park as this
will be our entrance after we have glimpsed Clovelly. So
turn right and descend the cobbled path as far as you
want to go.* The drinking fountain by the 90-degree
bend is a good place to decide if a further descent is
desired, and 45 minutes must be added to the estimated

walk time. Clovelly owes its existence to the
massive quay which provided some shelter on this
inhospitable coast. All supplies and rubbish have to
be manhandled on sleds, though a back road
Landrover service does ply between the Red Lion
by the harbour and the top car park.

*Now return to the Park gate and enter Clovelly
Court Park. As on the outward walk, this stretch is
well signposted and waymarked and is easily followed
all the way to the beach at Mouth Mill.* The path
loops in and out of woodland, passing a
summerhouse and a pagoda-roofed seat called
Angels' Wings. It then climbs to the top of
Gallantry Bower, which has a sheer drop to the
beach of over 350ft. Behind the beach is a ruined
limekiln, once kept supplied with coal and
limestone by sailing craft.

*Now climb the steep coast path westwards, and follow
the field edge after the National Trust property sign. At
the signpost to Brownsham and Beckland leave the coast
path and head inland.* This is a charming valley,
wonderful for bluebells in spring. The Iron Age
fortification of Windbury is on the opposite
hilltop.

*Enter the woods, and at a seat take the path marked
Brownsham Farm. The car park is reached in about 5
minutes.*

SCALE 1:25 000

Index

Page numbers in bold type indicate main entries. See also Directory, page 73.

Acknowledgements

The Automobile Association wishes to thank the following photographers, organisations and libraries for material reproduced in this book.

Anthony Blake Photo Library 25 Cream teas, 27 Cider making; *Dartmoor National Park* 20 Corndon Ford; *Devonport Royal Dockyard* 33 Dockyard; *English Heritage* 69 Totnes Castle – A Sorrell's reconstruction; *Derek Forss Cover* Gt Burland rocks; *Francis Frith Collection* 34 Plymouth Barbican; *The Mansell Collection* 19 Cockington Forge, 33 The Hamoaze; *Mary Evans Picture Library* 31 Bowls match, 32 Fishing, Plymouth, 33 Devonport, 112 Buzzard, 115 Blue tit; *Nature Photographers* 13 Puffin (C B Carver), Painted Lady (F V Blackburn), 14/15 Gt Mis Tor (A J Cleave), 14 Marsh Helleborine (A Warton), 15 Ring Ouzel (A K Davies), 16 Red Deer (W S Paton), 17 Grey Wagtail (P R Sterry), Dipper (D Hutton), Western Gorse (A J Cleave), 18 Buzzard (H Clark), Buzzard on nest (M E Gore), Tawny Owl (D A Smith), Barn Owl (E A Janes); *National Maritime Museum* 30 Sailing ship, 34 The Susan Vittery; *National Portrait Gallery* 31 Sir Francis Drake; *The National Trust Devon Regional Office* 20 Seaside farmhouse, 21 Farm; *City of Plymouth Museums* 31 Drake's Drum; *Brian Shuel* 27 Wassailing; *West Air Photography* 7 Plymouth, 8 Teignmouth, 60 Plymouth, 71 Salcombe

The following photographs are from the Automobile Association's Photo Library:

M Adelman 99 Ottery St Mary; *J Cady* 22 Cathedral Close, Exeter; *A Lawson* 1 Clovelly, 3 The Cygnet, 5 Combestone Tor, 6 Ashburton, 8 Prawle Point, 13 Red campion, 19 Thatcher, 21 Rendered building, 22 The Cherub, 23 Budleigh Salterton, 24 Bovey Tracey, 27 Cheeses, 28 Mackerel, 29 Beer, 35 Tomb, 35 Exmoor, 36 Appledore, 37 Barnstaple bridge, Flower pots, 38 Brentor, Bickleigh, Beer, 40 Brixham, 41 Budleigh Salterton, 41 Pilchard Inn sign, 42 Screen, 42 Clovelly, 43 Coombe Martin, 44 Crediton, 45 Cullompton, 46 Ashburton, sheep, Dartmoor, 46/7 Dartmoor, 48 Door, Dartmouth castle, Sailing boats, 50 Exeter Cathedral, 51 Craft fair, Bridge, 53 Lighthouse, Hartland, Holsworthy, 54 Lace making, Harbour, 56/7 Morwellham, 57 Newton Abbot, 58 Museum, 59 Paignton, 61 Killerton gardens, 62 Widecombe in the Moor, Salcombe, 63 Tram stop, Tram, Steam engine, 64 Sidmouth, 65 South Molton, 66 Teignmouth, Tavistock, 67 Lydford, 68 Torquay, 69 Totnes castle, Fore street, 71 Beach, Woolacombe, 73 Potter, Tapestry, Bovey Tracey, 74 Dulverton, Crediton, 75 Signs, 77 Bigbury-on-Sea, 78 Pony riders, 79 Sign, 99 Exeter; *S & O Mathews* 8 Valley of the Rocks, 11 Landacre bridge, 20 Dartmouth ceiling, 23 A la Ronde, Exmouth, 23 Beach house, 24 Maritime Museum, 46/7 Haytor Rocks, 55 Lydford, 60 Drake's statue, 66 Teignmouth, 95 Plymouth Hoe, 108 Castle Drago; *R Newton* 94 Princetown, 96 Buckland in the Moor, 97 Widecombe in the Moor, 98 Cliff Railway; *H Williams* 9 Hembury Hill Fort, 11 Tarr Steps, 39 Branscombe, 49 Dunster Castle, 52 Malmesmead, 55 Lydford Gorge, 56 Lynmouth, 60 Saltram House, 65 Slapton Ley, 76 Saltrim House, 98 Oare Church, Lynmouth, 100 Sidmouth; *J Wyand* 6/7 Hound Tor, 9 Merrivale, 10 Grimspound, 50 Exeter Cathedral, 61 Packhorse bridge, 72 Buckland Abbey, 94 Merrivale

Other Ordnance Survey Maps of Devon and Exmoor

How to get there with Routemaster and Routeplanner Maps

Reach Devon from Truro, Dorchester, Gloucester and Swansea using Routemaster sheet 8. Alternatively, use the Ordnance Survey Great Britain Routeplanner Map, which covers the whole of the country on one sheet.

Exploring with Landranger, Tourist and Outdoor Leisure Maps

Landranger Series
1¼ inches to one mile or 1:50 000 scale

These maps cover the whole of Britain and are good for local motoring and walking. Each contains tourist information such as parking, picnic places, viewpoints and rights of way. Sheets covering Devon are:

180 Barnstaple and Ilfracombe
181 Minehead & Brendon Hills
190 Bude and Clovelly
191 Okehampton and North Dartmoor
192 Exeter and Sidmouth
201 Plymouth and Launceston
202 Torbay and South Dartmoor

Holiday Map Series
1 inch to 3 miles

The West Country, covering the popular area of the West Country (Cornwall, Devon and part of Somerset). This map is invaluable to the visitor.

Tourist Map Series
1 inch to one mile or 1:63 360 scale

These maps cover popular holiday areas and are ideal for discovering the countryside. In addition to normal map details, ancient monuments, camping and caravan sites, parking facilities and viewpoints are marked. Lists of selected places of interest are included on some sheets and others include useful guides to the area.

Tourist Map Sheet 4 covers Dartmoor and Sheet 5 Exmoor

Outdoor Leisure Map Series
2½ inches to one mile or 1:25 000 scale

These maps cover popular leisure and recreation areas of the country and include details of Youth Hostels, camping and caravanning sites, picnic areas, footpaths and viewpoints.

Outdoor Leisure Map Sheet 28 covers Dartmoor and Sheet 20 South Devon

Other titles available in this series are:

Channel Islands	Isle of Wight	Peak District
Cornwall	Lake District	Scottish Highlands
Cotswolds	New Forest	South Downs
Forest of Dean & Wye Valley	Northumbria	Wessex
Ireland	North York Moors	Yorkshire Dales